COLUMBIA UNIVERSITY STUDIES IN ENGLISH
AND COMPARATIVE LITERATURE

CHAUCER
AND THE
ROMAN DE LA ROSE

CHAUCER
AND THE
ROMAN DE LA ROSE

BY
DEAN SPRUILL FANSLER, Ph.D.

GLOUCESTER, MASS.

PETER SMITH

1965

*Barry College Library
Miami, Florida*

Copyright, 1914
By Columbia University Press
Reprinted, 1965 by Permission of
Columbia University Press

This Monograph has been approved by the Department of English and Comparative Literature in Columbia University as a contribution to knowledge worthy of publication.

A. H. THORNDIKE,
Executive Officer.

To
My Father and Mother
This book is affectionately dedicated

PREFATORY NOTE

I take pleasure in acknowledging in print my indebtedness to Professor Harry M. Ayres, Professor George P. Krapp, and Professor William W. Lawrence, of Columbia University, who have generously read both the manuscript and the proof-sheets of this book and have made many suggestions of value. My greatest obligation is to Professor Lawrence, under whose immediate direction this dissertation has been prepared. He has unselfishly at all times given me the benefit of his wide acquaintance with medieval literature, and has been most courteous and helpful. I am also grateful to Professor William E. Mead, of Wesleyan University, for a number of useful bibliographical references. D. S. F.

Manila, 1913.

TABLE OF CONTENTS

	PAGE
Introduction	1
Chapter I. The Influence of the *Roman de la Rose* on Chaucer's Reading	11
Chapter II. Allusions to Historical and Legendary Persons and Places	24
Chapter III. Mythological Allusions	48
Chapter IV. Chaucer's Style as Affected by the *Roman*	73
Chapter V. Situations and Descriptions	123
Chapter VI. Proverbs and Proverbial Expressions	175
Chapter VII. Influence of the *Roman de la Rose* on Chaucer's Philosophical Discussions	203
Conclusion	229
Bibliography	235

Appendices for Reference:
  A. Comparative Table of Meon's, Michel's, and Marteau's Numbering of the Lines of the *Roman de la Rose* 240
  B. Table showing corresponding lines in Ellis's translation of the *Roman de la Rose*, the Middle English *Romaunt of the Rose*, and Marteau's edition of the Original French text 244

Index of Passages from Chaucer's Works and the English *Romaunt of the Rose* quoted or referred to in the text 249

Index of Passages from the *Roman de la Rose* quoted or referred to in the text 261

INTRODUCTION

Much has been written on the subject of Chaucer and the *Roman de la Rose;* but there is considerable diversity of opinion on the relative influence of Guillaume de Lorris and Jean de Meung upon the English poet. Some commentators hold that the author of the first part of the *Roman,* around whose work a large school of followers sprang up, exercised a dominating effect on the minor and earlier poems of Chaucer; others maintain that only the part written by Jean de Meung appealed to Chaucer, and that Guillaume's production was made little use of not only by the author of the *Canterbury Tales* but even by the comparatively young and inexperienced poet of the *Book of the Duchess.* As illustrations of the contradictory views held, we may glance at the conclusions a few of the investigators have reached.

Sandras was the first to make a wholesale attribution of Chaucer's work to the influence of the early French poets. Near the beginning of his *Etude* he says: "Il imite les poëtes latins, Virgile, Ovide, Stace, Lucain, Juvénal; il fait des emprunts à Dante, à Pétrarque, à Boccace; il traduit une grande partie du *Roman de la Rose,* et, à chaque page, à chaque ligne de ses écrits, se trahit, tantôt déguisée, tantôt manifeste, une reminiscence de nos trouvères." But what the French savant had to say about Chaucer and the authors of the *Roman de la Rose* is more to the point for our study, and may be repeated here: "Il [Chaucer] en traduisit une partie, et il y prit des inspirations continuelles. C'est au point que ce poëte, qui sentait les beautés de la nature, qui savait les peindre, se content souvent dans ses descriptions d'être la copiste de G. de Lorris; que cet érudit, qui certainement avait lu des Décades de Tite-Live, alors mises en faveur et par Pétrarque et par le traduction de Pierre Bercheure, reproduit l'histoire romaine telle que J. de Meung la lui transmet, altérée par l'imagination des conteurs; que cet homme de génie, qui mérite d'être placé entre Aristophane et Molière, arrive à la vieillesse, toujours sous le joug de l'imitation, et n'ayant guère composé que des poëmes allégoriques. Quand il renonce à cette poésie de cour si fausse, si maniérée, et qu'il écrit le Pélerinage de Canterbury, drame vivant et populaire, on retrouve dans son œuvre les traits saillants qui caractérisent la seconde partie du *Roman de la Rose,* de longues tirades contre les femmes, et le ridicule jeté à pleines mains sur les ordres religieux. Sans doute il remonte aux sources premières où ont puisé ses maîtres, sans doute il étudie les ouvrages de leurs disciples, ses contemporains; mais c'est à l'école de G. de Lorris que son gout s'est formé ou, si l'on veut, altéré; c'est à l'école de Jean de Meung que s'est façonné son esprit."[1]

Eighty years before Sandras wrote, Tyrwhitt had called attention to the fact that a number of passages in the *Canterbury Tales* appear to have been taken from the *Roman de la Rose.* He did not discuss his parallels, how-

---

[1] *Etude sur G. Chaucer considéré comme imitateur des trouvères,* by Etienne Gustave Sandras (Paris, 1859), p. 36.

ever; they took the form of brief notes on the text. It is really with Sandras's bold and sweeping assertions that critical investigations into the relations of Chaucer and his French contemporaries and predecessors started. Students in other countries began to look for proofs of Chaucer's indebtedness to the *Roman de la Rose,* and as a result of diligent search, the number of parallels has grown to a very large total. But the emphasis in nearly every case has been on the side of the influence either of Jean de Meung or of Guillaume de Lorris; the critics apparently have not been able to reconcile Chaucer to both at once.

Van Laun writes: "Of his two originals, Chaucer decidedly preferred the first [Lorris], both from the natural bent of his mind and also because he would readily perceive that Englishmen would not tolerate the license of Jean de Meung. . . . Indeed, his genius was cast in a different mould from that of Jean de Meung, who was natural philosopher first, and romancist afterwards. Chaucer, like Guillaume de Lorris, was before all a romancist."[2]

Lounsbury, writing some ten years later, remarks: "It ought to be said that it [i. e., the *Roman de la Rose*] is his [Chaucer's] favorite work, as regards adaptation, only so far as it is the composition of Jean de Meung. The portion of it composed by Lorris receives from him scant attention in this respect. From that part of the poem that exists for us in the English translation, he drew but little, and that little consists of nothing more than single words and phrases."[3]

[2] *History of French Literature* (London, 1883), I, pp. 183, 184.
[3] *Studies in Chaucer,* by T. R. Lounsbury (London, 1892), II, p. 220.

Skeat refers the student to Lounsbury for a discussion of the learning of Chaucer, but in his brief account of Chaucer's authorities, says: "He [Chaucer] was perfectly familiar with the French of the continent, and was under great obligations to Guillaume de Lorris and Jean de Meung, and to Guillaume de Machault."[4]

On the whole, criticism since 1890 has tended to make prominent Chaucer's borrowings from Jean de Meung and to reduce his debt to Guillaume de Lorris. Koeppel, writing in 1892 on Jean de Meung's influence on Chaucer, concludes: "So sind wir unserem dichter an zahllosen stellen auf den wegen Jehan de Meung's begegnet. Aber weder des meisters noch des schülers andenken hat durch die volle erkentniss ihres verhältnisses gelitten. Chaucer's kunst, die feine mässigung, mit welcher er die schonungslose weisheit der Franzosen verwertet, fordert unsere aufrichtige bewunderung, und Jehan de Meung's bedeutende, aber wenig anziehende gestalt wird von dem strahl, der von Chaucer's glänzender erscheinung auf sie zurückfällt, verschönernd getroffen."[5]

Miss Cipriani believes that the influence of the *Roman de la Rose* on Chaucer shows itself more distinctly in the *Troilus* than in any other single poem; of the *Troilus* she says in summary: "(a) There is an indirect influence of the *Roman de la Rose* through Boccaccio, which introduces elements characteristic of the first part of the French poem. (b) The changes in the character of Pandarus all show tendencies which coincide with the satirical attitude of

---
[4] *Complete Works of Chaucer*, VI, pp. xcviii, c. (1894).
[5] *Chauceriana*, by E. Koeppel, in Anglia, XIV, p. 267.

Jean de Meung toward love. The additions of Chaucer to the *Filostrato* are also primarily in the spirit and with the method and material used by Jean de Meung. (c) But the influence of Jean de Meung on Chaucer is most important in the ethical teaching with which Chaucer ends the love story, making the *Troylus* a *Tendenzroman,* in which the folly of love is shown in order to lead the reader to the love of Christ and eternal salvation."[6]

Miss Hammond does not mention Guillaume de Lorris, but emphatically writes: "The depth of de Meung's influence upon Chaucer is unsurpassed by that of any writer except Boethius."[7]

It is perhaps not inappropriate that this list of critics should end, as it began, with a Frenchman. Legouis, who has recently written a most readable book on Chaucer, emphasizes, like Sandras, the influence of Guillaume de Lorris on the English poet, and devotes eleven pages to a discussion of "Chaucer à l'école de nos trouvères." But the second part of the *Roman* is not overlooked, even if Jean de Meung's name is. For, after speaking of the sources of the *Canterbury Tales,* Legouis says: "Encore ne sont-ce là que les plus notables emprunts faits par Chaucer, ceux des sujets ou des genres. Dans l'intérieur même de ses cadres, il continuera de déverser abondamment, selon son usage, les maximes et les images, les développements et l'érudition qui lui viennent de ses lectures, surtout de ces

---

[6] *Studies in the Influence of the Roman de la Rose on Chaucer,* by Lisi Cipriani. Publ. Mod. Lang. Assoc. 1907.

[7] *Chaucer: a Bibliographical Manual,* by Eleanor P. Hammond (Macmillan, 1908), p. 79.

deux livres dont il faisait sa société constante: le *Roman de la Rose* et les *Consolations* de Boëce.''[8]

So it may be seen that although critics agree in the main on the extraordinary influence which the *Roman de la Rose* as a whole exerted upon Chaucer, they are by no means at one on the relative debt of the English poet to Lorris and Meung. We might naturally suppose that Chaucer borrowed more from Jean de Meung since Meung wrote more than four-fifths of the long French poem. But such an inference, without any other premise than that of proportional number of lines, would be absurd. For if Chaucer had liked Lorris's work and had not liked Meung's, Jean might have written a hundred thousand lines not one of which Chaucer would have used; whereas he might well have referred to Guillaume's four thousand constantly. Clearly, the work of each poet, unlike as Guillaume and Jean were, appealed to Chaucer for one purpose or another, as numerous unquestioned adaptations by the English poet from *both* parts of the *Roman* attest.

What was Chaucer's opinion of the *Roman de la Rose?* What parts of it appealed to him most? What is the nature of his borrowings from the French poem? How did he adapt and use the passages that he took over? These are pertinent questions, and as such are worthy an answer. They have not been answered by the critics we have quoted from, except in a most general way. Nor have they, indeed, been answered by any of Chaucer's commentators. Those investigators who have pointed out the largest number of

[8] *Geoffroy Chaucer,* by Emile Legouis (Les grands écrivains étrangers, Paris, 1910), p. 151.

parallel passages have given us the least discussion of them. Moreover, the usual method of procedure in the study of the relations between Chaucer and Guillaume de Lorris and Jean de Meung has been what we may call the chronological method; that is, to take up Chaucer's poems in the order in which they were written, so far as their dates have been established, and to cite from the *Roman de la Rose* parallels to the English lines. A different method, which we may call the topical method, that is, to classify Chaucer's borrowings from the *Roman de la Rose* according to the nature of the passages taken over, has not been followed hitherto, though it might well have been. Each has its advantages and disadvantages, obviously; and the chronological method would naturally precede the topical. For in tracing the sources of a poem or group of poems, one ordinarily reads that poem or that group of poems as a whole. And it goes without saying that before one can classify a miscellaneous collection of parallels, one must first get the parallels. But the topical method has a distinct value, once the parallels have been collected so that the critic may classify them, for it furnishes definite information as to the nature of the poet's interests.

It is perhaps unnecessary to remind ourselves here that there are parallels and parallels. The Tropics of Capricorn and Cancer are parallels, but they are not very close! In the question of Chaucer's borrowings from the *Roman de la Rose*, of his use of the *Roman de la Rose*, it is imperative, if we are to come to any useful conclusion, to determine first what he *actually* did consciously adapt from the French poem. Specific adaptations must be distinguished from slight correspondences. It is true that many a slight correspondence may be the result of deliberate adaptation and change of the borrowed material, but such a case is extremely difficult to prove. On the other hand, the fact that two passages are alike may be accidental and the result of entirely independent thinking. Furthermore, it should not be forgotten that Chaucer was very well-read for his time, and that his library was considerably larger even than Jean de Meung's. Moreover, Chaucer read many of Jean de Meung's sources in the original. Nevertheless, there is value in a collection of reminiscences and echoes; and in the case of two poets one of whom we know read and admired the other, even vague resemblances between the later man's work and the earlier man's are not without significance. But first we must always attempt to establish the conscious imitations. The unconscious make fairly good supporting evidence, but have little probative force.

The object of the present volume is three-fold: (1) To examine all the parallels between Chaucer's work and the *Roman de la Rose* that have hitherto been recorded, and to separate from doubtful or fortuitous resemblances what we may in all reason be sure are deliberate borrowings; (2) to present new parallels, of both kinds, that have hitherto not been recorded; and (3) to attempt to determine from the evidence at hand Chaucer's attitude toward the *Roman de la Rose,* the use he made of the poem, and the effect that it had, as the work of two entirely different authors and as a whole, on the English poet's literary production. The method of procedure is fundamentally topical, although I have endeavored to keep the advantages of the chronological method by following within the chapters the order of poems or sections of poems as we think Chaucer wrote them.

All references to Chaucer are made to Skeat's six-volume edition of the Complete Works (Oxford). References to the *Roman de la Rose* are to Michel's two-volume edition (Paris, 1864) unless otherwise stated. I have used Michel's text, not because it is the best—in many ways his edition is the poorest of the three nineteenth-century editions—but because it is the most convenient and accessible. Meon's edition in four volumes (Paris, 1814), which Sandras, Koeppel, and Skeat used, is rare; and Marteau's edition in five volumes in the Bibliothèque Elzévirienne (Orléans, 1878-80), although it is the best of the three, seems to be little known and almost never cited. For the reader's convenience in verifying in these three editions references that he may find to any of them, I have appended at the end of this book a comparative table of the numbering of the lines.

In some cases, references to parallel passages pointed out by Miss Cipriani, Koeppel, and Skeat are followed by the initial of the investigator: thus, (C) (K) (S). The (C) so used should not be confused with the reference to the third division of the *Canterbury Tales*, where the letter always precedes the number. The abbreviation RR. always signifies the French text; Rom., the Middle English translation.

Chaucer and the Roman de la Rose

CHAPTER I

The Influence of the Roman de la Rose on Chaucer's Reading

Chaucer's early literary career is more or less direct proof that the poet meant what he said when he wrote

> And as for me thogh that I can but lyte,
> On bokes for to rede I me delyte,
> And to hem yeve I feyth and ful credence,
> And in myn herte have hem in reverence
> So hertely, that ther is game noon
> That fro my bokes maketh me to goon,
> But it be seldom, on the holyday.   (L. 29-35)

Later on (Prol. A. 273-274) we have a reference to the size of the poet's library, when the god of Love says to Chaucer,

> Sixty bokes olde and newe
> Hast thou thy-self, alle fulle of stories grete.

In a poem which all critics agree is one of the earliest, if not the earliest, of Chaucer's genuine poems that have come down to us—the *Book of the Duchess*—the poet is revealed as a man already acquainted with a considerable body of literature. This poem furnishes incontrovertible evidence that Chaucer had read in Ovid, Machault, the authors of the *Roman de la Rose,* and other minor writers. There are a number of passages in the *Book of the Duchess* that go back ultimately to Boethius, though it is clear, as Skeat has shown,[1] that Chaucer got all these illustrations at second hand from the *Roman.* Except for Machault, whose influence does not appear to have made itself felt upon Chaucer to any great extent after the *Book of the Duchess* was written (if we disregard metrics), these writers and books—Ovid, the *Roman de la Rose,* and Boethius—had a permanent effect on our poet throughout his life. As Legouis says, the *Roman* and the *Consolations* were his constant companions. It is significant that in this youthful work we should find use made of the one book that was to be, perhaps, Chaucer's favorite volume above all others—the *Roman de la Rose.* It was probably his favorite volume in 1369. And if it be true, as Skeat conjectures and as appears very probable, that Chaucer's attention was first drawn to "Boece de Confort" through his perusal of the French poem,[1a] the English poet owed Jean de Meung no small additional debt for introduction to so fine a book as the *Consolations.* Of course, it is almost certain that if Jean de Meung had not mentioned Boethius, had not used him at all, Chaucer would have heard of the Latin philosopher through some other source. Machault, for instance, makes a complimentary allusion to Boethius

---

[1] *Chaucer,* II, xix-xxi.
[1a] Especially RR. 5757-61. See *Chaucer,* II, pp. x, xx-xxi.

by name in the *Confort d'Ami,* written about 1356.[2] Moreover, Boethius was well-known and his book revered all through the Middle Ages. But it is absurd to think of the *Roman de la Rose* without Boethius. Jean de Meung did make great use of the *Consolations,* a work which was directly or indirectly responsible for more than five thousand lines of the second part of the French poem. On the whole, the circumstantial evidence is strong that the late fifth-century philosopher was introduced to Chaucer by the thirteenth-century satirist and encyclopedist—Jean de Meung.

But Guillaume de Lorris must not be deprived of his share of the glory that every good teacher, merely by his information-giving qualities, is entitled to. The only book that Guillaume mentions—Macrobius's commentary on the *Somnium Scipionis*—was not overlooked by the student Geoffrey. Chaucer's earliest reference to this treatise occurs in the *Book of the Duchess:*

> Ne nat scarsly Macrobeus (284)
> (He that wroot al the avisioun
> That he mette, king Scipioun,
> The noble man, the Affrican . . .) (287)
> I trowe, a-rede my dremes even. (289)

[2] See Tarbé, pp. xxvi-xxvii, for a discussion of the date. The reference to Boethius, which can be found in Tarbé, p. 97, runs as follows:
> Et vues tu clerement savoir,
> Sans riens enclore, tout le voir
> Dont vient richesse et noblesse;
> Resgarde en livre de Boesse
> Que te dira, se oir le vues,
> Que tous les biens que perdre pues
> Sont de fortune, qui moult tost
> Le bien qu'elle a donné tout tost.

The lines in the *Roman de la Rose* run:

> Un acteur qui ot non Macrobes,
> Qui ne tint pas songes a lobes;
> Ançois escrist la vision,
> Qui avint au roi Cipion.   (7-10)

Clearly the English poet was following Guillaume de Lorris's lines almost literally. The fact that Chaucer adds the information that Scipio was "the Affrican"—a point that Guillaume does not mention—does not affect the soundness of the theory that Chaucer first heard of Macrobius and *Scipio's Dream* through the French poet. Scipio Africanus was the common name of the Roman general, whom Chaucer had possibly heard of in his school-days. Just as Guillaume appeals to Macrobius as an authority on dreams, so Chaucer says that this Latin writer would be put to considerable difficulty to interpret the wonderful vision the account of which is to follow in the *Book of the Duchess*. Before he wrote the *Parlement of Foules,* however, Chaucer had certainly looked into Macrobius for himself.

These two probable cases of the English poet's becoming acquainted through the *Roman de la Rose* with books which he used later in his work—one of them, indeed, becoming a life-long friend and the other a convenient authority to allude to, as in the *Nonne Preestes Tale,*—lead us to believe that perhaps other authors were either introduced to Chaucer by Jean de Meung, or at least recommended by him as worth reading. To be sure, in the absence of external proof, it is hazardous to insist on the theory, especially as it is pretty certain that Chaucer's opportunities for extensive reading were as great as Jean de Meung's. But the fact that, as we shall see in later chapters of this book, the English poet went to the Frenchman for every sort of illustration, seemingly regarding the *Roman* as a sort of universal cyclopedia of useful knowledge, and the fact that of the twenty-four writers Jean de Meung mentions and uses, Chaucer knew either at first or second hand all but four—these two facts give us courage to suggest that in a pretty real sense Jean de Meung was Chaucer's schoolmaster.

Let us look briefly at the literary history of the poem which the English poet knew so early and so intimately. The *Roman de la Rose* was finished nearly sixty years before Chaucer was born.[3] There are to-day several hundred manuscripts of it in existence. The British Museum alone has thirteen, five of which date from the fourteenth century.[4] The fact that so large a number of hand-written copies should have been preserved in addition to the twenty-one printed editions between 1480 and 1538 is indicative of widespread favor. Another significant phenomenon in the history of the *Roman de la Rose* is this, noted by

[3] Langlois, in Petit de Julleville's *Histoire de la langue et de la littérature française* (Paris, 1878-1900), says that Guillaume de Lorris's portion of the poem was finished somewhere between 1225 and 1230 (Vol. II, p. 108), and that Jean de Meung took up the work about 1270 (p. 127). Pierre Marteau has shown by internal evidence that the poem must have been completed by 1282 (in his edition of the *Roman*, I, p. xxiii), for in lines 7373-7381 Charles of Anjou is mentioned as the reigning king of Sicily. Now, Charles of Anjou died in 1285, but he had been driven out of Sicily in 1282.

[4] See F. W. Bourdillon: *The Early Editions of the Roman de la Rose* (London, 1906. Printed for the Bibliographical Society).

Ellis: "Strange to say, except the translation made by Chaucer and either one or two other contemporary hands, of seven thousand six hundred and ninety-eight lines, no attempt has been made to present it (i.e., the French poem) in any other European language, with the single exception of a German rendering into verse of the first part, by H. Fährmann, printed in 1839."[5]

As a half-way exception to Ellis's statement we might mention an Italian poem of the thirteenth century, named *Il Fiore,* consisting of two hundred and thirty-two sonnets imitated from the *Roman de la Rose*—an indication that the French poem must soon have become known in Italy. Miss Cipriani has shown that Boccaccio knew the *Roman* and used it in his *Filostrato,* and Sandras tells us that Petrarch had a copy of the *Roman,* though he did not care for the poem.[5a] The very dearth of translations is, I believe, but another proof of a general knowledge of the French poem. The original material, which was presented in a language certainly understood by the educated classes of England and Italy, was so absorbed and adapted into the literature of the thirteenth and fourteenth centuries that no need of a translation was felt. And it was through Jean de Meung's influence that the *Roman de la Rose* as a whole became popular; for Guillaume de Lorris's portion of it lay practically unimitated for forty years.[6]

---

[5] *The Romance of the Rose,* Englished and Edited by F. S. Ellis (Dent), Vol. I, p. viii.

[5a] *Etude,* p. 68. Sandras cites Petrarch's *Carm.* Bk. I, ep. 30.

[6] See F. M. Warren: *On the Date and Composition of Guillaume de Lorris's Roman de la Rose.* Pub. Mod. Lang. Assoc., 1908. Warren misinterprets the fact that there is in existence only one MS.

One of the fundamental differences between the two parts of the *Roman de la Rose* is that the object of the earlier writer was primarily to amuse; the object of the second, to instruct. Guillaume de Lorris gave his century a hand-book of the art of love; Jean de Meung, a guide to almost everything else. Both evidently took their work seriously; though Jean appears to have regarded with not a little ridicule the production of Guillaume. The second half of the poem (if we may so speak of de Meung's eighteen thousand lines) was written in a period in many respects different from that forty years before, for in the last half of the thirteenth century new social and political conditions had arisen. For example, the orders of friars, founded during the first quarter of the century, had become powerful and, we may believe Jean de Meung, corrupt. There was a general movement to free science and learning from the yoke of the church. A kind of renaissance had begun in France during the last half of the thirteenth century, one result of which was the founding by 1320 of no less than six colleges for the common people. Teaching in the vernacular was taken up. Many cyclopedias of general learning appeared, the authors of which wished to let the laity share in part of the knowledge of the clergy.

of the first part of the *Roman de la Rose* not followed by the portion by Jean de Meung. He infers from this unique copy (B. N. fr. 12786) that the part written by Guillaume de Lorris was unknown until Jean de Meung produced his own continuation of the poem. As a matter of fact, the literary influence of the *Roman* appears to have been negligible until after the appearance of the whole poem; but Langlois is of the opinion that even before Jean wrote, the work of Guillaume de Lorris was widely read. See *Les Manuscrits du Roman de la Rose*, p. 235.

The continuation of the *Roman de la Rose* by Jean de Meung was one of these cyclopedias, says Langlois, and for the instruction of the people at large the poet inserted into his long poem the good things of as many Latin works as he could incorporate.

It is pertinent to ask, Why did Jean de Meung's cyclopedia become so popular if it was only one of a large number of works on general learning? There are several reasons that might be suggested, but the most probable seems to me this: Jean de Meung realized with Horace that

Omne tulit punctum, qui miscuit utile dulci;

for the Frenchman, speaking of the purpose of poets, says:

Profit et delectation
C'est toute lor entencion. (RR. 16179-80)

His good sense in recognizing that the educational pill must be sugar-coated and his judgment in selecting the flavor of the coating are responsible without doubt for the fact that the public eagerly took what he had to give it. To Guillaume de Lorris's "lovers' guide-book"—which, if we keep the figure, was the sugar-coating—was due in no small measure the success of the *Roman de la Rose* as a whole. Jean de Meung took up and continued his predecessor's work because he saw that his predecessor's work would promote his. And if we may judge from the literary imitations which the *Roman* inspired during the fourteenth and fifteenth centuries, the coating proved the more acceptable part of the medicine. The attacks which the court and clergy began to make on the poem at the end of the fourteenth century were all directed against Jean de Meung's portion.

Jean de Meung's authorities were numerous as well as esteemed. The investigations of Langlois into the origins and sources of the *Roman de la Rose* afford material for a comparison of the learning of Jean de Meung with the learning of Chaucer. Of the authors and books besides Boethius and the Bible which are mentioned and used by Jean, the following appear in Chaucer's work also:[7] St. Augustine,[8] Homer,[9] Plato,[10] Aristotle,[11] Theophrastus,[12] Ptolemy,[13] the *Almagest*,[14] Cicero,[15] Vergil,[16] Livy,[17] Ovid,[18] Lucan,[19] Suetonius,[20] Juvenal,[21] Claudian,[22] Vale-

[7] The numbers below refer to the *Roman de la Rose*. The references in Chaucer may easily be found by consulting Skeat's Index of Proper Names (*Chaucer*, VI, pp. 359-380).

[8] 12239.

[9] 7516, 14560.

[10] 7852, 7846, 13830, 19995.

[11] 9700, 18966, 19132.

[12] 9310.

[13] 7781, 14578.

[14] 7783, 19506.

[15] *Tulles* 5151, 5469, 6128; *Tules* 17132. Chaucer has Tullius seventeen times.

[16] 9758, 17262, 17523, 20101, 22327.

[17] 6329, 6369, 9365, 17274. The name always appears as Titus Livius in the *Roman*. Chaucer has Titus twice, Titus (or Tytus) Livius three times. He does not use Livy or Livius alone.

[18] 8737, 14560, 21113, 22443. J. de Meung does not use Naso, though Chaucer has the name three times.

[19] 6395.

[20] 7194.

[21] 9038, 9458, 9486, 9891, 22437.

[22] 7091.

rius,[23] Heloise.[24] Of the other writers whose names appear in the *Roman de la Rose*—Pythagoras, Sallust, Horace, Solinus, Justinian, Albumazar, Abelard—Chaucer mentions none, though he appears to have known Horace, Sallust, and Justinian at second hand. Chaucer does speak of Aleyn (PF. 316), but curiously enough Jean de Meung does not once refer by name to the author of the *De Planctu Naturae* and the *Anticlaudianus,* works to which he owed directly or indirectly more than two thousand lines. Jean de Meung used, moreover, many minor authorities whose names, for reasons of his own, he did not see fit to mention. And so did Chaucer. Indeed, Chaucer never speaks of Jean de Meung, and only once refers indirectly to the author of the *Roman,*—

> For out of doute, I verraily suppose,
> That he that wroot the Romance of the Rose
> Ne coude of it the beautee wel devyse.[25]

Finally, it should be remembered that Chaucer's use of the sources he has in common with Jean de Meung often differs from the Frenchman's use of them. This fact, however, does not constitute an objection to the theory that Chaucer heard of many of these very sources through Jean's reference to them. Of course, the English poet investigated for himself, and read at first hand where the originals were accessible.

We have seen that it is likely that Chaucer, acting upon

[23] 9440, 9470, 9478, 10168.
[24] 9507, 9554.
[25] Marchantes Tale (E), 2031-33. The *he* of line 2032 is Guillaume de Lorris, says Skeat.

definite hints thrown out in the *Roman de la Rose,* read in the Latin for himself Boethius and Macrobius. With some of the ancient writers it appears that Chaucer had to be satisfied with an indirect acquaintance, just as Jean de Meung had to be. As we shall see in the next chapter, there is no convincing evidence that either Chaucer or Meung knew Livy and Suetonius at first hand any more than they knew Theophrastus directly. Nor have we much reason to believe that either the English or the French poet had seen Ptolemy's *Almagest,* though both refer directly to it and ostensibly quote from it. Chaucer, in the Wife of Bath's allusions to Ptolemy, is clearly following Jean de Meung,[26] just as he was following the French

[26] Skeat, in his Index of Authors Quoted or Referred To (Vol. VI, pp. 384ff.), implies that Chaucer knew Ptolemy's *Almagest* at first hand. The only evidence is a gloss in the Ellsmere MS. to the *Man of Lawes Tale,* (B) 295ff., which says, "Unde Ptholomeus, libro I, cap. 8." But Chaucer's use of the *Almagest* elsewhere leads us to believe that he probably derived his information about the nine revolving heavens from some intermediate source, possibly Dante's *Convito,* Bk. II, chapters 3-4.

The citations from the *Almagest* which connect themselves directly with the *Roman de la Rose* are the two made by the Wife of Bath, (D) 182-3, 324-7. In a note to the first of these passages Skeat says, "With regard to its being written in Ptolemy's *Almagest,* Tyrwhitt quaintly remarks: 'I suspect that the Wife of Bath's copy was very different from any that I have been able to meet with . . . ' I have no doubt that the Wife is simply copying for convenience these words in the *Roman de la Rose:*

>Car nous lisons de Tholomee
>Une parole moult honeste
>Au comencier de s'Almageste, etc.   (7781ff.)

Jean de Meung then cites a passage of quite another kind, but the Wife of Bath did not stick at such a trifle." (*Chaucer,* V, p. 295.)

poet in the story of Nero, where he refers to "Swetonius," and in the story of Virginius, where he mentions "Titus Livius."

Chaucer's extensive use of many different parts of the *Roman de la Rose* in the *Book of the Duchess* makes it clear that before 1369 the poet was familiar with the French poem *as a whole;* that he had not only read thoroughly the part written by Guillaume de Lorris but also that by Jean de Meung. If this is true, we are justified in believing that the English poet's acquaintance with many of the writers he was to know more intimately later, was made through the authoritative pages of the *Roman*. For everyone's learning has to start somewhere; from the very beginning of his literary career, so far as a record of it has been preserved to us, Chaucer seems to have been familiar with the French poem. None of the other writers

Skeat does not mention the fact that the Duenna's glib allusion to

Tholomee,
Par qui fu moult science amee (14578-9),

and in fact all the references to him in the *Roman de la Rose* gave Langlois as much trouble as the Wife caused Tyrwhitt. The French critic writes, "J'ai vainement cherché dans les oeuvres de Ptolémée les trois passages cités sous son nom dans le Roman de la Rose (vers 7781-85, 14576-79, 19502-9); je n'en ai trouvé aucuns." (Sources et origines, p. 110.)

Can it be merely coincidence that both poets should credit Ptolemy with proverbs that two excellent critics have not been able to run down? One is tempted to believe that through some gloss in his MS. of the *Roman de la Rose* Chaucer was referred to a book that went under the name of Ptolemy during the Middle Ages and that has not come down to us. It could hardly be that the English poet was so well acquainted with the *Almagest* that he knew that Jean de Meung was "bluffing."

he drew upon for material in the *Book of the Duchess* could have furnished our poet with a list of authorities worthy of study.

CHAPTER II

ALLUSIONS TO HISTORICAL AND LEGENDARY PERSONS AND PLACES

NERO

Two of the stories included in the *Monkes Tale,* and the *Phisiciens Tale* of Apius and Virginius, are the only extended narratives which critics say Chaucer derived from the *Roman de la Rose.* And these are not attributed unreservedly to the influence of the French poem.

The first of these stories, the account of Nero (B. 3653-3740), according to Skeat, makes use of three sources particularly; Boccaccio's *De Casibus Virorum Illustrium,* lib. vii, cap. 4; the *Roman de la Rose,* ll. 6911-87, 7171 ff.; and Boethius's *De Consolatione Philosophiae,* bk. II, met. vi, bk. III, met. iv. Jean de Meung's information about Nero was probably not drawn from the *Lives of the Twelve Caesars,* although the French poet refers not only to this book by name, but to its author, Suetonius (RR. 7191-94). Chaucer, too, mentions Suetonius, but his line

  As telleth us Swetonius, (B. 3655)

was pretty clearly suggested by Jean de Meung's

  Si cum Suétonius l'escript, (RR. 7194)

for Boethius does not mention the author of the *Twelve Caesars.* Skeat says that Chaucer took some details in his account from Suetonius, but there is no evidence that our poet was familiar with this Latin author. Langlois says that as for Jean's narrative of Nero's crimes against his mother, brother, sister, the senators, and Seneca, "rien ne prouve que Jean ait connu Suétone" (p. 130). It would appear, then, that Chaucer's information concerning "Swetonius" was really third hand. Jean's allusion to the horrible circumstances and motive of the death of Agrippina is found neither in Boethius nor in Suetonius. Langlois observes, "Pendant tout le moyen âge on a cru et répété que Néron avait fait ouvrir le ventre de sa mère pour voir ou il avait pris naissance. C'est un passage de Tacite,[1] celui de Suétone que je viens de rappeler,[2] et un autre de Dion Cassius,[2a] qui ont donné naissance à cette légende" (p. 129). Moreover, neither Boethius nor Suetonius hints that Nero outraged his sister. Jean de Meung refers to this crime (RR. 6944), with which the Middle Ages often reproached the wicked emperor.[3] The murder of Seneca is alluded to in Boethius[4] and Vincent de Beauvais.[5] In this episode Chaucer is pretty clearly following the *Roman de la Rose;* for the motive of the crime is the same in both

[1] Adspexeritne matrem corporis exanimem Nero, et formam corporis eius laudaverit, sunt qui tradiderint, sunt qui abnuant. *Annales* XIV, ix.

[2] Ad visendum interfectae cadaver accurrisse, contrectasse membra, alia vituperasse, alia laudasse, sitique interim aborta bibisse. *Nero,* xxxiv.

[2a] *Historiae Romanae*, LXI, xiv.

[3] See Langlois, p. 130, for an enumeration of the medieval authors who refer to this incident. None of them was known to Chaucer, probably.

[4] *De Cons. Phil.*, III, pr. 5.
[5] *Speculum historiale*, X, 9.

accounts. Langlois remarks, "Nulle part je n'ai rencontré le motif indiqué par Jean de Meun, que Néron, jugeant indigne d'un empereur l'habitude qu'il avait prise dans son enfance de se lever en présence de son maître, ne trouva d'autre moyen de la perdre que de se débarrasser de Sénèque." (p. 130.)

Skeat, as noted above, names Boccaccio's *De Casibus* as a main source for the Monk's tale of Nero,[6] but he nowhere points out any definite borrowings. On examination of the story as Chaucer tells it, I find that the English poet had to go no farther than Boethius and Jean de Meung for his material, with the possible exception of stanza two.[7] Furthermore, the account in the *Roman de la Rose* follows Boethius so closely in places that it is practically impossible in some lines to decide which was Chaucer's immediate original. In a note to B. 3669 ff., Skeat says, "This passage follows Boethius, bk. II, met. 6, very closely, as is evident by comparing it with Chaucer's translation." But this translation, it should be observed, is eked out by many glosses, which Miss Cipriani has cleverly shown might have been derived from the *Roman de la Rose*.[8] Moreover, Boethius is silent about Nero's crime against his sister, and does not speak of the tyrant's commanding wine to be brought to him after he has looked on the corpse of his

[6] *Chaucer*, V, p. 242.

[7] Possibly taken from Eutropius: *Breviarum Historiae Romanae*, VII, ix.

[8] The following explanations which Chaucer has inserted in his translation of bk. II, met. 6, Miss Cipriani refers to the *Roman*:

Bo. 5-6 from RR. 6930-32,
Bo. 8 from RR. 6928,
Bo. 12-13, 15-16, 19, from RR. 6984-86.

mother. The *Roman de la Rose* has both details (ll. 6940-42, 6944). Koeppel's parallels, taken with what has just been said, prove conclusively that the Monk's story of Nero owes more directly to Jean de Meung than to Boethius.[9] If additional evidence is desired, it may be found in the agreement, hitherto unrecorded, I believe, of the two accounts describing the manner of Seneca's death. Chaucer writes:

>And thus hath Nero slayn his maister dere. (3708)
>But natheles this Seneca the wyse (3705)
>Chees in a bath to deye in this manere
>Rather than han another tormentyse. (3707)
>... he [i. e., Nero] in a bath made him to
>   blede (3699)
>On bothe his armes, til he moste dye.

The *Roman de la Rose* has it thus:

>Seneque mist-il a martire (6947)
>Son bon mestre, et li fist eslire
>De quel mort morir il vorroit. (6949)
>. . . . .
>Donc soit, dist-il, uns bains chaufes, (6952)
>Puisque d'echaper est néans,
>Si me faites seignier léans,
>Si que je muire en l'iaue chaude,
>Et que m'ame joieuse et baude,
>A Dieu qui la forma ge rende, (6957)
>Qui d'autres tormens la défende! (6958)

---

[9] The German critic has pointed out the following close correspondences:

B.	RR.	B.	RR.
3669-70	6926-27	3719-24	7163-70
3672-75	6929-42	3725-28	7173-79
3677-82	6944	3732-33	7171-72
3701-704	6975-81	3735-39	7183-88

For the phrase "on bothe his armes" I have found no previous authority. It is entirely possible that when writing this phrase Chaucer had before him, or in mind, a manuscript picture of the death of the philosopher.[10]

CROESUS

Tyrwhitt was the first to remark that this story (B. 3917-56) seems to have been taken from the *Roman de la Rose*. The French account, extending from line 7225 to line 7358, includes a good deal of moralizing digression, much more than Chaucer will admit into the thirty-four lines of his story. The English poet's narrative is straightforward enough, although the dénouement

> Anhanged was Cresus, the proude king,
> His royal trone mighte him nat availle   (3949-50)

comes very suddenly upon Phanie's interpretation of her father's dream. This abrupt ending suggests that Chaucer was tired of "swich ensaumples"—for the French text has a nineteen-line answer that the disgusted Croesus makes to his prophetic daughter. This, Chaucer passes by. Except for line 3918, where reference is made to Cyrus, Chaucer did not go outside the *Roman de la Rose* for material;

[10] The early editions and manuscripts of the *Roman de la Rose* were plentifully supplied with illustrations. Marteau (V) reproduces some of the woodcuts that appeared in Jean Dupré's edition (Paris, about 1493). In one of these Seneca is represented as sitting in a tub of water up to his waist. A surgeon is cutting the veins in the philosopher's right arm, while a benevolent-looking old man stands behind Seneca. The artist doubtless meant this third figure for Nero (it wears a crown), but he has not made of it the monster that the text would lead us to imagine.

line 3918 he took from Boethius, bk. II, pr. 2.[11] Skeat has pointed out definite lines in Chaucer that agree with Jean de Meung's account,[12] and more might be added to his list. Compare, for instance:

> Of which he was so proud and eek so fayn. (3931)
> Thus warned she him ful plat and ful playn (3947)
> Anhanged was Cresus . . . (3949)
> His royal trone mighte him nat availle. (3950)
> Dont si grant fiance acueilli, (RR. 7247)
> Que comme fox s'enorgueilli; (7248)
> Ainsinc le chastioit Phanie.[13] (7329)
> Qu'il ne se pot onques desfendre (7357)
> Qu'el n'el feist au gibet pendre. (7358)

Koeppel has noted that lines B. 3940-3945 correspond with RR. 7277-7283.

As is well known, Jean de Meung uses the histories of

---

[11] Nesciebas Croesum regem Lydorum Cyro paullo ante formidabilem, mox deinde miserandum rogi flammis traditum, misso caelitus imbre defensum?

[12] B. 3917-22 is from RR. 7226-30
    3934-38 " "   7243-45
    3941 " "   7283
    3948 " "   7249-50 But, as noted above, line 3918 is not from the *Roman de la Rose* but from *De Cons. Phil.*

Skeat, following Sandras, also compares HF. 103-108 with RR. 7225-27, and shows that Chaucer's form Lyde was taken from the French. (III, 248.)

[13] In *Chaucer* V, 246, Skeat says that Vincent of Beauvais's *Speculum Historiale*, iii, 17, seems to be the account which is followed in the *Roman de la Rose*. But Langlois observes (p. 134), "L'épisode de la mort de Crésus, tel qu'il est raconté dans Le Roman de la Rose, a pour point de départ une allusion de Boèce, mais ses développements, en particulier le rôle de Phanie, fille de roi de Lydie, ne se trouvent que dans les Mythographes" (I, 196, et II, 190).

Nero, Emperor of Rome, and Croesus, King of Lydia, to illustrate the caprice of Fortune. Chaucer uses these stories in the same way, and it should be noticed that throughout the *Monkes Tale* emphasis is laid on the fickleness and falseness of the goddess.[14] Just as the French poet cites from contemporary history the destruction of Conradin and Manfred in Sicily by Charles of Anjou, Chaucer recalls briefly the comparatively recent events in the lives of Peter, King of Spain, and Peter, King of Cyprus.

From what has been said, it will be seen that Boethius and Jean de Meung are entitled to a somewhat prominent place in the development of literature of the "Falls of Princes" type.

SAMSON

The story of Samson in the *Monkes Tale* does not emphasize so much the capriciousness of Fortune as the evil consequences of not keeping one's secrets. It is possible that what Jean de Meung says of Samson and Dalila influenced at least slightly the line of development and the emphasis of the Monk's story. To be sure, the account in the *Roman de la Rose* is very short, not more than a dozen lines (17614-17625), but it is used as a sort of exemplum to Genius's long sermon on the foolishness of husbands who cannot keep their own counsel, but are lured by deceitful mistresses and wives to disclose what should not be told.[15] The conclusion to the Monk's version—

[14] Cf. B. 3185-86, 3326, 3379, 3431-35, 3537, 3587, 3635-36, 3740, 3773, 3851-52, 3953-56.
[15] R.R. 17262 ff.

> Beth war by this ensample old and playn
> That no men telle hir conseil til hir wyves
> Of swich thing as they wolde han secree fayn,
> If that it touche hir limmes or hir lyves. (3281-84)

seems to be a succinct summary of the warning given in the *Roman* 17478-17637.[16] An explanation of Chaucer's form Dalida (B. 3253), which Skeat (V. 230) goes to some length to account for, may be found in Jean's spelling of the word, which is exactly the same as Chaucer's:—

> Ainsinc Sansons . . .
> Fu par Dalida deceus.   (RR. 9956)
> Dalida la malicieuse.   (RR. 17614)

Finally, compare B. 3253-57, 3261-62 with RR. 17614-26, 9953-56.

THE PHISICIENS TALE

Tyrwhitt characteristically remarks in his notes to the Phisiciens Tale, "In the Discourse, etc., I forgot to mention the *Roman de la Rose* as one of the sources of this tale; although, upon examination, I find that our author has drawn more from thence than from either Gower or Livy." Skeat agrees with Tyrwhitt, and says, "It is absurd to argue, as in Bell's Chaucer, that our poet must necessarily have known Livy 'in the original' and then to draw the conclusion that we must look to Livy only as the true source of the tale. . . The belief that Chaucer

---

[16] In his reference to Samson and Dalila (B. Duch. 738-739), among other stock pairs of woful lovers, Chaucer probably had in mind the passage in the *Roman*, 9945-9956, which Koeppel pointed out.

may have read the tale "in the original" does not alter the fact that he trusted more to the French text!"[17] Jean de Meung may have used the Latin historian's account, although, as Langlois says, "Il est probable que cette imitation est faite de mémoire, car Jean de Meung commet une inexactitude, en disant que Virginius a coupé la tête à sa fille."[18] Chaucer follows the French poet in having Virginius kill his daughter by cutting off her head.

Skeat is rather misleading in stating that the English poet "trusted more to the French text" than to the Latin; for there is, indeed, very little detailed narrative about Virginia in the *Roman de la Rose*. In this poem Reason is haranguing the Lover on various themes, and the subject of justice leads her to a discussion of corrupt judges: "Many a judge who hangs a thief," she says, "is the one who ought to be hanged for all the crimes he has done." And then she plunges right into the story of Appius's villainy:—

> Ne fist bien Apius[19] a pendre
> Qui fist a son serjant emprendre
> Par faus tesmoings, fauce querele
> Contre Virgine la pucele, etc.   (RR. 6324-27)

And having finished the narrative, which is after all

---

[17] *Works*, V, p. 260.

[18] Livy writes, "Data venia, seducit filiam ac nutricem prope Cloacinae ad tabernas . . . atque ibi, ab lanio cultro arrepto, 'Hoc te uno, quo possum,' ait, 'modo filia, in libertatem vindico.' Pectus deinde puellae transfigit, respectansque ad tribunal, 'Te,' inquit, 'Appi, tuumque caput sanguine hoc consecro.'" Bk. III, chap. 48.

[19] Jean de Meung, Gower, and Chaucer all spell the name *Apius*; Livy, of course, has Appius.

nothing more than incidental illustrative allusion, Reason returns to her theme that judges are scoundrels:—

> Briefment juges font trop d'outrages. (RR. 6394)

and goes on to quote a proverb from Lucan.

Chaucer's indebtedness to the French as source is very much less than Skeat's statements and parallels would lead one to think. The English critic calls attention to the following:[20]

C. 1	RR. 6329-30	C. 184	cf. RR. 6339-44
135-38	6331-33	203	6359-65
165	cf. 6335-38	255-276	6371-93
168-69	6347-49		

Let us examine these correspondences in detail. Chaucer's references to Livy (line 1) may very likely have been suggested by Jean's "Si cum dist Titus Livius"; but it does not necessarily follow, as Skeat would imply, that all Chaucer knew of Livy was this reference to him. It is hard to see how lines 135-38 can be derived from

> Por ce qu'il ne pooit donter
> La pucele, qui n'avoit cure
> Ne de li ne de sa luxure. (6331-33)

Nor, given the general situation, is there much resemblance between Chaucer's lines

> And seyde, "lord, if that it be your wille,
> As dooth me right upon this pitous bille." (165-66)

[20] I disregard for the present parallels drawn from other parts of the *Roman de la Rose*.

and the French

> Sire juges, donnes sentence
> Por moi, car la pucele est moie. (6335-36)

Lines 168-69 are clearly from the passage cited by Skeat. Line 184, which reads "Which fro myn hous was stole upon a night," is not much more like the French "De mon hostel me fu emblee" than like the Latin of Livy: "Puellam, domi suae natam, *furtoque inde in domum Virginii translatam.*" Lines 203 ff. somewhat resemble RR. 6359-65: the "worthy knight" does recall "Li bons prodons, bons chevaliers." The last passage (lines 255-276), or the summary of the events after the death of Virginia, follows the French text closely; but Skeat has not noted that 262-266 are Chaucer's own addition.

It will thus be seen that not more than a score of lines in the English story can be surely traced to the influence of the *Roman de la Rose*. Moreover, the French account does not explain the relation between Claudius and Appius except through what is said in 6325; and there is nothing to correspond with the long passage in Chaucer telling of Appius's conspiracy with the "subtil cherl" (139-164). The poet was evidently drawing upon his imagination or some unknown source, for he follows neither Livy, Gower, nor Boccaccio.[21] As Skeat has observed, the fine dialogue included by lines 207 and 253 appears to be entirely original with Chaucer. The placing of this scene between Virginius and his daughter in their own home is not found

[21] Gower, in *Confessio Amantis*, VII, 5131-5306, and Boccaccio, in *De Claris Mulieribus*, chap. 57, follow Livy essentially.

elsewhere before Chaucer. The description of Virginia, which, with the moralizing of the narrator, covers the first one hundred and twenty lines of the poem, is original; that is, originally introduced; many of the details are conventional and reminiscent enough.

The superiority of the Phisiciens Tale as a work of art, if we consider the story properly as beginning at line 105, is easily seen by comparing it with Gower's, Boccaccio's, and Jean de Meung's versions. Chaucer could not refrain from pointing a moral—a medieval propensity—but this is kept distinct from the narrative, once the story is under way.[21a] The events follow each other logically, the motives are clearly set forth, the various scenes are presented dramatically and vividly, and the conclusion hastens after the climax has been reached deliberately and feelingly. Altogether, there is a fine balance maintained, which one feels is lacking in the earlier poetic forms of this tragedy. And Chaucer is greatest in his original scenes and situations. Indeed, except for the summarizing passage at the end, we may say that the story is as much Chaucer's own as Shakespeare's Roman plays are his own. Furthermore, the Phisiciens Tale of Appius and Virginius may be remembered as perhaps the finest English telling of the story in substantially the form in which it has been popular in English literature even down to the nineteenth century.

In addition to the extended records of historical or

[21a] In his discussion of the *Phisiciens Tale*, Tatlock proposes and elaborates the theory that Chaucer was trying to make the story point a moral to Elizabeth, second daughter of John of Gaunt and Blanche. See *Development and Chronology of Chaucer's Works*, p. 154.

quasi-historical events just discussed, many of Chaucer's chance references to real or legendary persons and places have been attributed to his reading of the *Roman de la Rose*. As these are scattered throughout the poems and have no connection with one another, their consideration must be more or less haphazard. Our concern is simply to find out whether Chaucer in these cases was entirely dependent on the French poem, or could have obtained his information elsewhere. Most of the allusions of this class can be disposed of summarily; hence I have grouped together, first, those that it seems likely Chaucer adapted from the French poem, and, second, those of which the source is open to question.

I. Allusions Reasonably Supposed to Have Been Derived from the *Roman de la Rose*

(a) *Alcipyades,* B. Duch. 1057. Chaucer's spelling of the name (cf. RR. 9692-95) and the fact that at the time of writing the *Book of the Duchess* he does not appear to have known Boethius,[22] except through Jean de Meung, constitute the evidence.

(b) *Alocen* (Alhazen), F. 232, and *Aristotle,* F. 233. These two philosophers are mentioned within four lines of each other in the *Roman:* 18966, 18969. Alhazen's treatise on optics is also referred to. Koeppel has noted other close parallels between the French poem and F. 228ff, making

---

[22] Jean mentions Boece (9698) in connection with this passage about Alcibiades. See Skeat's note, I, 489. All the MSS. of B. Duch. read *Alcipyades,* the form in the most authoritative MSS. of the *Roman*. Langlois accepts this spelling.

it reasonable to suppose that the English lines are at least reminiscent of the French. With the English passage compare particularly RR. 18969-71, 18979-81, 19111, 19122, 19182-87.

(c) *Argus* (Algus), B. Duch. 435-440. Skeat's note (I, 475) is convincing. The passage imitated is RR. 13731-37.[23]

(d) *Absolon* (Absolom) Leg. G. W. 249. Koeppel called attention to RR. 14817, of which Chaucer's line is almost a literal translation. At the same time it must be remembered that Absalom's beauty was proverbial.[24] This fact accounts, doubtless, for the name of the handsome parish clerk in the Milleres Tale:—

> Now was ther of that chirche a parish-clerk,
> That whiche that was y-cleped Absolon,
> Crul was his heer, and as the gold it shoon.
> (A. 3312-14)

(e) *Helowys* (Heloise) W. B.'s Prol. (D.) 677-8. Skeat writes, "I have no doubt at all that Chaucer derived his knowledge of her from the short sketch of her life given in the *Roman de la Rose*" (7510-73). Inasmuch as the *Wife of Bath* devotes only two lines to this abbess, the English critic is probably right.[25]

---

[23] Langlois evidently did not understand these lines, which he says are from Ovid, *Ars Amatoria*, III, 618: "Quot fuerant Argo lumina, verba dabis."

[24] The color of his hair is not mentioned in the Hebrew Scriptures, but the abundance is. See 2 Sam., 14:25-26.

[25] Langlois may pertinently be quoted here. "On sait que Jean de Meung a traduit la correspondance d'Abailart et d'Héloïse; cette traduction est conservée dans un manuscrit assez fautif, de la première moitié du quatorzième siècle. Il est difficile de dire si elle

(f) *Penelope,* B. Duch. 1081. Lines 1080-85, with the rhymes *Grece: Lucrece,* and the reference to Titus Livius, seem to make it practically certain that Chaucer was following Jean de Meung, but not, as Skeat points out, lines 9404-05; rather lines 9358-61, 9365:—

> Pénélope néis prendroit (9358)
> Qui bien à li prendre entendroit;
> Si n'ot meillor fame en Grèce.
> Si feroit-il, par foi, Lucrèce.
> . . . . . .
> N'onc, ce dit Titus Livius, etc. (9365)

(g) *Saint Leonard,* HF. 117-118. The line "To make lythe of that was hard" seems to connect this allusion to the saint with RR. 9582-87.

(h) *Scipio,* HF. 916-918. Chaucer had surely by this time read for himself Macrobius's commentary on the *Dream;* but the compact account of Scipio in this poem strongly suggests that the poet was thinking of some lines near the end of the *Roman de la Rose:*

> Si cum fist Scipion jadis,
> Qui vit enfer et paradis,
> Et ciel et air, et mer, et terre, (19302-4)

—a resemblance hitherto overlooked.

(i) *Socrates,* B. Duch 717-719. Socrates was a classic example of patience, and medieval writers were fond of

est antèrieure au Roman de la Rose; du moins, il est certain que notre auteur connaissait déjà ces lettres lorsqu'il écrivait son poème" (p. 147). It is interesting to note that the account of these two lovers in the *Roman de la Rose* is older by thirty years than any existing manuscript of the original letters.

using his experiences as illustrative material. It is interesting to compare how Gower's Lover, Jean de Meung's Lover, and the Knight in the *Book of the Duchess* regard the old philosopher's stoicism. In the *Book of the Duchess* we read—

> Remembre yow of Socrates;
> For he ne counted nat three strees
> Of noght that Fortune coude do.
> "No," quod he, "I can not so." (717-720)

Jean's Lover says with much spirit—

> Ge ne priseroie trois chiches
> Socrate, combien qu'il fust riches,
> Ne plus n'en quier oir parler. (7652-54)

For Gower, see *Confessio Amantis*, III, 639-714 and following. Troilus is another lover who behaves very much as the hero of the *Roman*, though he is somewhat more dignified in his remonstrance with Pandarus and his tiresome saws:

> Freend, though that I stille lye,
> I am not deef; now pees, and cry no more;
> For I have herd thy wordes and thy lore;
> But suffre me my mischief to biwayle,
> For thy proverbes may me nought avayle.
> (T. i, 752–6)

But the situation was conventional enough among poets in Chaucer's day. The lines Chaucer was directly imitating in B. Duch. 717-719 were RR. 6581-86.[26] He appears to

[26] See Skeat's note, I, 481, where the French text is quoted. Langlois thinks that Jean took these verses from Solinus: "Inter alia Socratis magna praeclarum est, quod in eodem vultus tenore etiam adversis interpellantibus perstitit." *Sources et origines*, etc., p. 132.

have had them in mind also when writing a part of his poem on *Fortune:*—

> O Socrates, thou stedfast champioun,
> She never mighte be thy tormentour;
> Thou never dreddest her oppressioun,
> Ne in hir chere founde thou no savour. (17-20)

(j) *Zanzis* (Zeuxis), C. 16-18. Skeat (V. 261) shows conclusively that Chaucer derived his knowledge of Zeuxis from the *Roman*, 17113ff. "Jean de Meung is there speaking of Nature and of the inability of artists to vie with her, which is precisely Chaucer's argument here."

II. Allusions not Necessarily Inspired by the *Roman de la Rose*

Koeppel has drawn attention to the fact that many of the stock examples registered in the *Book of the Duchess* are used in a similar way in the *Roman de la Rose*. The correspondences he has noticed are these:

Helen and Lavyne,[26a] (B. Duch. 331)   (RR. 21818-19)
Daedalus, (B. Duch. 570)   (22365)
Echo and Narcissus, (B. Duch. 735)   (6574)
Dalida and Samson, (B. Duch. 738; D. 721-23) (9953-56)

[26a] The lines from the *Roman* are

> "N'onques Helaine ne Lavine
> Ne furent de color si fine."

The identical rhymes, *Lavyne: fyne* and *Lavine: fine*, besides the presence of the name Helen, seem to add weight to Koeppel's parallel. But there is nothing particularly striking about either passage; and the resemblance, it seems to me, may be nothing more than a coincidence.

Skeat contributes the following:

Dido and Æneas, (B. Duch. 732-33; HF. 239ff) (14115ff)
Hercules, (B. Duch. 1058) (9933, 9941)
Dejanira and Hercules, (D. 724-26) (9945-56)
The poisoned shirt, (HF. 1413-14) (9948)
Genelon, (B. Duch. 1121) (8617)
Hipocras and Galien, (B. Duch. 572, A. 431) (16895-96)
Razis, Constantine, Avicene (A. 431-2) (RR. 16897)
St. Julyan, (HF. 1022) (9583)
Gawain the courteous, (F. 95) (2103-4)

Also the *Romaunt of the Rose* (2205-12), for which there is no French original.

Euclid and Ptolemy, (D. 2289) (17107)

Compare Skeat's notes to all these references in Chaucer. Thus much should be said in support of Jean de Meung's influence on the *Book of the Duchess:* while no one reference cited above can be proved to have come from the *Roman,* the cumulative evidence is fairly strong; fifteen straws are harder to break in a bundle than separately. And yet it should not be forgotten that Ovid and Vergil and Hyginus are full of classic examples, and that the influence of Guillaume de Machault upon the *Duchess* was even greater than that of Jean de Meung.[27] In the later poems, written when Chaucer's acquaintance with literature was larger (though I suspect that as a boy and a

[27] Professor Kittredge has pointed out many significant parallels between this poem and *Le Jugement dou Roy de Behaigne* in Modern Philology, April, 1910. See also Lounsbury, I, 423, II, 212-15, III, 409; Ten Brink, *Studien,* 8ff.; Sandras, *Etude,* etc., 75ff. (288-294); Skeat, I, 63, 462, 464. But Machault's indebtedness to the *Roman de la Rose* must not be disregarded.

young man he had read far more than his critics seem to admit), it is more difficult to feel confident about sources. Gawain's courtesy, Ganelon's treachery, and St. Julian's hospitality were not infrequently alluded to. Indeed, no formal sources are needed for them.

Medea. Five early allusions to Medea are due to the *Roman de la Rose,* says Root.[28] These are B. Duch. 724-731; HF. 397-404, 1271-74; A. 1944-46; B. 72-74. Three of the five may be dismissed without much discussion. The reference in the *Book of the Duchess* is only one of a number of allusions to stock examples, which, as Skeat has observed, are all to be found in the *Roman.* But they also occur in Ovid and in Machault, poets whom Chaucer used freely while writing the *Book of the Duchess.* That the English poet had the French poem in mind when writing HF. 401 is simply a matter of opinion. As Skeat says, probably all the examples mentioned in ll. 388-407 were taken from Ovid's *Epistles,* a work that Chaucer refers to by name in line 379. It does not seem unreasonable to consider this enumeration of hapless women as an immediate anticipation or reminiscence of the *Legend of Good Women.* The coupling of the names of Medea and Circe as enchantresses in the *Knightes Tale,* A. 1944, does not appear to me conclusive evidence that Chaucer had in mind RR. 15350-54. Ovid links these two personages together in *Ars Amatoria,* II, 101-104.

The other two allusions seem to be connected more definitely with the *Roman de la Rose.*

[28] *Chaucer's Legend of Medea,* by Robert K. Root. Publ. Mod. Lang. Assoc., Vol. XXIV, p. 134.

> Ther saugh I thee, queen Medea,
> And Circes eke, and Calipsa;
> Ther saugh I Hermes Ballenus,
> Lymote, and eek Simon Magus.   (HF. 1271-74)

has been compared by Skeat with

> Que ja riens d'enchantement croie,   (15342)
> Ne sorcerie, ne charroie,
> Ne *Balenus,* ne sa science,
> Ne magique, ne nigromance   (15345)
> Onques ne pot tenir *Medeé*   (15349)
> Jason por nul enchantement;
> N'onc Circe ne tint ensement
> Ulixes qu'il ne s'en foist.   (15352)

But I feel by no means certain that the four English lines are any more due to the *Roman* than to Ovid; for Ovid mentions Medea, Circe, and Calypso in close proximity in Book II of the *Ars Amatoria.* The "sorcerer-sorceress list" may have been eked out from the *Roman,* which, like the *Ars Amatoria,* mentions only three of the names Chaucer mentions. For Chaucer's Hermes, Lymote, and Simon Magus there is no original either in Ovid or Jean de Meung. Moreover, it is not proved that Jean's *Balenus,* Chaucer's *Ballenus,* and Skeat's *Belinous* are the same person. Lantin de Damerey thinks it very probable that Balenus is meant for Helenus, son of Priam and Hecuba, who is mentioned at length in the third book of the Æneid. Helenus was a seer and priest of no mean ability; and proper names are often distorted in medieval manuscripts.[28a] Jean does not mention Hermes. If one insists

[28a] Lantin de Damerey is quoted by Marteau in the notes to his edition of the *Roman.*

on deriving Chaucer's reference from Jean de Meung's line, the English lines would better read,

> Ther saugh I Hermes, Ballenus,
> Lymote, and eek Simon Magus;

not leaving Hermes Ballenus a compound name, as Skeat makes it.

In the Introduction to the Man of Law's Prologue we find a catalogue of heroines similar to that in the *Hous of Fame*. The allusion to Medea—

> The crueltee of thee, queen Medea,
> Thy litcl children hanging by the hals
> For thy Jason, that was of love so fals! (B. 72-74)

especially the phrase "hanging by the hals," in which Chaucer "has cut loose from tradition," is directly connected by Root with the following passage from the *Roman:*

> Dont ses enfans, quant el le sot,
> Por ce que de Jason les ot,
> Estrangla de duel et de rage,
> Dont el ne fist mie que sage,
> Quant el lessa pitié de mere,
> Et fist pis que marastre amere. (14198-14203)

Root says: "It would be interesting to know whence Jean de Meung's *estrangla* is derived. This I have not been able to determine."

The similarity of "estrangla" and "hanging by the hals" is the strongest piece of evidence advanced for deriving the one passage from the other. But the evidence is not conclusive; for *estrangla* ordinarily does not mean *hanging by the hals,* and Chaucer is very fond of this pair of rhymes, *hals: fals.* No less than five other instances occur.[29] I should say that at most the Man of Lawe's allusion to Medea is but a vague reminiscence of the *Roman.* After all, why should one take the Man of Lawe's enumeration of the table of contents of the "Seintes Legende of Cupyde" so seriously? Chaucer continually laughs at the pilgrims, and makes fun of himself and his own work. The accuracy of the information the Man of Lawe vouchsafes is such as we should expect from him of whom Chaucer had already written, "And yet he semed bisier than he was." The Man of Lawe is advertising a book that he has evidently not read.

Phyllis. The brief account of Phyllis and Demophon in the *Hous of Fame,* 388-396, has been traced by Root to the *Roman,* on the strength of l. 392:—

And falsly gan his terme pace,

which is nearly a literal translation of the French

Por le terme qu'il trespassa, (14154)

But by the time Chaucer wrote the *Hous of Fame* he must have read Ovid's *Epistles,* for he speaks of Demophon as "duk of Athenis" (l. 388) and of Phyllis as "the kinges daughter . . . of Trace"—details that Jean de Meung does not mention. Line 392 might very easily have been taken from Ovid's

te . . .

---

[29] I.e., PF. 456-458; HF. 343-4; L. (a) 292-3; E. 2379-80; G. 1028-29.

Ultra promissum tempus abesse queror, (*Epist.* II, 1-2)
which Chaucer translated thus in his legend of Phyllis:

> Thy Phillis . . . upon yow moot compleyne,
> Over the terme set betwix us tweyne,
> That ye ne holden forward, as ye seyde. (L. 2497-2500)

Skeat first pointed out the close resemblance between HF. 392 and RR. 14154.[30]

Finally, a word or two should be said about a stanza in *Troilus* (IV, 222), where Criseyde apostrophizes the river Simois. Miss Cipriani thinks that the expression

> That thou retorne bakwarde to thy welle, (iv, 1553)

is copied from the *Roman de la Rose:*—

> Que Xantus s'en retorneroit
> Si tost cum il la lesseroit. (14166-67)

The ultimate source of this idea of the lover's being faithful until a river flows back to its fountain-head is Ovid.[31] But Criseyde addresses the Simois, not the Xanthus. Jean de Meung does not mention the Simois. Ovid, however, writes of this river many times, and, once at least, in connection with the Xanthus (*Heroides,* xiii, 53). I believe that the first two lines of the stanza in question—

> And thou, Simoys, that as an arwe clere
> Thorugh Troye rennest ay downward to the see,
> (1548-49)

---

[30] *Chaucer*, III, 252.
[31] *Heroides*, v. 29-30:

> Cum Paris Oenone poterit spirare relicta,
> Ad fontem Xanthi versa recurret aqua.

were written by the poet with his eye on Ovid,—

> Dum rapidas Simois in mare volvet aquas,
> (*Amores* I, xv, 10)

and that Chaucer deliberately applied the legend of the Xanthus (which there is no more reason to think he got from Jean de Meung than from Ovid) to the Simois, to make Criseyde's oath all the stronger.

CHAPTER III

Mythological Allusions

Mythology in Chaucer's writings has not been made the subject of special investigation, I believe, though Miss Hammond has called attention to the need of such a study, and Skeat has thrown out a few hints. In this chapter no attempt will be made to cover the whole field; only those references to gods and goddesses that were probably suggested by the *Roman de la Rose* will be considered.

As everyone who has read the French poem knows, it abounds in allusions to Saturn, Jupiter, Mars, Venus, the Furies, Apollo, etc., etc. The god of Love is a most necessary personage at all times; without him, the Lover would never have been shot with the arrows of desire and longing; without the aid of his mother, "sainte Venus," the Rose could never have been won. Side by side with pagan mythology goes the poet's Christianity. The Lover swears by the Catholic saints and prays to Cupid. Altogether, the *Roman de la Rose* is an amazing jumble of heathen divinities, allegorical vices and virtues, realistic duennas and hypocrites—so confusing that one well-nigh loses his way in the bewildering labyrinth. Everything, in fact, is there. Moreover, Guillaume de Lorris and Jean de Meung present all their learning and imagination in the garb of the Middle Ages. For instance, Cupid is a liege lord, and all lovers owe him fealty; Virginius is a "bons chevaliers," Venus dresses like a fine lady of the thirteenth century, and so on. This leveling, medievalizing, anachronizing— whatever one may choose to call it—is illustrated particularly well in the case of Venus and Cupid, or the god of Love, as he is usually called. Although it is impossible here to make any detailed study of the attitude of the Middle Ages toward love, or of its treatment in literature,[1] the examination of the points of mythological contact between Chaucer and the *Roman de la Rose* will set forth some of the most distinguishing latter-day traits of the winged blind god and his mother. We shall reserve the end of the chapter for these notables, and consider first the deities who have less important rôles to play.

Æolus. The only mention of this god in Chaucer is in the *Hous of Fame*, where his name occurs no less than eleven times. He is the god of winds and is called the "king of Thrace" (1789). With line 1571 Skeat suggests a comparison of RR. 18941,—"Car Eolus le diex des vans," —of which it is almost an exact translation. But the expression is commonplace enough;[2] ask almost anyone who Æolus was, and the answer will be, "The god of the winds." Moreover, Jean de Meung says nothing of Triton

[1] For a general introduction to the subject, the reader may be referred to Langlois: *Origines et sources*, Part I; Neilson: *Origins and Sources of the Court of Love;* Mott: *System of Courtly Love;* and Myrrha Borodine: *La femme dans l'œuvre de Chrétien de Troyes.*

[2] Cf. Strabo I, 2; VI, 2, and *Æneid*, I, 52; VIII, 417, where the home of the wind-god is placed in the Liparean Islands. See also Ovid, *Heroides*, X, 66; XI, 65, 74, 95. Gower speaks of Æolus as "the god of wynd," *Conf. Aman.*, V, 977-79. See also Skeat's note to line 1571 (*Chaucer*, III, 280).

or Thrace in connection with Æolus, and there is no further resemblance between the two passages.

Furies. Chaucer speaks of these three goddesses both as Furies and as the Herines. In his Proemium to Book IV of *Troilus,* the poet summons the "Herines, Nightes doughtren three" (line 22) to be his muses. Miss Cipriani thinks that Chaucer's reference to Night as the mother of the Erinys is due to RR. 17872-73. This investigator also adds that Alecto, Tisiphone, and Megæra are mentioned in RR. 20767-69. But Chaucer did not need to take these names or this genealogy from the French poem. In the first place, a gloss in the MS. to T. iv, 22-24, implies that the name Herines was taken from Lucan.[3] Although ancient authorities do not agree on the parentage of the Erinys, the majority make them the children of Night.[4] It is clearly unnecessary to settle upon the *Roman de la Rose* as the source of these details in Chaucer. Elsewhere in *Troilus* (i, 6; ii, 436) is reference made to these goddesses. In the later passage Pandarus calls on them thus:

"O Furies three of helle, on yow I crye!"

As hell was the regular abiding place of the Furies, there is no object in hunting for a source for this line. But the

[3] *Chaucer,* II, lxxiii.

[4] According to Empedocles they are the children of Kronos. Hesiod (*Theog.,* 182-185) refers to the Erinys as the daughters of Earth, and sprung from the blood of the mutilated Uranus. For the Furies as daughters of Night, see Æschylus, *Eumenides,* 317, 413; Sophocles, *Œd. Col.,* 40, 106; Ovid, *Metam.,* iv, 451. Compare also Vergil, *Æneid,* vi, 250; vii, 320; xii, 845; Ovid, *Heroides,* xi, 103. The Orphic Hymns assign the Furies the rulers of Erebos for parents. See Keightley, p. 196.

reader might compare RR. 20771: "Ces trois en enfer vous atendent," and especially Dante's *Inferno*, IX, 38: "tre furie infernal di sangue tinte." This reference in Dante, which Skeat does not call attention to, leads me to say a word about Chaucer's address to Pity:

"Have mercy on me, thou Herenus queen!"[5]

Skeat asserts that Herenus is merely an error for Herines, and that "Pity may be said to be the queen of the Furies in the sense that pity (or mercy) can alone control the vindictiveness of vengeance." In giving the Erinys a queen who was pitiful, Chaucer may have had in mind Proserpina, who, when she was goddess of spring, was benevolent to man, but when the goddess of death, directed the Furies and was "cruel, unyielding, inimical to youth and life and hope."[6] Compare also *Inferno*, IX, 43-45:

E quei, che ben conobbe le meschine
Della regina dell' eterno pianto,
"Guarda," mi disse, "le feroci Erine."

In the next three lines of the *Inferno* appear the names Megera, Tesifone, and Aletto. Chaucer's *Alete* (T. iv, 24) is probably due to the Italian form; it is hardly from the French *Alecto*. Moreover, Dante uses the word *Erine;* the *Roman* has *les trois forceneries*.

The reference in the *Legend of Philomela* to "The furies three, with alle hir mortel brond," line 25, is borrowed, of course, from Ovid's story of Progne and Philomela, *Metam.*,

[5] *The Compleynte unto Pite*, 92.
[6] See Gayley's *Classic Myths*, p. 53 (Boston, 1911).

VI, 430. Exactly the same thought is to be found also in the *Heroides*, VI, 45-46.

The Fates. There are but two references to the Fates, both in *Troilus*.

And Attropos my threed of lyf to-brest,   (iv. 1546)

might be compared with RR. 20702-3:

> Mes Atropos vont et descire
> Quanque ces deus pueent filer.

And this line:

Til Lachesis his threed no longer twyne,   (v. 7)

suggests RR. 20701:

> Et Lachesis qui les filz tire.

Chaucer does not mention Clotho. To the passages just quoted from the *Roman,* I do not imply any obligation on Chaucer's part; for doubtless the various offices of the three Destinies were as carefully differentiated and as well known in the fourteenth century as they are to-day.[7] Besides, see Skeat's note, Vol. II, p. 495.

Hymenaeus, the god of marriage, appears twice in Chaucer. The reference to him in the *Legend of Philomela* (L. 2250) is probably from *Metamorphoses*, VI, 429. Here, as in the Legend, he is mentioned along with Juno. The same coupling of these two deities as regular attendants upon weddings occurs in the *Roman de la Rose:*

[7] Cf. the refrain stanzas in Lowell's Villa Franca: "Spin, spin, Clotho, spin! Lachesis, twist! and Atropos, sever!"—Quoted by Gayley, p. 481.

> Ymeneus et Juno m'oie;
> Qu'il voillent a nos noces estre. (22004-5)

The only noteworthy fact about this quotation is the spelling of the name of the god—a spelling that Chaucer follows also in the *Marchantes Tale* (E. 1730).

Lucina in Chaucer is usually identified with Diana or the moon; e. g., T. iv. 1591; v. 655; F. 1045. In the *Knightes Tale*, in a passage not derived from the *Teseide*, she is invoked as the goddess of childbirth:

> A womman travailinge was hir biforn,
> But, for hir child so longe was unborn,
> Ful pitously Lucyna gan she calle,
> And seyde, "help, for thou mayst best of alle."
>
> (A. 2083-86)

With this may be cited the following from the *Roman:*

> Pri-ge Lucina la deesse
> D'enfantement, qu'el doint qu'il nesse
> Sans mal et sans encombrement,
> Si qu'il puist vivre longement. (11388-91)

But beyond the fact that Lucina is supplicated to the end that birth may be made easy, there is no significant resemblance between the two quotations. Lucina, of course, was a Roman epithet, which was given sometimes to Juno, sometimes to Diana. References in Ovid to her are not infrequent.[8]

Flora and *Zephirus* are mentioned together in B. Duch. 402-3 and Prol. B to the *Legend*, 171-174, as the deities

---

[8] *Heroides*, VI, 122, XI, 55; *Ars Amatoria*, III, 785. See Skeat's note, V, 84.

of the flowers. Skeat justly calls these two passages reminiscences of the *Roman de la Rose:*

> Zephirus et Flora, sa fame,
> Qui des flors est deesse et dame,
> Cil dui font les floretes naistre,
> Flors ne congnoissent autre mestre.   (9160-63)

and compares also RR. 6674-77. Zephyrus, the "sweet-breathed" west wind, is spoken of elsewhere in Chaucer; in Boethius (though without this epithet); and many times in Ovid, where it is called "leni Zephyro."[9] In the *Fasti*[10] Ovid tells the story of Flora and Zephyrus, and writes that Flora was an ancient Italian deity, and was loved by the west wind.

Echo and *Narcissus*. Chaucer does not independently tell the story of Narcissus, but in two places he alludes to Echo and her death. The poet, in the *Book of the Duchess*, seems to express contempt for those who kill themselves or die because of unrequited love.

> And Ecquo dyed for Narcisus
> Nolde nat love hir; and right thus
> Hath many another foly don.   (735-37)

Here the spelling Ecquo is very much like the French Equo. Koeppel thinks that Chaucer took this reference from RR. 1447ff, and Skeat agrees. In the *Frankeleyns Tale* Aurelius compares himself to Echo:

And dye he moste, he seyde, as dide Ekko
For Narcisus, that dorste nat telle hir wo.   (F. 951-2)

[9] *Amores*, I, vii, 55; *Heroides*, XIV, 39.
[10] Book V, 183ff.

In a note to line 951 Skeat says, "Chaucer probably took this from *Le Roman de la Rose*, 1447. But he had learned by this time that the true original was Ovid (*Metamorph.*, iii, 407). Hence the side-note in MS. E—'Methamorposios'." But the MS. knew better than the learned professor. This reference must have been put down with Ovid's story in mind, not Guillaume de Lorris's. For Chaucer says "that dorste nat telle hir wo." In the French narrative, it is Echo who prays the gods that Narcissus may feel the torture of loving and not being loved: she "tells hir wo." In the Latin account, Echo, after being repulsed by the arrogant boy, hides herself in the woods and shrivels up until nothing is left but her voice. It is some unnamed damsel that prays for vengeance.

Jupiter. I have detected only one sure case in which Chaucer follows the *Roman de la Rose* in the characterization of this deity. At the close of the poem on the *Former Age* occur the lines:

> Yit was not Jupiter the likerous,
> That first was fader of delicacye,
> Come in this world;   (57-59)

In his note to these lines, Skeat seems to be again on the wrong track. He says: "Jupiter is mentioned in Ovid's *Metamorphoses* immediately after the description of the golden, silver, brazen, and iron ages." But the Jupiter described by Ovid is the righteously indignant ruler of the world:

> Ingentes animo et dignas Iove concipit iras,
> Conciliumque vocat.   (*Metam.*, I, 166-67)

In the *Roman de la Rose* it is the pleasure-loving Jupiter who destroys the golden age. Surely Chaucer had in mind these lines when he wrote "Jupiter the likerous":

> Jupiter, qui la monde regle
> Commande et establit pour regle,
> Que chascuns pense d'estre aaise;
> Et s'il set chose qui li plaise,
> Qu'il la face s'il la puet faire,
> Por solas a son cuer atraire. (RR. 21027-32)

And Jean de Meung goes on to say (lines 21042-46) that Dan Jupiter practiced what he preached.

Venus. Throughout his poetry Chaucer has occasion constantly to refer to Venus, but he appears to know little about her genealogy. Or rather, he has read much about her parentage,—so many different reports that he is confused. His doubt and inconsistency are brought out in the *Knightes Tale*, where, in line (A.) 2222, the goddess of Love is called "doughter to Jove," and later she is daughter to Saturn:

"My dere doughter Venus," quod Saturne. (A. 2452) This last detail Chaucer very likely took from the *Roman de la Rose*. In lines 6270-75 of the French poem, Reason speaks of Jupiter's mutilation of Saturn, and says that from the member, which was thrown into the sea, "Venus la déesse issi." (l. 6276.) Several thousand lines farther on, we find this more definite statement (Cupid is speaking):

> Mes, par sainte Venus ma mere,
> Et par Saturnus son vieil pere,

Qui ja l'engendra jone touse,
Mes non pas de sa fame espouse. (11592-95)

Reason asserts that the story is true, "Car li livres le dit ainsi" (6277). Langlois has shown that Jean de Meung got his information from the *Mythographes*.[11]

Among the epithets most frequently applied to Venus are Cyprian and Cytherean. She is twice called Cipris in Chaucer (HF. 518; T. iii, 725) and twice Cipryde (PF. 277; T. v, 208). Miss Cipriani has referred the HF. allusion to RR. 22234, "Bien avisa dame Cypris," which in turn was taken from *Li Tornoiemenz Antecrit* of Huon de Meri.[12] But if Chaucer had not known that Cypris (*Cipris* is the form used in all the MSS. of Chaucer) meant Venus, the line in the *Roman de la Rose* would not have conveyed the idea.

Koeppel first discovered that Chaucer's mention of Cithaeron as the dwelling place of Venus (A. 1936-37) was derived from a description of that mountain in the *Roman*

---

[11] See *Origines et sources*, etc., p. 134.

This account, tho Langlois has not noticed the fact, seems to have resulted from a confusion or contamination of two older stories. In Hesiod (*Theog.*, 188ff.) Venus is said to have sprung from the foam that gathered around the mutilated member of Uranus. According to Empedocles, Aphrodite was daughter of Kronos (Saturn), and Keightley comments thus: "There does not appear the slightest allusion to this strange genealogy anywhere else."—*Mythology*, p. 69 n. Hyginus tells an entirely different story in Fabula cxcvii.

[12] Cf. Langlois, pp. 151-153. The form Cipryde (PF. 277) Chaucer found in Alanus de Insulis. See *Chaucer*, I, 514. In his story of Pygmalion, Ovid says, "Festa dies Veneris tota celeberrima Cypro venerat."—*Metam.*, X, 270-271.

(16596-604).[13] The English poet also gives the goddess the name Citherea, an appellation very common in Ovid.[14]

In the *Roman de la Rose,* Venus is the mother of Love (4032), the mortal enemy of Chastity (4030-31); she urges youths day and night to "pluck roses" (2862-64). She is described as clad in wondrous robes and carrying a flaming torch in her right hand (4040ff., 4034-36).[14a] However pleasure-loving she is, she is not mercenary (11559ff.). In the *Knightes Tale,* after the reference to Venus's dwelling at Cithaeron, the author goes on to describe the statue of the goddess in her temple. The picture is conventional enough; perhaps it is not necessary to go farther than Skeat's note (V, 78). Idleness, for instance, like Venus, wears a garland of fresh roses and bears in her hand a mirror. When Chaucer speaks of so many folk caught in Venus's net—

> Lo, alle thise folk so caught were in hir las,
> Til they for wo ful ofte seyde "allas"! (A. 1951-52)

he may have had in mind a couplet from the *Roman*—

---

[13] Langlois has been unable to trace the source of this passage, but conjectures that it was some "poète ancien." p. 171.

[14] See particularly the *Ars Amatoria,* II, 15-16:

> "Nunc mihi, siquando, puer et Cytherea, favete,
> Nunc Erato! nam tu nomen amoris habes."

[14a] Jean de Meung speaks of her bow and torch:

> Ge ne doi prisier ung landon
> Moi, ne mon arc, ne mon brandon. (16712-13)

Skeat refers to these lines in connection with PF. 114 and E. 1777. (I, 509.)

Si pueent en lor laz cheoir,
Qu'il lor en devra mescheoir. (11664-65)

which had been translated in the English *Romaunt* thus:

If that they falle into hir laas,
That they for wo mowe seyn "Allas!" (6029-30)

though here not Venus's net is meant, but the snares that women lay for rich lovers. In the French poem, it is Cupid who entangles lovers;[14b] Venus's net is of a different sort. With Chaucer, as with Jean de Meung, Venus is the mother of Cupid, who calls her "Saint Venus";[15] she carries a torch;[16] she is the enemy of chastity;[17] Palamon prays to her and promises never to be chaste if he win his love—just as Pygmalion prays.[18] Chaucer also probably took the Wife of Bath's phrase, *chambre of Venus* (D. 618), from RR. 14277.

Venus, in both poets, is the goddess of voluptuous love, just as Jupiter is the "likerous."[19] This conception, however, was not peculiar to Jean de Meung and Chaucer; it is Ovidian also. She is much more sensual than Cupid, her son. He has courtliness, at least, and insists on being

[14b] Ge qui estoie pris où laz
Ou Amors les amans enlace. RR. 16046-47.

With these lines Koeppel compares L. 600 and A. 1817, 1951.

[15] T. iii. 1255. Legend 338; cf. RR. 11592—*K*. See also WB. Prol. (D. 604) and RR. 22080.

[16] *Marchantes Tale*, E. 1777.

[17] A. 2235-36. Cf. also D. 611.

[18] A. 2233-37, imitated from RR. 22087-94. *Skeat* and *Koeppel*.

[19] Guillaume de Lorris very fittingly makes Idleness the gate-keeper in the garden of delight (RR. 584). Chaucer seems to be following him in A. 1940.—Sk. In PF. 261 the porter of Venus is Richesse.

sovereign: he commands respect. The Roman deity Venus ever had less dignity and nobility than Aphrodite, her Greek counterpart. By the thirteenth century she had degenerated into the fitting patron of such a person as La Vieille. Jean de Meung tells at length of her escapade with Mars (RR. 14785-14815, 15100-15129, 18996-19024), and Chaucer refers to the incident (A. 2388-90).[20] All in all, Chaucer and Jean de Meung appear to have viewed the goddess of Love in much the same light, but, except for a few details, Chaucer probably did not owe anything essential in his conception to the French poet. Chaucer's acquaintance with the classics (i. e., Latin, of course; neither appears to have known much, if any, Greek) was broader than the French poet's. At least, Chaucer had a finer, more scientific feeling for antiquity. He was both classical and medieval in his sympathies, and oftentimes modern. Jean de Meung was through and through medieval.

Cupid. The god of Love is by no means the least interesting of Chaucer's characters. If for no other reason, he is worth studying because he had appeared before the last half of the fourteenth century many times in the literature of France, and can therefore be cross-examined and made to give an account of himself here. He had ruled the

---

[20] Ovid tells the story twice. Jean de Meung undoubtedly followed the account in *Ars Amatoria*, II, 561-600. Skeat (V, 87) calls attention to the narrative in *Metam.*, IV, 171-189. Both authors emphasize the foolishness of Vulcan in exposing the shame of his wife, and the laughter and coarse jests of the other gods at the expense of the wronged husband. Chaucer's *Compleynt of Mars* appears to owe nothing to the *Roman de la Rose*.

dreams of many a poet before Chaucer; we should expect to find him treating our poet in much the same way as he treated the others. After we have looked somewhat closely at his bearing toward earlier authors, we shall be able to compare his conduct toward Chaucer.

In the *Roman de la Rose,* the god of Love is a very distinct person. He deals to lovers happiness or sorrow, as seems best to him; he casts down pride, and makes high-minded men humble, and proud ladies meek. He wears, not a robe of silk, but a variegated garment of flowers, covered with representations of all manner of beasts. He is crowned with a garland of sweet-scented roses, and around his head fly birds of every sort. Altogether he appears to be one of God's angels. His attendant, Sweet-Looks, bears in each hand a Turkish bow,—one black and gnarled, the other white and graceful, and richly carved. In his right hand he also carries five golden, brilliantly feathered arrows, named Beauty, Simplicity, Franchise, Companionship, and Fair-Seeming. In his left hand Sweet-Looks holds five other arrows, made of iron "blacker than the devil of hell." These are Pride, Felony, Shame, Despair, and New-Thought or Infidelity (RR. 869-988).

After the god of Love has pierced the dreamer with the five beautiful arrows, he claims him as his prisoner: "Vassal, pris ies, noient n'i a Du contredire ne du defendre" (1884-85), and tells how the homage rendered to him has often been false, how his courtesy has been repaid by deceit and strife. The dreamer—now become the Lover—offers to have his heart locked up by Love as a pledge of faithfulness. The god thinks the suggestion a fair one, and drawing forth a little gold key, presses it to the Lover's side and adroitly and painlessly seals his heart. After swearing eternal loyalty, the Lover claims instruction from his master, whereupon the god of Love enumerates his precepts (2087-2274). He next recounts the toils and griefs the Lover will have to suffer (2275-2568). On the Lover's expressing serious doubts as to his ability to endure such torments, the god gives him, in addition to Hope, three gifts,—Sweet-Thought, Soft-Speech, and Sweet-Looks,—who are to help him win his desire. Cupid then departs, and does not reappear until verse 11198. After learning of the difficulties the Lover has experienced for the last eight thousand lines and how in spite of his suffering he has turned a deaf ear to Reason and has remained faithful to his lord, Love assembles his barons for a council of war. Of these, Dame Idleness bore the largest banner (11208-9). After interminable digressions into every conceivable subject, from free-will to alchemy, the author finally tells how Cupid, aided by his mother, Venus, successfully storms the castle that imprisoned the Rose. The flower is suddenly changed to a beautiful maiden and given to the Lover.

What is the character of the god of Love in the Prologue to the *Legend of Good Women?* As in the *Roman,* he here appears to the poet in a dream; but it is to be noted that all the description of the beauty of spring with its flowers and birds *precedes* the vision. The *whole* of the French poem is a dream except the first forty-four lines. Chaucer "mette" how he lay in the meadow to enjoy the daisy that he so loves and fears. From afar came walking the god of Love, leading by the hand a queen dressed in gold and white, to resemble the flower that the poet had been admiring. As for her companion—

> Y-clothed was this mighty god of love (226)
> In silke, enbrouded ful of grene greves,
> In-with a fret of rede rose-leves, (228)
> The fresshest sin the world was first bigonne.
> His gilte heer was corouned with a sonne, (230)
> Instede of gold, for hevinesse and wighte;
> Therwith me thought his face shoon so brighte (232)
> That wel unnethes mighte I him beholde;
> And in his hande me thoughte I saugh him holde (234)
> Two fyry dartes, as the gledes rede;
> And aungellyke his winges saugh I sprede. (236)
> And al be that men seyn that blind is he,
> Al-gate me thoughte that he mighte see; (238)
> For sternely on me he gan biholde,
> So that his looking doth myn herte colde. (240)

After this description, the poet introduces his balade in praise of the "lady fre":

> Hyd, Absolon, thy gilte tresses clere, etc., (249)

for had it not been for the comfort of her presence, the dreamer

> had been deed, withouten any defence,
> For drede of Loves wordes and his chere. (279-280)

Love is followed by a countless throng of fair women—more numerous than the poet ever thought lived in the world—

> And trewe of love thise women were echon. (290)

(One feels like putting an exclamation point after this statement; Chaucer could not resist the opportunity for a thrust.) The god of Love seats himself, and the ladies group themselves around him. After a long silence (suggestive of the dulness of his court), the god looks about him, sees the poet kneeling by the daisy, and asks abruptly, "Who kneleth ther?" The dreamer's meek "Sir, hit am I," does not seem to turn away wrath, for the tyrant says:

>What dostow heer
>So nigh myn owne flour, so boldely?
>For it were better worthy, trewely,
>A worm to neghen neer my flour than thou. (315-18)

(The *thou* that the god of Love always uses when addressing the poet is significant of the social relationship between the two; the poet replies with *you*. The god and Alceste use *you* to each other.) The poet is accused of being the foe of Love for having translated the *Romance of the Rose* and having written of Criseyde in such a way as to make men lose confidence in women. And, says Love,

>By seynt Venus, that my moder is,
>If that thou live, thou shalt repenten this
>So cruelly, that hit shal wel be sene! (338-40)

The lady then speaks up, and says that it is the part of a deity to be gracious and merciful; and that the poet wrote nothing in malice—only thoughtlessness; that king or lord

>oghte nat be tiraunt ne cruel
>As is a fermour, to doon the harm he can.
>He moste thinke hit is his lige man,

> And is his tresour and his gold in cofre. (377-380)
> . . . .
> For . . . hit is no maystrie for a lord
> To dampne a man withoute answere of word;
> And for a lord, that is ful foul to use. (400-402)

The poet is given an opportunity to justify his conduct, but he has no more than finished one short defense when the lady interrupts him with

> lat be thyn arguinge;
> For Love ne wol nat countrepleted be
> In right ne wrong; and lerne that of me! (475-77)

She then imposes the penance for the trespass committed,— the poet must spend the best part of his remaining years on a "glorious Legende of Gode Wommen." The god of Love considers the penalty light, and asks the dreamer if he knows who his judge is. But the condemned man replies, "No, Sire; I only see that she is good." The god, becoming more contemptuous, says:

> That is a trewe tale, by myn hood,
> . . . and that thou knowest wel, pardee,
> If hit be so that thou avyse thee. (507-509)

If this be a court of love, one feels like saying justice is administered in a most eccentric way. Here is a humble man who is called to account by an overbearing lord who will not be contradicted. A gentle lady pleads for the accused, and defends him quite logically. She then imposes a heavy sentence on him for his fault! The irony of the whole situation is delicious; there is nothing particular attractive in the service of such a tyrant as is here presented. Chaucer winks at his reader and says, "I told you so; it was always thus; keep out of it!" At length, after a few leading hints have been given him, the poet guesses that the lady is Alceste. Whereupon he launches into such a eulogy of her that she blushes for shame "a lyte." (535) The god of Love says to the dreamer, "You did wrong in not mentioning Alceste in your balade of 'Hyd, Absolon.'"

> But now I charge thee, upon thy lyf,
> That in thy Legend thou make of this wyf,
> Whan thou hast other smale y-maad before;
> And fare now wel, I charge thee no more.   (548-551)

But before he goes, he gives more minute directions about the stories to be written. The poet is allowed thus much liberty, however: he can make the meters as he pleases.[20a]

Now, it is obvious that we have got far away from mythology. The god of Love no longer resembles Cupid; and though he still calls Venus his mother, he is a disagreeable despot, Chaucer will not let us forget. Are there any points of contact between the god of Love and Guillaume's and Jean's Amors?

Koeppel has called attention to line 338 and RR. 11592:

> Mes, par sainte Venus ma mere,

in which the epithet *saint* as applied to the goddess of Love seems to be of some significance. As for Venus being the mother of Love, that was a commonplace. In RR. 22080

[20a] Professor Kittredge (in Mod. Phil., April, 1910, pp. 471-474) has shown that the general situation of a poet judged and punished by a king for having offended ladies occurs in Machault's *Le Jugement dou Roy de Navarre*.

we find the phrase "Sainte Venus," and the Wife of Bath thus accounts for her amorous nature:

> I hadde the prente of sëynt Venus seel. (D. 604)

M. Bech[21] compared the description of Cupid in L. 226-240 with RR. 880-907. But there are essential differences between the two. One has only to recall Chaucer's beautiful apology (lines 73-82) for treating his theme conventionally, to realize that so far as the poet can he is going to treat it unconventionally. Now, literary influence is manifested in two ways: imitation or conscious variation. Both imply a thorough acquaintance with the model. *Don Quixote* is a case in point. When Chaucer writes

> And I come after, glening here and there,
> And am ful glad if I may finde an ere
> Of any goodly word that ye han left, (75-77)

he has been interpreted to mean, "I am going to write a poem in praise of the daisy. Many of my contemporaries and predecessors have already done this, so I shall have to say that they have said. My method will be to select from this large body of poetry, lines and sentiments—if there are any good ones—and work them up into my piece." This, or substantially this, Chaucer meant by his "glening," it has been said. But an examination of lines 75-77 and the three that follow—

> And thogh it happen that me rehercen eft
> That ye han in your fresshe songes sayd,
> For-bereth me, and beth not evel apayd (78-80)—

[21] In "Quelle und Plan der Legende of Good Women," *Anglia*, V, p. 359.

make it clear that the poet's endeavor was to write something that had *not* been written by the others—something that "had been left," i. e., overlooked[22]—although he realizes that he will have to "rehercen eft" much of what has already been well said in the "fresshe songes"; that is, the first songs of this type. Consequently, we must be on the lookout for deliberate departures from preceding conventions. Here, only those relating to the god of Love will be noticed.

Clearly, Chaucer followed no one author in the description of Cupid. The English poet's fundamental conception of the god of Love, in this poem at least, as a cross-grained, irritable king, would not permit of the monarch's being clothed in flowers; he must have silk. But the flowers must be worked in somewhere, so they are embroidered into the garment. In the B-text, no garland is mentioned; but in the A-text, the god of Love wears a garland of roses stuck full of lilies. In any case there are no birds flying about his head. The line, "And aungellyke his winges saugh I sprede," which may have been suggested by

> Il sembloit que ce fust uns anges
> Qui fust tantost venus du ciau. (RR. 906-907)

---

[22] The editors of the New English Dictionary appear so to understand the meaning here:

Glean.—1. *Intr.*—To gather or pick up ears of corn which have been left by the reapers.

c. 1385—Chaucer L. G. W. Prol. 75.

2. *Trans.*—To gather or pick up [ears of corn or other produce] after the reapers, etc.

1387-8.—T. Usk *Test. Love* I, Prol. 112 (Skeat's Chaucer, VII, p. 4): "Yet also have I leve . . . to come after . . . these great workmen, and glene my handfuls of the shedynge of their handes."

is certainly less of a compliment than the French couplet. The *Roman de la Rose* says nothing of the "fyry dartes," of Love's blindness, or of his stern countenance, which chilled the heart of the dreamer. Altogether I can find little or no resemblance between Chaucer's description and Guillaume de Lorris's. Nor does the French poet speak of Love's wings or of the train of followers who render homage to the deity. Some of these details Chaucer probably took from an early poem of Guillaume de Machault—*Le Dit du Vergier*—which students have almost altogether overlooked because they have kept their eyes too steadily fixed on the "marguerite" poems of Deschamps, Machault, and Froissart. As the *Dit du Vergier* has not been examined in this connection before, so far as I know, we may consider it briefly here.

In *Le Dit du Vergier,* the author tells how one beautiful spring morning he took a stroll through a woods. The nightingale was singing the return of spring; the flowers were gorgeously in bloom; and everything breathed gladness and love. Machault abandoned himself to pleasant dreams, and finally sank into a slumber. Suddenly a delightful apparition greeted his eyes. He saw, in a little meadow, the most beautiful company of young people he had ever seen—six youths and six maidens. On a little tree was sitting a marvelous creature:

> Car nulle goute ne veoit
> Et en sa dextre main tenoit
> Un dart qui bien estoit ferré
> De fer tranchant et acéré;
> Et en l'autre avoit un brandon

> De feu que gettoit grant randon;
> Et s'avoit pour voler ii eles
> Si belles, qu'onques ne vi telles.
> La face avoit clere et moult belle,
> Et la couleur fresche et vermeille;
>
> . . . .
>
> Mais encore vi je de rechief
> Qui tuit li gentil Damoisel
> Qui estoient plain de revel
> Et les Damoiselles aussi,
> Tous ensamble et chascuns par li,
> Li faisoient feste et honneur
> Comme a leur souverain signeur,
> Et com leur Dieu l'aouroient,
> Graces et loenge li rendoient.[23]
> Et quant j'eus tout cela veü
> Ymaginé et conceü
> J'en os en moy moult grant freour
> Pour le feu, doubtance et paour,
> Qu' adès vraiement me sambloit
> Que vers moy lancier le voloit.
> Pour ce ne savoie que faire,
> D'aler avant on d'arrier traire.[24]

But the dreamer makes bold to approach the group, to learn about this youth who could not see a "goute." Drawing near, he salutes them and begins to ask many questions.

> Et quant je li eus ma prière
> Toute dicte en tele manière,
> Lors parla gracieusement,[25]

---

[23] Tarbé, p. 15, lines 8-17, 25-33.
[24] Hoepffner's edition of Machault (Soc. des anc. textes franç.), I, pp. 19-20, lines 193-200. Tarbé does not print this passage.
[25] Tarbé, p. 16, lines 29-31.

i. e., the unknown youth spoke, but does not tell his name until more than a hundred lines later:

> Et si te diray de mon non,
> Se tu le vues savoir ou non.
> Je ne te le queir j'ai celer:
> Diex d'Amours me fait appeller.[26]

Except for some of the allegorical passages, the rest of the *Dit du Vergier* has no particular bearing on the Prologue.

It will be seen that Machault's dream opens abruptly with an account of the appearance of Love and his company. The god carries in his hands an iron barbed dart and a fiery brand—Chaucer's "fyry dartes." He has two wings, is blind,—cannot see at all,—and is surrounded by a beautiful company who do him homage. Chaucer refers to this tradition about Love, and asserts (L. 237-249, 311) that Love can see; but Machault's god gives a long explanation of why he is blind.[27] Machault's god of Love is accompanied by twelve allegorical personages—six youths and six maidens. Chaucer's god of Love is accompanied by thousands of beautiful women who have been true to love. Here is a departure from convention, then. On the whole, *Le Dit du Vergier* clearly furnished the English poet with not a little of the situation and external description in the Prologue, both for imitation and for variation.

Chaucer's god of Love, however, after all has been said, still remains the poet's own creation; and although he has been identified as Richard II, these claims have been ably

---

[26] Tarbé, p. 20, lines 8-11.
[27] Ibid., p. 20, lines 20ff.

refuted.[28] Alceste's defense of the dreamer against the charges preferred by the deity has some resemblance to False-Seeming's defense of the Lover against Evil-Tongue's accusations (RR. 13215-13264)—a passage that appears in the *Romaunt of the Rose* (7608-7666). With L. 410-11 compare also RR. 11688-9:

> Si vous prions trestuit, biau sire,
> Que vous li pardonnes vostre ire.

To sum up: In the god of Love as he is represented in the Prologue to the Legend, we have a character who, externally described in part by a cento of lines and phrases taken from fourteenth-century French poets, in part by original features contradicting what previous "makers" had said, is essentially a new individual in literature. Chaucer's inventiveness here, as usual, has enabled him to convert, through the crucible of his genius, somewhat shadowy, allegorical figures into one lifelike person—one not very agreeable, to be sure, but nevertheless vivid and interesting.[29]

---

[28] See Lowes's discussion in Publ. Mod. Lang. Assoc., XIX, pp. 668-669 and 674-675.

[29] Some other facts are recorded about Cupid elsewhere in Chaucer. In HF. 609, 617, he is called the "blind nevew of Jupiter"; in HF. 668 he is the "reccheles." Two conventional descriptions of him as blind, winged, provided with bow and arrows, and as the companion to his mother, Venus, occur in HF. 137-138 and A. 1963-66. Following Boccaccio's *Teseide*, Bk. VII, stanza 54, Chaucer gives the god a daughter (named Voluttade in the Italian poem) in PF. 211-217. Criseyde (T. v. 1590) speaks figuratively of Troilus as "Cupydes sone." But none of these details has anything to do with the *Roman de la Rose*.

For classical genealogies of Eros (Cupid), see Keightley, p. 146.

CHAPTER IV

Chaucer's Style as Affected by the *Roman*

It is impossible to separate the *Roman de la Rose* from the poems of its day in the matter of style, especially as it is the work of two authors so different as Guillaume de Lorris and Jean de Meung, who together represent nearly every thirteenth-century tendency in poetry. The *Roman* was epoch-making, and appears to have had an extraordinary effect on Italian as well as French writers. It is possible, consequently, that some influence from this poem descended to Chaucer indirectly through Boccaccio and Dante, and Machault, Froissart and Deschamps. But one must not forget the English poet's acquaintance with medieval romances, medieval Latin writers, and, not least of all, Middle English literature in general; for it is inconceivable that such a varied, idiomatic, correct use of our language as the author of the *Canterbury Tales* displays could have resulted merely from following foreign models. Therefore, one must proceed cautiously, even skeptically, in a search for the sources of Chaucer's style.

Koeppel cites a number of parallels which he says are not without significance for a knowledge of the influence of the *Roman de la Rose* on Chaucer's diction, although they can be found here and there in other English authors of that time(!).[1] Koeppel's illustrations, together with those furnished by other commentators, we may classify somewhat arbitrarily under the following heads: (1) picturesque negation, (2) exclamations and imprecations, (3) figures of speech—allegory, simile, metaphor, anaphora, (4) rhymes and vocabulary, (5) various other devices of expression, such as the use of emphatic repetition in interrogative form, emphasis by a series of contrasts, the employment of extended lists of objects; catalogues, and transitional and summarizing sentences.

(1) PICTURESQUE NEGATION

By picturesque negation, or "gemeinschaftliche ausdrücke der geringschätzung," as Koeppel calls it, is meant the undervaluation of some person, thing, attribute or quality, by means of a *reductio ad absurdum* comparison with a common, well-known object of little or no worth; as, "Swich talking is nat worth a boterflye" (B. 3980). This form of phraseology is said to have been introduced into early Middle English from the French; it is fairly common in Latin and Middle High German, but does not appear to have been used in Old English.[2] Chaucer seems to have been fond of such expressions, for they occur no

[1] Anglia, XIV, p. 262ff. The critic seems to imply by this that Chaucer deliberately chose the French poem as a model.

[2] See *French Elements in Middle English*, by Frederick H. Sykes (Oxford, 1899), esp. pp. 24-25, 36, 39. We have no *proof* that picturesque negation was unknown to the Anglo-Saxons. The mere fact that no examples of it occur in A.-S. literature is of no particular significance, for A.-S. literature is never colloquial. Picturesque negation is distinctly a characteristic of colloquial speech.

less than sixty-five times throughout his work, and the comparisons are drawn from more than a score of different objects.[3] The device was a favorite one with Jean de Meung, too, for it is used at least forty-six times in his portion of the *Roman,* and in Guillaume's but once. Twenty-five separate objects furnish the comparisons.[4] We find not

[3] The following list is, I believe, complete. Willi Haeckel, in *Das Sprichwort bei Chaucer* (Erlanger Beiträge, viii), printed a number of examples, but he overlooked many. The enumeration below does not include mere exclamations such as "Strawe!" G. 925, or indeed any sentiment that does not contain the statement, "is noght worth a," "he yaf nat a," "as much as a," "counte nat a," "sette nat a," "avayleth noght a," "dere y-nough a," or its equivalent.
BEAN. MB. 29, 39; T. iii 1167; T. v 363; A. 3672; B. 94, 4004; E. 1263, 1854. BEAN-STRAW. E. 1421. BUTTERFLY. B. 3980; E. 2303-4. CRESS. A. 3756. CORN (a grain). C. 863. FLY. PF. 501; A. 4192; B. 1360-61; F. 1132; G. 1150. GNAT. T. iv 595; D. 347; H. 254-5. GROAT. T. iv 586. HAT. T. iii 320. HAY. H. 14; cf. E. 1567. HAW. T. iii 854, iv 1397-98; D. 659. HEN. A. 177; D. 1112. JANE (a small Genoese coin). E. 999. LEEK. HF. 1708; D. 572; E. 1350; G. 795. MITE. CM. 126; AA. 269; T. iii 900; T. iv 684; L. 741; A. 1558; D. 1961; G. 511, 633, 698. MOTE. T. iii 1603. OYSTER. A. 182. RAKE-HANDLE. D. 949. RUSH. T. iii 1161. SHOE. D. 708, STRAW. B. Duch. 671, 718, 887, 1237; HF. 363; B. 2526, 4280; I. 601. TARE. T. iii 936; A. 1570, 4000, 4056. TORD. B. 2120. (WHILE. T. v 882.)
Chaucer also has "ne . . . worthy unbokele his galoche." F. 555. This phrase was doubtless imitated from St. Mark, i, 7, or St. John, i, 27.

[4] The verbs or adjectives most often used in the French form of the expression are "ne vaut un," "ne prisent un," "il n'en donroient un," "pas vaillant un," "il ne valent un," "ne vaudroit-il pas un." AIL (garlic). 13859-60, 15513-14. BILLE (piece of wood). 7303, 10084-85. BOUTON (button). 9239, 10413-14, 15152-53. CHASTENGNE (chestnut). 15255. CHICHE (chick-pea). 7652-53, 10518-20. CIVE (onion or chive). 6062, 17407. COQUE (cock). 7255. COUTEL TROINE (a white wooden knife). 11822-24. DENIER (a small coin). 5379, 13965, 14560-61, 20327. ESCORCE (piece of bark). 8440-41, 13162-3, 14652, 19784-5. FESTU (straw). 5395-96, 6870-71, 9926, 12897, 18858-

more than five of these common to Chaucer and the two French poets. In spite of the fact that this device of emphatic undervaluation was frequently used in France (other than in the *Roman de la Rose*) and in England, before Chaucer's day,[5] I cannot help thinking that the

59. GRAIN DE MOSTARDE (mustard). 15401. GRAIN DE POIVRE (pepper). 6481. GUIMPLE (wimple). 18167. LANDON (stick of wood). 16712. LORAIN (strap). 6060. MAILLE (a small Genoese coin). 5717. NAVEZ (turnips). 18843-44. OEF (egg). 13792-93. PIPES. 5775. POIS (pea). 2273, 15429-30. POME (apple). 4747-48, 6019, 7290-91, 9954-55, 13563-64, 19525, 19682. PRUNE. 6581-82, 8822-23. SECHE (cuttle-fish). 12174. SERAN (flax-comb). 15481-82. TARTRE (tart). 14163.

[5] For illustrations of the use in French, see Rutebeuf (*Œuvres*, ed. Jubinal): "Je ne pris mie .ij. festus," II, p. 63, l. 4; "Mes cele ne done une bille," II, p. 69, l. 132; "Ne priseroit vaillant .i. oef," II, p. 210, l. 103; "Ne m'est remez vaillant .i. sac," II, p. 231, l. 5; "et teil qui ne valent .ij. ciennes," II, p. 99, l. 11. Guillaume de Machault (*Œuvres*, ed. Tarbé): "Ne delit qui vaille un festu," p. 99; "Que je ne prise sa franchise une truit," p. 89; "Ne je ne prise un bec de jay," p. 7; "Qu'il ne vaut I pourroit ongnon (rotten onion)," p. 82; "N'il ne doit or prisier II chiches," p. 103. Gower's *Mirour de l'Omme* (ed. Macaulay): "Ne t'en redorroit une prune," 6648; "je ne douns un festu," 12098; "Mais la value d'un botoun," 25629, etc. In the French *Roman de Guillaume de Dole* occurs this rather striking example:

> Qui ne prisent mauves dangier
> La coue d'une violette. 288-289

As illustrations of the use in English, the following might be cited from the romances: "Sir, therof yive y nought a slo!" *Amis and Amil*, 395;

> He alone ayens us thre
> Nys naght worth a stre. *Lyb. Disc.* 421-22;

"By his sar set he noght a stra." *Ywain and Gawin*, 2655;
"Heo seide, Mahoun ne Appolin
Were not worth the brustel of a swyn,
Ayeynes my lordes grace." *King of Tars*, 776-78.

"He ne yaf a note (i.e., nut) of alle his othes," *Havelok the*

English poet's predilection for this trick of diction came from his reading of Jean de Meung; for by no other two writers is it so frequently used as by Chaucer and the author of the second part of the *Roman de la Rose*. I do not mean to say that the phrases were translated directly out of the French poem; such copying would be unnecessary. For, once a writer had the idea, he could ring all the changes of both verb and noun. So it was with Chaucer. All he needed, I should say, was a literary sanction of the usage (if, indeed, he would stand on ceremony), and he found authority in the *Roman*. Beyond this somewhat liberal admission of the French poet's influence on the Englishman it is unsafe to go. The most probable particular case of indebtedness has been cited in another connection. Koeppel compares Chaucer's *straw* with Jean's *festu;* but says nothing of *leek* and *cive, hawe* and *pome, janne* and *denier*. Not even in the case of unusual expressions, however—and these, if any, would most likely be the ones to be taken over literally—can we say that Chaucer was following one poet and not another.[6]

Dane, 419; see also lines 465, 820, 314-15, 966, 1331, 2051. Gower in his English poem also uses the device: see *Conf. Aman.*, II, 42, III, 588, 1652, 667. The *Owl and the Nightingale* furnishes two of the earliest examples in English: ''þat nis wurþ on of hire heare,'' 1550, and ''A tord ne yeue ic for eu alle,'' 1686.

If the reader cares for more, he should consult Sykes and his bibliography.

[6] I wonder if Chaucer was thinking of False-Seeming's lines,

''Cist argument est trop fieus
Il ne vaut pas un coutel troine,'' RR. 11822-23,

when he has Criseyde say to Troilus:

''Swich arguments ne been not worth a bene.'' T. iii 1167.

(2) EXCLAMATIONS AND IMPRECATIONS

Cursing, anathematizing, swearing by the saints or by the soul of one's father or of oneself, seem to have been a very common habit of the Middle Ages. The French and English romances are full of it. Chaucer's poor parson preaches against it in sections 35-38 of his Tale. The speech of Frenchman, Spaniard, Italian, Englishman, fairly bristled with "by saint Johns" or any other saint—adjurations harmless enough, perhaps, because of their frequency. It would be hard to trace this whole tendency to the French; it would be many times as hard to trace Chaucer's use of such expressions to the influence of the *Roman de la Rose*.

Let us consider Koeppel's specific parallels. The German critic compares Chaucer's "By Seynt Gyle," HF. 1183 and G. 1185, with RR. "par saint Gile," 14676; also the oath "bi seint Denys of Fraunce," B. 1341, with RR. "par saint Denis," 9438. In *King Horn*, 1189, we find "bi seint gile," and Hall in a note shows that this was a common pilgrim's oath.[7] It occurs not infrequently elsewhere in early literature.[8] The same remark may be made of "Bi Seint Denys," the patron saint of France.[9] There is no need of mentioning any more of the saints whose names were used in this way,[11] except, perhaps, the Wife of Bath's

[7] *King Horn*, ed. by Joseph Hall (Oxford, 1901), p. 162.

[8] E. g., *Lyb. Disc.*, 567, 756, 1060; *Amis and Amil*, 952.

[9] For other references to him, see *Lyb. Disc.*, 57, 64; *Amis and Amil*, 1567; Rutebeuf, II, p. 74, l. 248.

[11] The most common seem to have been JOHN: *Lyb. Disc.*, 1688, 715; *Seven Sages*, 2630; *Degore*, 728; *Amis and Amil*, 832, 956, 1336, 1918, 1936, 1960, etc. MICHAEL: *Seven Sages*, 1602, 2163; *Lyb. Disc.*,

vehement and triumphant "But he was quit, by god and by seint Joce!" (D. 483), which, as Skeat shows, was evidently taken from Jean de Meung's *Testament*.[12] It is perfectly clear that the habit of thus swearing by the saints was well-nigh universal in medieval literature—at least after the twelfth century. And it is also believable that the custom was even stronger in the spoken language. So Chaucer was not following Jean de Meung; he was following his own times.

Likewise, when we find such expressions as "by myn heed" (A. 2670, HF. 1875), "by my pan" (A. 1165), "by my crown" (A. 4041, 4099), we are not obliged to infer that they were suggested by Jean's *par mon chief*[13] or *par ma teste*,[14] for these occur elsewhere as well as in the *Roman*.[15] Again, swearing by one's own soul or that of one's father in Chaucer has been referred by Koeppel to the *Roman de la Rose*. He compares with RR. 15218 and 2609, A. 781, E. 2265, 2393; B. 3127, 1178, in all of which Chaucer has "by my fader soule." Although the appearance of this type of oath in English does not seem to be general, nothing definite can be proved about the source of Chaucer's use of it.[16]

740, 811, 1494, 1355; *Ywain and Gawin*, 701. SIMON: *Seven Sages*, 1104; *Yw. and Gaw.*, 2661, etc. And there are also JAMES, THOMAS, MARTIN, MARY, BLANCHART DE VITRE, JULIEN, REMI, and a host of others.

[12] See *Chaucer*, V, 303.

[13] RR. 2004, 4894, 7488, 10052, 11135, 11816, 13523.

[14] RR. 9444.

[15] E. g., in *Yw. and Gaw.*, 521. Cf. *Seven Sages*, 3413; *Chev. au Lyon*, 579.

[16] Neither Godefroy nor the New English Dictionary furnish examples; though I dare say that on examination the Old French

The expression "A wylde fyr upon thair bodyes falle," A. 4172, says Skeat, means "may erysipelas seize them and torment them." If this is the sense of "wylde fyr," the word is one translation of the French *mal feu,* as Koeppel would have it. The curse "mal feu l'arde!" is spoken at least three times in the *Roman de la Rose,*[17] and seems to have been common among the French.[18] Marteau explains the phrase *mal-feu* thus: "On appelait *mal feu* ou *mal des ardens* une épidémie charbonneuse qui fit de nombreuses victimes à Paris en 1131, sous Louis VI." The wild-fire which means a composition of materials very combustible, readily inflammable and hard to extinguish, was often mentioned in the romances.[19] Then again, "wild-fire," like

contes, fableaux, and *chansons de geste* would yield many instances. Machault in his correspondence with Agnes of Navarre uses *par m'ame* constantly. (See Tarbé, pp. 135-154.) The phrase undoubtedly was colloquial. In *Ywain and Gawin* occurs a couplet which combines both swearing by one's own head and the soul of one's father:

> He swar by his owyn crowne,
> And his fadersowl, Uter-Pendragowne. 521-22

[17] I. e., RR. 8152, 9030, 11488. Michel translates *mal-feu* simply as *mauvais feu.*

[18] Cf. "Renarz, la male flambe t'arde!" from the *Roman de Renart* in Paris-Langlois's *Chrestomathie,* p. 168. The editors translate this line as "Renard, que le feu d'enfer te brule!" Also from *Aimeri de Narbonne:* "De mal feu soit ele arse!" Ibid., p. 77, translated in the same way. In *Le Roman de Guillaume de Dole* we find "Que male flambe puisse ardoir!" 3979; and in Marie de France's *Guigemar* (ed. Warnke, 1900), "ceo doinse deus que mals feus l'arde!" 348.

That some distinction was felt between *mal feus* and *male flambe* would appear from RR. 22289, "Mal feus et male flambe l'arde."

[19] See Skeat's note, V, p. 301. Cf. also *King Alisaunder,* 1615, 1903, 2783-4, 2883, 3032.

mal-feu, possibly also meant "hell-fire." Chaucer's phrase may connote all three ideas of erysipelas, Greek fire, and hell fire. If erysipelas was known as "wilde-fyr" as early as Aelfric's day,[20] the term did not have to be reintroduced into England from France. But even if it did come from France, the frequency of its use there makes is impossible to prove Chaucer's indebtedness to Jean de Meung for this detail. The malediction "A wilde fyr upon thair bodyes falle" certainly belongs in kind with "The devel set hem on fuyre! (*King of Tars*, 646), "The deuel of helle him sone take!" (*Havelok*, 446) and "The devil sette hir soules bothe a-fyre!" (Leg. of G. W., 2493)—curses to be found everywhere in medieval literature.

The exclamation "Avoy!" occurs once in Chaucer (B. 4098). The situation is this: Chaunticleer is groaning uneasily in his sleep, when Pertelote, frightened, awakens him and asks what is his trouble. The cock then narrates his bad dream about the fox. Pertelote answers,

"Avoy." . . . "fi on you, hertelees."
"Alas!" quod she, "for, by that god above,
Now han ye lost myn herte and al my love;
I can nat love a coward, by my feith." (4098-4101)

Skeat glosses *avoy* very nearly correctly, I think, when he interprets it as *fie!* But as Pertelote uses the word, she expresses disgust as well as indignation. What she really says is, "Begone! fy on you, coward!" The fact that Chaucer repeats the "quod she" in the following line, with the interjection "Alas!" seems to be proof that *avoy* does

[20] See Skeat's note to A. 4172 (Vol. V, p. 125).

not connote "alas." Koeppel implies that *avoy*, as used here, was taken from the *Roman de la Rose*, where the word occurs twice.[21] But Chaucer's *avoy* is not equivalent to the French *avoi*, unless the latter be derived from the English *away*, as Marteau suggests.[22] Besides, the word occurs in English and Latin before Chaucer,[23] as well as elsewhere in Old French.[24] And so altogether nothing definite can be said as to the source of this hapaxlegomenon in Chaucer. It would be just as fair to say that *harrow!* came from the *Roman de Renart* as *avoy!* from the *Roman de la Rose;* and upon whom, pray, might not such expressions as *alas! par foy!* be fathered?

(3) FIGURES OF SPEECH

Allegory, or Personification

"On a souvent accusé les auteurs du Roman de la Rose d'avoir mis à la mode l'allégorie, qui a gâté la poésie des siècles suivants. C'est une erreur semblable à celle du geographe qui attribuerait exclusivement l'existence d'un fleuve à l'un de ses nombreux affluents. Le Roman de la

---

[21] L. 7998, glossed by Michel as *holà;* and l. 17369, where it clearly means *hélas*.

[22] The editors of the New English Dictionary leave the etymology unaccounted for: "Avoy—(OF. *avoi, avoy!* of uncertain origin). Exclamation of surprise, fear, remonstrance." Marteau (V, 106) gives his guess: "Avoi—allons, eh quoi! Racine angl. away." Constans, in his *Chrestomathie*, p. 174, defines the word as an "interjection marquant l'étonnement et l'indignation; oh!"

[23] See N. E. D. for instances, s. v.

[24] Godefroy (I, 536) gives nearly two columns of illustrations. He defines *avoi* as an "exclamation de surprise, de terreur, d'affirmation énergique, d'exhortation, de commandement, de prière."

Rose s'est jeté dans le courant des allégories, dont la source remontait très haut et qui s'était grossi depuis longtemps d'un grand nombre d'œuvres antérieures; il en a été, certainement, l'affluent de beaucoup le plus important, il en a augmenté la force plus que tout autre, mais pas à l'éxclusion des autres."[25]

Speaking of the influence of the *Roman de la Rose*, Professor Neilson writes: "A direct knowledge of that poem by any later mediaeval author is to be presumed about as certainly as a knowledge of the Bible; and even though a writer had not himself read the book, its influence would still appear in his work if he followed the allegorical tradition at all. And this tradition, it has sufficiently appeared, every allegorist did follow."[26]

The kind of allegory in the *Roman* which seems to have been most used by Chaucer was nothing more than personification of abstractions. Such characters as Pity, Cruelty, Gentilesse, Pleasance, and Delight are usually introduced into the English poet's work simply to fill out a situation, to elaborate a description, to turn a compliment, or perhaps to enforce a bit of satire. A complete list of the personified abstractions employed by Chaucer would

---

[25] Langlois, p. 46. The critic goes on to discuss the different kinds of allegory, and to show that by the end of the twelfth century allegorical poetry was in full bloom: "C'est l'époque ou parurent *l'Anticlaudianus* et le *de Planctu Naturae*, d'Alain de Lille; le *Besant de Dieu*, de Guillaume le Clerc; le *Roman des Eles*, le *Songe d'Enfer*, la *Voie de Paradis*, de Raoul de Houdan; le *Tournoiement d'Antechrist*, de Huon de Meri; les deux romans de *Carité* et de *Miserere*, du reclus de Molliens; les *Bestiaires*, . . . et une foule d'autres compositions du même genre." p. 53.

[26] *Court of Love*, p. 228.

run into the scores, I dare say; and a catalogue of those occurring in the *Roman de la Rose* would contain as many items.[27] Guillaume de Machault enumerates in *Le Dit du Vergier* alone at least twenty-two.[28] Common sense should give sufficient assurance of the absolute futility of attempting to trace the source of such mushroom growths as personified abstractions. Even more than the device of picturesque negation can this be carried on indefinitely. And yet Skeat boldly asserts that the allegorical personages in these lines from the Prologue to the *Legend*,

[27] Personification appears to be most abundant in the *Compleynt to Pite* and the *Parlement of Foules*. In the former are mentioned Pite, Crueltee, Beautee, Lust, Jolitye, Maner, Youthe, Honestee, Wisdom, Estaat, Dreed, Governaunce, Bountee, Gentilesse, Curtesye, Trouthe, Desire. In the latter, in addition to seven already named, we fine Plesaunce, Aray, Craft, Delyt, Fool-hardinesse, Flatery, Messagerye, Mede, Pees, Pacience, Art, Behest, Jalousye, Richesse, Nature. In these two poems alone, then, occur thirty-two different personifications.

For a goodly list of some in the *Roman de la Rose* compare the following:

    Dame Oiseuse la Jardiniere
   I vint o la plus grant baniere;
   Noblesce de cuer et Richesce,
   Franchise, Pitie et Largesce,
   Hardemens, Honors, Cortoisie,
   Delis, Simplesce et Compaignie,
   Seurte, Deduis et Leesce,
   Jolivete, Biaute, Jonesce,
   Humilite et Pacience,
   Bien-Celer, Contrainte-Astenence,
   Qui Faux-Semblant o li amaine;
   Sans li i venist-ele a paine. 11208-11219

[28] Voloirs, Pensers, Dous plaisir, Loiaute, Celers, Desir, Grace, Pitie, Esperance, Souvenir, Franchise, Atemprance, Dangier, Paour, Honte, Durtez, Cruautez, Doutance, Dous Penser, Espoir, Dangiers, Hardiment.

> Al founde they Daunger for a tyme a lord,
> Yet Pitee, through his stronge gentil might
> Forgaf, and made Mercy passen Right (160-162),

were suggested by the *Roman de la Rose*.[29] Moreover, it must be indiscriminating enthusiasm for the French poem which will lead another investigator [29a] to say, referring to this passage in the *Book of the Duchess*,

> For that tyme Youthe, my maistresse,
> Governed me in ydelnesse. (797-798),

that "ydelnesse is not perhaps without relation to Oiseuse,"—the maiden who opens the wicket to the dreamer in the *Roman de la Rose*. Surely Chaucer had seen youths reared in idleness, and knew the effects of such early training. Besides, there is no personification of "ydelnesse" here.

The characterization of "ydelnesse" (G. 3) as "porter of the gate of delyces" was taken from the *Romaunt*, 528-594, says Skeat. Chaucer repeated the idea in the *Knightes Tale*, A. 1940, and in the *Persones Tale*, I, 714. There is no doubt that this allegory was due originally to Guillaume de Lorris.

It is no more safe to say that Chaucer took two or three personified abstractions from the *Roman de la Rose* than that he took all those that are common to him and the French poem; unless, of course, other defining characteristics are also present. As, for example,

> "jelousye,
> That wered of yelwe goldes a gerland." (A. 1928-29),

[29] See Vol. III, 295. The rest of his note is more convincing. For the phrase, "Mercy passen Right," cf. T. iii 1282 and A. 3089.
[29a] Miss Cipriani.

which is surprisingly like

> Especiaument Jalousie
> O tout son chapel de soussie   (RR. 22816-17),

as Koeppel showed. But Jean de Meung says nothing about "a cokkow sitting on hir hand" (A. 1930), a capital and distinctly Chaucerian touch.

Similes

Guillaume de Lorris seems to have been fond of short similes used descriptively. These are seldom more than a half-line in length. Very rarely, indeed, does either he or Jean de Meung employ the extended comparison which later was so characteristic of Dante. By Chaucer's day many similes had become stereotyped and so commonplace as to have lost almost all suggestiveness. Their use was subconscious, so to speak; at any rate, we may consider it as a stylistic trait, because such similes were thrown in to fill out a line or to carry forward a narrative or descriptive passage. Often, however, they only marked time: they were chiefly used, at least by Chaucer, I think we may say, as literary "padding."

To the ears of most of us to-day, a comparison like "She was as simple as a dove, or as a bride," sounds fresh; but on fourteenth-century ears it probably fell with little effect, if, indeed, it was noticed at all. In the first part of the *Roman de la Rose* we continually meet with such phrases as "vert com une cive" (200), "nue comme vers" (554), "la face comme une pomme" (808), "plus noirs que mores" (918), or "que deables d'enfer" (964), "clere comme la lune" (1000), "tendre comme rousee" (1003), "blanche comme flor de lis" (1005), "blanche comme nois" (1199), "plus clere qu'argens fins" (1535). These have all been translated accurately and tastefully in fragment A of the *Romaunt of the Rose*.[30] Jean de Meung adds to Guillaume's list; he speaks of foolish men who believe the fawning words of flatterers ("Ansinc cum ce fust Evangile," RR. 5600), and he describes Vulcan's net as "Plus soutile que fil d'araigne" (19007).

Chaucer, for his part, is not behind these French poets in the use of short similes. For the larger number of them, however, equivalents can be found in the romances and other early French and English poems. Such expressions as "true as steel," "hair like gold," "dead as a stone," "still as a stone," "cold as a stone," "color like the sun," "fresh as a rose," "white as milk," had become platitudes. And we may use a hackneyed comparison to express the futility of the search for their source: it is like hunting for a needle in a hay-stack.

Let us take even a somewhat more elaborate case to show the extent of this convention. Chaucer's figure describing Blanche—

> That as the someres sonne bright
> Is fairer, clerer, and hath more light
> Than any planete, [is] in heven,
> The mone, or the sterres seven,
> For al the worlde, so had she
> Surmounted hem alle of beaute
> 　　　　　　　(B. Duch. 821-826)—

[30] Rom. 212, 454, 819, 928, 974, 1010, 1013, 1214, 1556-57.

is compared by Miss Cipriani to Guillaume de Lorris's picture of Courtesy—

> El fu clere comme la lune
> Est avers les autres estoiles,
> Qui ne ressemblent que chandoiles.
>
> (RR. 1246-48; also 1000-02)

A later critic, however, says that Chaucer was following Machault:—

> Si en choisi entre les autres une
> Qui, tout aussi com li solaus la lune
>   Veint de clarte,
> Avoit ella les autres seurmonte
> De pris, d'onneur, de grace et de biaute.[31]

But this figure is used in exactly the same way in German, Scandinavian, and Oriental literature.[32] It seems, therefore, to have been the common property of poets.

---

[31] *Le Jugement dou Roy de Behaigne*, ll. 286-290. See Professor Kittredge's *Chauceriana* in Mod. Phil., April, 1910. This parallel was pointed out by Sandras, although he mistook the poem for the *Fontaine Amoureuse*. Skeat perpetuated Sandras's error.

[32] Cf. this from the *Nibelungenlied*, Aventiure V, stanza 19:

Sam der liehte mane	vor den sternen stat,
des scin so luterliche	ab den wolken gat,
dem stuont si nu geliche	vor maneger frouwen guot
des wart da wol gehoehet	den aieren heleden der muot.

Or this from the *Volsunga-Saga*:

"Gudrun had a daughter by Sigurd hight Swanhild; she was fairest of all women, eager-eyed as her father, so that few durst look under the brows of her; and as far did she excel other woman kind as the sun excels the other lights of heaven." Chapter XI, Morris's translation, p. 151. For other examples in M. H. G. literature, see Ballerstedt, p. 23.

Or this from *The Arabian Nights*:

"The women encompassed her, and appeared like stars; she, in the

When Chaucer says of Nature's forming Virginia,

> For right as she can peynt a lilie whyt
> And reed a rose, right with swich peynture
> She peynted hath this noble creature   (C. 32-34),

he is merely using conventional similes with an allegorical twist of the figure. Skeat compares with this passage RR. 17178-80; but examples of the juxtaposition of the rose and lily to describe beauty are common enough.[33] Thirteenth

midst of them, being as the moon when the clouds have withdrawn from before it." The Arabian Nights' Entertainments, translated by Edward William Lane (New York), Vol. I, p. 384. In Vol. II, p. 10, we read, "The bride came forward among the female slaves like the moon among the stars, or the chief pearl among the minor pearls of the string."

In another part of the *Roman de la Rose* from that cited by Miss Cipriani occurs a much closer parallel to the description of the Duchess. Faux-Semblant says:

> Autant cum par, sa grant valor,   (12751)
> Soit de clarte, soit de chalor,
> Sormonte li solaus la lune,
> Qui trop est plus troble et plus brune   (12754)
>
> .   .   .   .
>
> Tant sormonte ceste Evangile   (12758)
> Ceus que li quatre evangelistres
> Jhesu-Crist firent a lor tistres.
> *De tex comparoisons grant masse*
> *I trovast-l'en, que ge trespasse.*   (12762)

(The lines that I have italicized form an interesting bit of literary criticism.) Chaucer makes use of this figure of the brightness of the sun to describe the goddess Nature, in PF. 298-301.

[33] *King Horn*, 15-16; *Roman de Guillaume de Dole*, 696-7; and Machault's rondeau, "Blanche com lys, plus que rose vermeille" (Tarbé, p. 51). For a woman's color compared to the rose, see *Lyb. Disc.*, 1244, 880; *King of Tars*, 14; *Le Jug. dou Roy de Beh.* 358-9; Marie de France's *Eliduc*, 1011-12; and RR. 844-45. Also *Knightes Tale* (A) 1037-38, which seems to be reminiscent of *Rom.*, 855-56. The rhymes are identical. For "white as a lily," compare RR. 1005;

and fourteenth century poets—and reading public (!) as well—had definite requirements that the lady of romance must meet to be considered beautiful. First of all, she must have blonde hair,—yellow or golden,—gray eyes, rose-red complexion, arched eyebrows, long and straight nose, and small, ivory-white neck.[34] Her whole countenance

Emare, 205; *Sir Tryamour*, 649; *Knightes Tale* (A) 2178. For numerous examples in French and Latin poetry, see Langlois, pp. 40-41.

[34] It seems superfluous to record instances since such usage was almost universal; and once for all it may be said that such descriptions were entirely conventional. It is this kind of details that I wish to dispose of here; variations from them will be discussed in Chapter V.

HAIR. References to golden hair are many in Chaucer: B. Duch. 858; PF. 267; HF. 1387; A. 3314; D. 304, etc. Yellow hair is mentioned in L. 1672, 1747; A. 675, 1049, 2166. Doubtless there were different shades of yellow meant, too; certainly the Pardoner's hair, "yelwe as any wax," is not to be put in the same class with Emily's. Golden, I suspect, was used sometimes to describe red hair—not brick red, but golden red—for gold was regularly given the epithet red in English and Germanic literature. Professor Carpenter, in his translation of the *Nibelungenlied* (World's Great Classics), in a note on p. 391 says, "The comparison of the brilliant color of a blooming northern beauty to gold, 'red gold,' as it is constantly called in Old German and Old English poetry, forms a curious contrast with the phrases of Catullus, 'inaurata pallidior statua,' 'magis fulgore expalluit auri,' and that of Statius 'pallidus fossor redit erutoque concolor auro,' not to mention the saying of Diogenes that gold was pale through fear of those who had a design on it." At any rate, a typical beauty's *hair* was blonde. Michel, in a note to RR. 527 (Vol. I, p. 18) says, "Dans le moyen âge, ni homme ni femme n'était réputé beau s'il n'avait les cheveux blonds. Voyez à ce sujet une note de *Théâtre français au moyen âge*, p. 58. Les cheveux noirs étaient rare à la fin du XIIIe siècle; cependant il est question de combattants blonds et *mors*, de 'personnes noires et blondes,' dans une chronique de l'époque, dans la *Branche des royaux lignages*, de Guillaume Guiart, v. 2756 et 6925."

EYES. Skeat in a note to A. 152 (Vol. V, p. 17) says, "This

must shine as the sun. Such descriptions could be, and probably were, written automatically by the poets of the "courtly school" of Chaucer's day, and it is useless to attempt to find an original for them.

(grey) seems to have been the favorite color of ladies' eyes in Chaucer's time and even later,'' and he cites a number of instances. Grey was used to translate the French *vair*, as may be seen by comparing A. 152 and 3974 with

Les iex ot vairs come cristal (Fab. de Gombert et des deux clercs).

Absolon's eyes "greye as goos" were doubtless the color of Dame Idleness's:

"Les iex ot plus vairs c'uns faucons,'' (RR. 533). Compare also Rom. 546 with RR. 533, and Rom. 862 with RR. 850. *Vair* was the conventional color of eyes in early French poetry. Cf. RR. 811, 1202, 1581, etc. But the word also meant scintillating, shining, as well as grey. Compare *Roman de Guillaume de Dole*, 705, where the word cannot signify gray or blue. See also Marteau's note 16 to Vol. I.

COMPLEXION. "Bright, fresh, rosy, new,'' are the adjectives commonly used to describe a beauty's complexion, or *rode*. See note 33.

EYEBROWS. Eyebrows must be arched and must not run together. In the description of Oiseuse we read,

> Son entr'oil ne fu pas petis, (RR. 530)

which means that the space between her eyes and the space between her two eyebrows was not small; in other words, it was well marked. In line 529 Oiseuse is said to have "sorcis votis.'' So also again in line 1202. With RR. 849,

> Les sorcis bruns et enarchies,

we might compare what is said of the Carpenter's dainty wife:

> Ful smale y-pulled were hir browes two,
> And tho were bent, and blake as any sloo. (A. 3245-46)

In the *Roman de Guillaume de Dole* are mentioned,

> Sorcils bien fez, lons et tretiz,
> Non pas joignans, c'est veritez. (706-707)

(Cf. also l. 362.) Chaucer evidently considered joined eyebrows no mark of beauty:

However, when Chaucer says that Fortune is like "filth over y-strawed with floures," B. Duch. 628-9, he is using a rarer figure, and may be following RR. 9656-62, as Koeppel noted.[35] The poet's comparison of the deceitful Dame

> And, save hir browes joyneden y-fere,
> Ther nas no lak, in ought I can espyen. (T. v. 813-814)

See Krapp's article in Mod. Lang. Notes, Vol. XIX, p. 235.
In the *Court of Love* Rosiall's eyebrows are thus described:

> . . . lovelich browes, flawe, of colour pure,
> Bytwene the which was mene disseveraunce
> From every brow, to shewen a distaunce. (782-84)

In fact, the whole full-length portrait of this maiden is worth reading because of the conventionalities it makes use of (778-833). But complete word-pictures in color of ideal beauties were frequent in literature long before Chaucer's day.

NOSE. The Prioresse's nose is "tretys." See Skeat's note to A. 152. Pug-noses were clearly not in style even in Guillaume de Lorris's day. Compare

> Et si n'ot pas nes d'Orlenois,
> Aincois l'avoit lonc et traitis, (RR. 1200-1201)

although there seems to have been plenty of them in real life to make fun of. See Michel's note on the proverbial Orleans nose (Vol. I, p. 39). Also compare *Lyb. Disc.*, 885.

NECK. In the English metrical romances necks were usually white as "swan, whale-bone, snow, flower on the hill, milk, etc." Compare Chaucer's B. Duch. 939ff.; A. 238; *King of Tars*, 16; *Lyb. Disc.*, 889. In French poetry, RR. 539-40; *Rom. de Guil. de Dole*, 713-714; Machault's *Confort d'Ami* (Tarbé, p. 99, line 32), etc., etc.

ADORNMENTS. Nearly all the beautiful women in early French poetry wore crowns of gold and jewels or wreaths of flowers. Chaplets appear in literature long before Guillaume de Lorris's *Roman*. Cf. *Roman de Guillaume de Dole*, 199, 204-5, 1537-8, etc. Chaucer's description of Alcestis, L. 215-217, which Skeat compares with *Roman*, 1108-9, is founded upon a conventional idea; it probably owes nothing directly to Guillaume de Lorris.

[35] Langlois points out no analogue to this passage in the *Roman*.

Fortune to a scorpion, B. Duch. 636-641 and E. 2058-64, Koeppel thinks was inspired by RR. 7480-82. But as Chaucer more than once elsewhere likened false women to scorpions and appears to have had abundant literary and popular tradition to copy,[36] it is unnecessary to look to the French as original.

A very curious note of Skeat's to E. 880,—

Lat me nat lyk a worm go by the weye,—

may be reproduced here as a sample of a scholar's confusion: "These lines (i.e. 880-882) are Chaucer's own; l. 880 is characteristic of him. The phrase in l. 880 seems to have been proverbial . . . But Chaucer got it from *Le Roman de la Rose,* 445; see his translation, l. 454." Now, the similitude in the *Roman* forms a part of the description of Povrete; and there is no suggestion of "go by the weye" in

Qu'ele iere nue comme vers.

As Skeat says, the comparison was doubtless proverbial. Why, then, should Chaucer necessarily have had to learn it from the French poem?

Haeckel (p. 57) shows that "strokes as thikke as hail" (L. 655) was proverbial. There is no need of assuming with Koeppel that this simile was taken from RR. 16558-59. Nor can it be proved that the innocent clause "As

---

[36] Cf. B. 360, 404, and Skeat's notes, III, 479, and V, 153; also D. 1994-95, which Skeat says is from RR. 17528 and 10547-50. His note (V, 337) is not altogether convincing. Sandras compares B. Duch. 633-37 with a passage from Machault's *Remède de Fortune;* see *Etude,* etc., p. 291, and *Chaucer,* I, 479.

craft countrefeteth kinde" (HF. 1213) was imitated directly from RR. 16967—a parallel of Skeat's.

Again, Skeat compares "Singeth ful merrier than the papejay," E. 2322, with RR. 10845-46. The parallel is close, but the figure is not unusual in early poetry. "The papejay," as Mead has noted, "seems to have held a place by a sort of prescriptive right in the lists of medieval birds,"[37] and references to it are not infrequent. Machault, for instance, speaks of the "jolis papegaus."[38] Chaucer himself mentions this bird several times.[39]

The proverbially beautiful voices of mermaids, which furnished Chaucer with this characterization of Chaunticleer,

> Song merier than the mermayde in the see,   (B. 4460)

are mentioned in the *Roman*, ll. 675-678, but the resemblance is probably of little significance.

A comparison of the figure found in T. iv, 519-520:—

> This Troilus in teres gan distille,
> As licour out of alambyk ful faste,

with the passage that probably suggested it—

> Je vois maintes fois que to plores
> Cum alambic sus alutel,   (RR. 7118-19)

will reveal the superiority of the English turn of the words. It seems more appropriate to speak of the person distilling tears than to speak of an alembic weeping. The effective-

---
[37] *Squyr*, etc., p. lix.
[38] Tarbé, p. 45, l. 20.
[39] PF. 359; B. 1559, 1957.

ness of the scene is enhanced, moreover, by the implied silence of Troilus's grief. With line 519 we might also compare *King Horn*, 676:—

And horn let the teres stille.

Miss Cipriani says that Reason's speech (RR. 7118-7143) is to be considered in connection with Chaucer's humorous conception of Troilus and Pandarus. So it is, but not here in Book IV. Pandarus has become all sympathy, and does not feel in a jocular mood. Nor does he during the rest of the story.

The circumstances under which Pandarus uses the simile "Alday as thikke as been flen from an hyve," (iv, 1356), are so unlike those under which the Amis, quoting from *Valerius,* speaks of wicked women, who

Sunt essains plus grans que de mouches,
Qui se recuillent en lor rouches   (RR. 9472-73),

and the figure is so familiar that we will leave Koeppel to prove Chaucer's indebtedness for it to the French poem. Koeppel also, by the way, equates this couplet from the *Roman* with T. ii, 193-94.

The simile in PF. 148-151 appears to owe nothing to *Rom*. 1182 ff. (RR. 1164 ff.), where the attractive powers of silver and gold are compared with the well-known property of "adamaunt."

Metaphors

A few metaphors in *Troilus* and the *Canterbury Tales* have been traced to the *Roman de la Rose,* and there the scent seems to have been lost. For instance, Pandarus's cheering words to Troilus—

"Stand faste, for to good port hastow rowed," (i, 969)—

is said to translate RR. 13700-701. But the expression was very common. It occurs at least fifty years before the *Roman*.[40] Chaucer expresses the same idea in the line

"And do that I my ship to haven winne." (AA. 20)

The Wife of Bath's reply to the Pardoner, who has interrupted her in her Prologue,

Nay, thou shalt drinken of another tonne
Er that I go, shal savoure wors than ale (D. 170-171),

Skeat says is probably due to the *Roman de la Rose*, 7549-56. Koeppel adds RR. 11396-99, which is a much closer parallel:—

> Des tonneaus qu'il a tous jors dobles,
> Dont l'un est cler et l'autre trobles,
> (Li uns est dous, et l'autre amer
> Plus que n'est suie ne la mer).

[40] I. e., in the *Roman de Guil. de Dole:*

> Bien est a droit port arrivez. (l. 1393)

As early as Ovid we come across the same thought:

> Contigimus portus, quo mihi cursus erat.

(*Rem. Amor.*, 812.) This figure runs all through the *Ars Amatoria*. Cf., for instance, *Ars Amat.*, II, 9-10, with Pandarus's words of restraint to Troilus. Rutebeuf has the following couplet, which is worth comparing in this connection:

> Arivez fusses a mal port
> Ou il n'a solaz ne deport;

(*Œuvres*, II, p. 259, ll. 590-91.)

In the Wife's boast,

> I made him of the same wode a croce (D. 484),

Skeat clearly shows that Chaucer was copying Jean de Meung's *Testament*.[41] Koeppel draws attention to a similar expression in RR. 15162-63:—

> Puisque vous m'aves faite coupe
> Ge vous ferai d'autel pain soupe.

But this type of figure is very ordinary, is thoroughly colloquial, and was doubtless of popular origin.

Miss Cipriani compares the following line and a half,

> For she, that of his herte berth the keye,
> Was absent   (T. v, 460-461),

with RR. 2018-20, and might pertinently have added AA. 323-24—

> Arcite hath born awey the keye
> Of al my worlde and my good aventure.

The lines referred to in the *Roman*,

> Lors la me toucha au coste,
> Et ferma mon cuer si soef,
> Qu'a grant poine senti la clef,

record how the god of Love locks the dreamer's heart as a pledge of loyal and constant service. There is only a general similarity between this situation and that expressed in the two passages quoted from Chaucer—one where

---

[41] The French goes, "Si li refait sovent d'autel fust une croce." See note in Vol. V, 303.

Criseyde, who is represented as having the key of Troilus's heart, has deserted her lover and is soon to prove false; the other where Anelida is bemoaning the fact that the faithless Arcite has run off with the "key of her worlde," that is, her love, honor, peace of mind. An explanation of the significance of the lines in *Anelida and Arcite* may be found, I believe, in Machault's *Le Livre du Voir Dit*. When the lover, who is the poet himself, comes to part with his mistress, she takes a key of gold, hands it to him, and says, "Guard it well, for it is the key of my treasure."

> Si attaingni une clavette
> D'or, et de main de maistre faite
> Et dist: ceste clef porteres,
> Amis, et bien la garderes;
> Car c'est la clef de mon tresor.
> Je vous en fais seigneur des or;
> Et desseur tout en serez mastre,
> Et si l'aim plus que mon oeil destre:
> Car c'est m'onneur; c'est ma richesse;
> C'est ce dont je puis faire largesse.
>
> (Tarbé, pp. 49-50[42])

These lines from the French and the passage in *Anelida*

---

[42] Tarbé's note (s. v. *clavette*, p. 161) explains a little more definitely and may be quoted in part: "Parmi les usages singuliers en vigueur au moyen âge, il faut certainement compter celui des ceintures de chasteté. Les jeunes filles et les jeunes dames en portaient . . . L'usage de ces ceintures était alors assez general: on en montre encore dans les musées d'Italie. Eustache Deschamps y fait allusion dans un de ses virelais: s'il s'agit d'une jeune fille qui fait l'énumeration de ses appas:

> Que quinze ans n'ay, je vous dis.
> Moult est mes tresors jolis;
> S'en garderay la clavette, etc."

and Arcite are not unlike a couplet in *Ywain and Gawin:*—

> Thou ert the lok and kay also
> Of al my wele, and al my wo.   (2681-82)

The figure of the cold sword of winter, which cuts down the flowers and drives away the birds, is both personification and metaphor. Chaucer uses it twice—L. 127 and F. 57. It occurs in the *Roman de la Rose,*—

> Il fauche
> Les florettes et la verdure
> A l'espee de sa froidure.   (6678-80)

but Jean de Meung took it directly from the *Anticlaudianus* of Alanus de Insulis, says Ballerstedt:—

> Sicque furens Aquilo praedatur singula, flores
> Frigoris ense metit, et pristina guadia delet.
> (VII, 8, 21-22)

Three lines from Machault's *Jugement dou Roy de Navarre* resemble the RR. passage very closely:—

> Car bise l'avoit tout desteint
> Qui mainte fleur a decopee
> Par la froidure de s'espee.   (34-36)

It is uncertain to whom Machault and Chaucer were indebted; possibly Jean de Meung, possibly Alanus. De Meung's figure is much finer than Machault's.

Criseyde's determined line,

> Shall noon housbonde seyn to me "Chekmat,"
> (T. ii. 754)

which Koeppel refers to RR. 7388-89,—

> Eschec et mat li ala dire
> Desus son destrier auferrant,

has just as close a parallel in Rutebeuf's *Le Miracle de Theophile:*—

> Bien m'a dit li evesque: "Eschac,"
> Et m'a rendu mate en l'angle:
> Sanz avoir m'a lessie tout sangle.   (6-8)

Even if B. Duch. 660-661 is taken from the *Roman de la Rose*,[43] one should remember that Rutebeuf, the author of the *Roman de Poire,* Deschamps, and Machault all used the figure of a game of chess. It is only fair that they, too, be allowed to have had some influence on Chaucer in this detail! The figure seems to have been often employed by medieval poets, and may well have been colloquial.

An almost literal translation of the *Roman* that Koeppel and Skeat have both missed is Chaucer's

> Taketh the fruyt and lat the chaf be stille.   (B. 4633)
> G'en pren le grain et laiz la paille.   (RR. 11986)

Elsewhere Chaucer uses this metaphor of the grain and the chaff, or straw, as in

> Me list nat of the chaf nor of the stree
> Maken so long a tale, as of the corn.   (B. 701-2)
> But yit I sey, what eyleth thee to write
> The draf of stories and forgo the corn?   (L. (a) 311-12)
> Let be the chaf, and wryt wel of the corn.   (L. (a) 529)

But the comparison was very old.[44]

[43] See Skeat, I, 480, 478.
[44] See Jeremiah, xxiii, 28, and St. Matthew, iii, 12. Rutebeuf uses *grain* and *paille* in juxtaposition in

> "Je sui li grains, il sont la paille."

(*Œuvres,* II, p. 283, l. 559.)

CHAUCER AND THE ROMAN DE LA ROSE 101

I doubt very much if Troilus's beautiful apostrophe in the lines

> O sterre, of which I lost have al the light,
>   With herte soor wel oughte I to bewayle,
> That ever derk in torment, night by night,
>   Toward my deeth with wind in stere I sayle;
>   (v. 638-41)

is reminiscent of a passage Miss Cipriani quotes from the *Roman*, 8300-305. For variety, I cite Ellis's translation of the lines:—

> The mariner who steers his bark
> Through unknown seas, when night falls dark,
> Regardeth not one only star
> To guide his course, nor would he far
> Entrust his ship with one poor sail,
> But try what others might avail
> 'Mid storm and tempest.   (7935-7941)

The reader can judge for himself. This figure of the mariner steering by the stars, it might be remarked, occurs again in the *Roman*, 16871-74.

The legend of the Phoenix was so common in the Middle Ages that there is no need of deriving the knight's characterization of the Duchess,—

> Trewely she was, to myn yë
> The soleyn fenix of Arabye,
> For there liveth never but oon;   (B. Duch. 981-83)

from the account of this *rara avis* in the *Roman de la Rose*.[45]

---

[45] Lines 16913 ff. See Skeat's note, Vol. I, p. 485. Compare also *The Pearl*, ed. Osgood, ll. 429-432.

The French poet says,

> Tous jors est-il un seul Fenis;

but he also quotes from *Valerius,* in another place:—

> Prodefame, par saint Denis,
> Dont il est mains que de fenis. (RR. 9438-39)

The deduction is unavoidable. Surely Chaucer did not have this passage in mind!

Anaphora

Anaphora need not detain us long, as this rhetorical device was freely used in the older literature. Professor Mead[46] recalls the fact that Chaucer "begins sixteen consecutive lines in the *Hous of Fame,* iii, 871-886 (misprinted 876), with *Of,* and twenty-four lines in the *Parlement of Foules,* 337-364, with *The.*" Mead also mentions T. v, 1828-1832, 1849-1854. Although this usage is very common in the *Roman de la Rose,* it is found elsewhere in early French and Middle English literature.[47]

---

[46] In his edition of *The Squyr of Lowe Degre* (Boston, 1904), p. 90, note to lines 941-954.

[47] Cf. RR. 4910-27, 5074-79, 5095-5100, 5785-88, 9340-47, 9680-86, 11836-11840, 12515-21. In Rutebeuf's *Du Secrestain et de la Famme au Chevalier,* 49-60, ten lines out of twelve begin with the word *Envie.* The identical passage, with the exception of the last line, is repeated in *La Voie de Paradis,* 344-354. In *La Vie Sainte Marie l'Egiptianne* occur seven consecutive verses beginning with the emphatic *Por toi.* Compare Machault (ed. Tarbé), pp. 42, 78; *Roman de Guillaume de Dole,* 361-63, 370-73, 431-435, etc.

For instances in Middle English, see, besides Mead's note, *King Alisaunder,* 2212-15, 3418-22; *Moral Ode* (B-text, ed. Morris), 82-87; *Owl and Nightingale* (MS. Jes. Coll., ed. Wells), 66-69, 89-91, 776-780; 796-801, etc. In the *Confessio Amantis,* Bk. III, 279-285, seven consecutive lines begin with *O.*

Rhymes and Vocabulary

No scholarly investigation into the question of the influence of the *Roman de la Rose* on Chaucer's rhymes and vocabulary can be made until there appears a critical text and complete glossary of the French poem. It is to be hoped that Langlois's long-promised edition will supply the want soon. The Chaucer Society has furnished accurate enough material for a study of the English poet's half of the comparison; but Michel's text of the *Roman* is far from adequate. Kaluza's painstaking reconstruction of the parts of the French poem that correspond to the English *Romaunt*[48] gives a starting-ground at least, and in a later work[49] he gives tables in which we find that there are a hundred and eight identical rhymes in Chaucer's genuine work and the part of the French poem corresponding to fragments A and C of the English translation. While this information is interesting enough, and while it is not impossible that Chaucer used the *Roman* as a sort of rhyme-dictionary as well as encyclopedia of facts, it cannot be proved, except in a few cases that are discussed in other connections in the present work, that the English poet owed any particular rhymes to the French poem. Nor can we prove, until we have an Old French dictionary of the type of the New English Dictionary, Chaucer's indebtedness to the *Roman de la Rose* for words that he uses elsewhere than at the ends of verses.

---

[48] Max Kaluza: *The Romaunt of the Rose*, from the Glasgow MS., parallel with its original, Le Roman de la Rose, Part I.—The Texts. Ch. Soc., 1891.

[49] *Chaucer und der Rosenroman* (Berlin, 1893), pp. 84-123.

Koeppel instances a few cases of identical words and phrases which he thinks owe something to Jean de Meung.

> Neporquant il vous tient en lesse   (RR. 8056)

is to be compared with

> And sin that slouth her holdeth in a lees (G. 19).

The investigator also cites Jean de Meung's *Codicile:*

> Povrete, qui si vous compresse,
> Qu'elle vous maint com chien en lesse.   (34-35)

Lesse and *lees* here mean the same thing, "leash—a thong or line in which hounds are held." This word is found in English as early as 1300, and the phrase "in a lees" appears to have been not uncommon.[50] Certainly the idea of comparing a person held in restraint to a hound straining in the leash, could have occurred originally to scores of sport-loving Englishmen. There is no doubt that *lees* was taken over from the French; but it had been adopted long before Chaucer's day.

The phrase "do [make] no fors," meaning "to take no account of, attach no importance to," is used several times by Chaucer: B. 4131; D. 1234, 1512; H. 68; I. 711, etc. Other verbs such as *let, give, take, have,* were equivalent to *do* or *make* in this expression, which we find in English as early as Robert of Brunne, 1303.[51] Godefroy[52] gives a few instances of *ne pas faire force d'un chose*, meaning "n'en être pas effrayé, n'en pas faire difficulté," but he

[50] See N. E. D., s. v., definition 1, for examples.
[51] See N. E. D., s. v. *force*, definition 21.
[52] Vol. IV, p. 65.

does not cite examples from the *Roman de la Rose*. Koeppel parallels these lines in Chaucer with RR. 14219 and 21016; but enough has been said to show that the phrase was not unusual. Indeed, the wealth of synonyms for "do" as opposed to the single French "faire" seems to indicate a special English development of this kind of expression.

The earliest recorded occurrence in English of *nacioun*, meaning "family, kindred," is in the *Wife of Bath's Tale* (D. 1067). Koeppel derives Chaucer's use of the word from RR. 19545—"Par noblece de nacion." But Godefroy[53] gives many early examples of this regular meaning of "naissance, extraction, rang." So, even if we are certain (which we are not) that Chaucer introduced this meaning into English—a meaning now obsolete—we can by no means be sure that he got it from the *Roman*.[54] Critics seem to forget that a poet's experience or learning is not *all* derived from *books,* and it is perfectly possible that Chaucer anglicised many French words that he had never seen in print, but had only heard on the Continent, or in London, for that matter.

The phrase "to love par amour" is defined in the New English Dictionary thus: "(usually) to love by way of (sexual) love, to love (a person of the opposite sex), to love amorously or as a lover, . . . sometimes, to have a clandestine or illicit amour with," and examples are given from *Floris and Blanchfleur, Cursor Mundi,* Wright's *Lyric Poems,* and Barbour's *Bruce*. In Chaucer, "par

---

[53] Vol. V, p. 462.
[54] Machault uses the word in this sense in a poem that Chaucer undoubtedly knew, *Le Jugement dou Roy de Navarre* (3861).

amours" is often used adverbially to mean "passionately, longingly."[55] Machault uses the phrase in the same sense:

> Se par amours n'amiez autrui ne moy,
> Ma grief doulour en seroit assez mendre.[56]

Chaucer's perfect familiarity with the expression makes it manifest that the English poet did not have to go to the one, almost chance, appearance of it in the *Roman*.[57]

The word "chevisaunce," which appears three times in the *Shipmannes Tale* (B. 1519, 1537, 1581) and which means a "borrowing" according to Skeat, has been attributed by Koeppel to the influence of RR. 14714:—

> Metra tantost main a la borse,
> Ou fera quelque chevissance
> Dont li gage auront deliverance.

Outside the *Roman de la Rose* the occurrence of *chevissance* is rare in OF., if one can judge from Godefroy's quotations. The Oxford Dictionary gives one or two instances in English before 1380. Chaucer uses the word in the *Legend of*

---

[55] B. 1933, A. 2112, "That loveth paramours, and hath his might," a line which Skeat most unwarrantedly asserts is from RR. 21715, and L. (a) 260. See Skeat's note to this last line (*Chaucer*, III, 301). This critic himself says (V, p. 67—note to A. 1155), "To love *par amour* is an old phrase for to love excessively. Cf. Bruce, xiii, 485."

[56] The first two lines of a rondeau that may be found in Tarbé's edition, pp. 53-54.

[57] For other examples of the expression, "to love paramours," outside of Chaucer, see Kittredge: *Authorship of the Romaunt of the Rose* (Studies and Notes in Philology and Literature, Vol. I) p. 17.

Phillis (L. 2434), with the meaning "provisions, substance," and rhymes it with *mischaunce:*—

> And maken in that lond som chevisaunce,
> To kepen him fro wo and fro mischaunce.

Curiously enough the *Roman* has the same rhymes in the following couplet:

> Et quant el voit la mescheance
> Si quiert honteuse chevissance, (6893-94)

a resemblance not noted by Koeppel. Elsewhere, *chevissance* is rhymed with *remembrance* (3113-14), *poissance* (8179-80), and *deliverance* (14714-15). Chaucer rhymes *chevisaunce* with *countenance* (B. 1581-82), *reconissaunce* (B. 1519-20), and *governance* (A. 281-82). The identical rhymes in the *Legend* and the *Roman* suggest an indebtedness to the French poem; but I do not attach any special significance to the parallelism. As to the use of *chevisaunce* in the *Shipmannes Tale,* I am satisfied to believe that Chaucer found the word in some French source for the story, if he did not already know it.

The use of the words "piment and clarree" in a gloss to Boethius, bk. II, meter v, was due to RR. 9129-30, says Skeat. "Chaucer uses these two words here in conjunction, for the simple reason that he was thinking of the parallel passage in the French *Rom. de la Rose,* which is imitated from the present passage in Boethius" (Vol. II, p. 432). Let us see how the translation of Boethius runs: "They ne coude nat medly the yifte of Bacchus to the cleer hony; *that is to seyn, they coude make no piment nor clarree*" (ll. 5-6). Obviously, to anyone who knows how piment is made, there is enough in the quotation preceding the italics to suggest the name of the wine. Furthermore, these two words, "piment" and "clarree," had appeared in conjunction many times in English and French before Chaucer's day.[58]

As for the phrases in Boethius II, pr. viii, line 31 and III, pr. viii, line 26 *(the knowing of thy verray freendes* and *the beautee of thy body,)* Miss Cipriani supposes the influence of the *Roman de la Rose,* 5682-83 and 9063-64 respectively. While I cannot bring forward "counter-parallels," as in the case above, I believe that the italicized explanations of Chaucer could without any trouble have been suggested by the context. At least, the question is decidedly an open one.

Finally, the following words used by Chaucer have been attributed to their appearance in the *Roman:*

atempre, (B. Duch. 341, L. 128)	(RR. 125)
estres, (L. 1715, A. 4295)	(RR. 13456)
fers, (B. Duch. 654)	(RR. 7400)

Skeat also implies that *carole* (B. Duch. 849) was due to the influence of the *Roman* (747-48), etc.

Atempre, meaning "temperate, moderate, well-regulated," appears in English as early as 1340. The more common form of the word in the *Roman* is *atrempe,* 4505, 6811, 6826, etc. In fact, I believe that *atempre* occurs only once. But it was in general use elsewhere in Old French

---

[58] Mead, in a note to line 760 of the *Squyr of Lowe Degre,* cites a number of instances; *Rich. Coer de Lion,* 3481, 2625, 3601; *King Alisaunder,* 7581-82. See also *Life of St. Alexis,* 72, and *Havelok,* 1728. See Godefroy for examples in Old French.

poetry. Machault uses it. However, as Chaucer was following Guillaume de Lorris for other material in this part of the *Book of the Duchess,* he probably took over *atempree* from him.

Estres, meaning "apartments, dwellings, quarters; the inner rooms of a house," was known in English nearly a century and a half before Chaucer. The New English Dictionary furnishes these examples: *Anc. Riw.* 296, *Curs. Mundi,* 2252, *K. Alis.* 7611, *Art. and Merl.* 816, *Wm. of Pal.* 1768. In French the word was not unusual.

Fers, "the piece of chess now known as the queen," is recorded only twice with this meaning in the New English Dictionary—Chaucer's use of it here, and Surrey's. The Old French form is *fierce, fierche,* or *fierge,* and appears not infrequently. The English spelling is so different from the French that Chaucer may have used the word as he *heard* it, not as he *read* it.

Carol, meaning originally "a ring dance with an accompaniment of song," was used in English as early as 1300.

The uselessness of dogmatizing about where Chaucer *must* have found his French words is easily apparent. In the *Roman of Guillaume de Dole,* for instance, we find *estre* no less than eight times, *fierce* once, and *caroler* six times.

(5) VARIOUS OTHER DEVICES OF EXPRESSION

(a) *Emphatic Repetition in Interrogative Form*

"Der Französe liebt es, sich selbst zu verbessern, indem er das anstössige wort am anfang der verszeile fragend wiederholt, um es mit allem nachdruck ablehnen zu können," writes Koeppel;[59] then proceeds to enumerate instances of this device in the *Roman de la Rose*, viz.: lines 8776, 15034, 16199, 17103. Examples of the same sort of thing are to be found in Chaucer, he has noticed:—

>"Bet? ne no wight so wel," quod he. (B. Duch. 1045)
>"Repentaunce! nay fy," quod he. (Ibid. 1115)
>"Nede!" nay, I gabbe now,
>Noght "nede," and I wol telle how. (Ibid. 1075-76)
>Servage? nay, but in lordshipe above. (F. 795)
>Jason? certes, ne non other man. (F. 548)

This trick of emphasis by repetition is to be found in much other French poetry.[60] Besides, it is a common enough colloquial device to express doubt, astonishment, or ridicule. It is employed by these early writers, particularly, in dialogue that is meant to be brisk. Chaucer probably did not have to go out of his own home to become thoroughly acquainted with all the uses of the artifice.

(b) *Emphasis by a Series of Contrasts*

The oratorical effectiveness of a list of antitheses has always been recognized, from classical times to *Euphues*, from *Love's Contrarieties*[61] to the *Tale of Two Cities*.[62]

---

[59] *Anglia*, XIV, p. 265.

[60] Compare *Chev. au Lyon* (extract in Paris-Langlois *Chrestomathie*), 145-46, 199-200, 493-4, 618, 619, which is particularly full of examples of this usage. Also these lines from Rutebeuf:

>Dirai-je lui? nenil, sanz doute. (II, p. 122, line 233)
>Pourquoi? qu'il s'en estoit fuiz. (II, p. 127, line 376)
>Bien ferme? quar, i prenez garde! (II, p. 127, line 387)

[61] A slight twenty-one line poem in *Davison's Poetical Rhapsody*, ed. Bullen (London, 1891), Vol. II, p. 41.

[62] See the first paragraph of this novel.

In the Prologue to the *Confessio Amantis,* Gower speaks of the fickleness of the times, and uses a long series of contrasts (ll. 921-941). The force of such a device was often dissipated in the case of the mediaeval poets by the undue extension of the catalogue; three or four lines would make a much more powerful effect than twenty. But an author of the thirteenth or fourteenth century took pride in making a display of his ingenuity—the more antitheses he could bring together, the finer the passage. We notice this same inability to stop in the elaborate tree-lists, flower-lists, bird-lists, musical instrument-lists, and lists of all kinds with which poets—and prose writers, too—padded their work.

Chaucer was fond of using series of contrasted ideas, but was not uniformly happy in the instances. A comparison of the vivid picture conjured up by Pandarus in not more than seven lines:—

> For thilke ground, that bereth the wedes wikke,
> Bereth eek thise holsom herbes, as ful ofte
> Next the foule netle, rough and thikke
> The rose waxeth swote and smothe and softe;[63]
> And next the valey is the hil a-lofte;
> And next the derke night the glade morwe;
> And also joye is next the fyn of sorwe.   (T. i, 946-952)

---

[63] Lines 946-949, it has not been noted hitherto, I believe, are a literal translation of Ovid's *Remedia Amoris,* 45-46:

> Terra salutares herbas eademque nocentes
>   Nutrit, et urticae proxima saepe rosast.

with the tiresome complaint of the knight in the *Book of the Duchess* (599-616) would certainly give the palm to Troilus's friend. As he grew more mature in his art, Chaucer himself must have realized the value of brevity, for Troilus's lament (at least the inventory of opposites), so similar to the Knight's of the early poem, is only two-fifths as long.[64]

The enumeration of the "rouninges and jangles" in the *Hous of Fame* (1960-1976) is little more than a collection of words with their antonyms. There is ingenuity but no poetry displayed in the passage.

Jean de Meung and Guillaume de Machault have been suggested as the originals for B. Duch. 599-616. There is nothing to disprove the assumption that both poets inspired the lines—Machault immediately and Jean indirectly. Sandras says (p. 292), "Cette kyrielle d'antithesis est un emprunt malheureux fait à G. de Machault." Skeat compares RR. 4910-4951. (RR. 5018-58, verses which Meon thinks were added by a scribe of the fifteenth century, continue the list of the contrarities of love.) Chaucer may well have taken the passage, or the idea for it, from Machault,[65] who took it from Jean de Meung, who took it from Alanus de Insulis,[66] who took it from—? It is but fair to add that the antitheses of not only love, but money, women, fortune, are to be found catalogued in trouvère poetry. Even Richard Rolle of Hampole can think of

---

[64] T. v. 1373-1379.
[65] *Le Jugement dou Roy de Behaigne* (ed. Hoepffner), 177-187.
[66] See Langlois, p. 149.

twenty-two contrasted states of man in this unstable life here below.[67]

(c) *Lists of Birds, Trees, Spices, Musical Instruments*

Closely related to the enumeration of objects or conditions and their opposites is the enumeration of species belonging to the same genus, whether it be, as noted above, musical instruments, wines, weapons, trees, flowers, spices, fish, birds, beasts, or what not. And the device was not only well-established by Chaucer's day, but had probably already begun to decline in popularity. Tree-lists, for instance, had flourished in literature since the days of Ovid.[68] This Latin poet started out with the respectable number of twenty-five species mentioned within the space of fourteen lines. Statius, Seneca, Claudian, and Lucan add very few new names. Not until we get to the *Roman de la Rose*, tracing the device chronologically, do we find a list of specimens that will vie with Ovid's in length. Guillaume de Lorris, in thirty-one lines (1338-1368) records thirty-six different kinds of trees. The first twenty-three are the names of trees bearing fruits, spices, and nuts; the rest of the list, with the exception of *oliviers* (olive), consists of trees valuable only for shade and wood.

[67] See *Pricke of Conscience* (in Morris-Skeat's Specimens, II) ll. 1450ff:

> For now es mirthe, now is murnyng,
> Now es laghter, and now es gretyng;
> Now er men wele, now er men wa,
> Now es a man frende, now es he faa; etc.

[68] See Skeat's notes, I, 511, and V, 92.

As is well known, Chaucer has two tree-lists—PF. 176-182 and A. 2921-23. Skeat, in a note to the first reference, says, "Chaucer's list of trees was suggested by a passage in the *Teseide*, xi, 22-24; but he extended his list by help of one in the *Roman de la Rose*, especially ll. 1363-68. . . . This list contains seven kinds of trees out of Chaucer's thirteen." It is very easy to make an item by item comparison of Chaucer's catalogue with all the tree catalogues that had preceded him, and to show what is common to the English poet and his predecessors. But is one to infer that because Chaucer mentions *beeches,* he had to take the idea from the French *fos*? Skeat does not insist, on the same reasoning, that *box-tree* (178), which is not mentioned in the *Roman,* is from the Latin *buxum,* which appears both in Ovid and Claudian! Of Chaucer's thirteen trees, the names of all but three—cypress, olive, and laurel—had existed as English words since Anglo-Saxon times. Is it to be supposed that our poet could not think out a few things for himself? It would not be a difficult task for any person of fair education to sit down and write out, merely from his own observation and experience, the names of a score of trees that he knew. I admit that it is probable that Chaucer took the *idea* of characterizing the trees in the garden from the *Roman de la Rose,* whether directly or indirectly through the *Teseide;*[69] likewise the trees forming the funeral pyre of Arcite. But the idea was all he needed; he had sufficient ingenuity to select his own woods.

[69] Sandras points out parallels between the *Teseide* and the *Roman* (p. 61ff.).

A comparison of Chaucer's bird-list, which the poet purposely made as long as possible, with its source, Alanus de Insulis's *De Planctu Naturae*, shows that even here the English poet did not exhaust the possibilities of his original. For of the thirty-six birds mentioned in PF. 330-364, eleven, or nearly one-third, are not found in the *De Planctu*, while the Latin work enumerates nine (ten, including the bat) that Chaucer is silent about. Five of Chaucer's extra eleven he could have taken from the *Roman de la Rose* (647-674), where thirteen different kinds of birds are named. Chaucer's list is the longest of the three and contains the names of six birds—cuckow, cormorant, lapwing, robin, goose, feldefare—not in Alanus or Guillaume. As in the case of the trees, we must admit that the English poet knew for himself a few birds and their traits.

Much as Chaucer appears to have been indebted to Alanus, it must not be forgotten that, when using the Latin writer, the English poet was merely refreshing his mind on information he had acquired before. For instance, the belief in the owl as the foreboder of death is common to all folklore, and is not originally a literary tradition.[70] Even in the case of the birds common to the *De Planctu*

[70] Compare what the nightingale says of the owl in *O. and N.* (Jesus MS.), 1137-1164. Skeat states that PF. 343 is from the *De Planctu*: "Illic bubo, propheta miseriae, psalmodias funereae lamentationis praecinebat." He also adduces as parallel RR. 6709-14. But the French lines, as Ballerstedt has shown, are not based on the *De Planctu*, but the *Anticlaudianus*, lib., VII, chap. 8, ll. 41-43:

> Hic raro philomena canit, cytharizat alanda:
> Crebrius hic miseros eventus bubo prophetat.
> Nuntius adversi casus et praeco doloris.

A dozen other references in literature to the owl might be given.

and the *Parlement*,—twenty-four or five in all,—Chaucer does not use what Alanus said about the falcon, quail, lark, dove, heron, sparrow, nightingale, swallow, pheasant, raven, and crow. By adding these eleven to Chaucer's eleven that Alanus does not mention at all, one can see that for twenty-two of his thirty-six birds, or nearly two-thirds of the whole number, the English poet was not under obligations to any one writer. The *Roman de la Rose* need not have served him at all.

The short spice- and bird-lists in *Sir Thopas*, (B) 1950-1961, are disposed of by Mead as follows: "Any one who recalls Chaucer's habit of gathering, perhaps unconsciously, choice phrases from his favorite book, the *Roman de la Rose*, will find nothing difficult in the position that he gleaned everything he needed for this passage from the *Roman*. This does not conclusively prove that he drew upon the French poem, familiar though he certainly was with it, for he could have found the same collocation in *Kyng Alisaunder* (ll. 6790-6799), in a passage possibly, though not probably, based on the more extended catalogue in the *Roman de la Rose*."[71] Speaking of the birds mentioned in B. 1956-61, Mead further observes: "So far is this list from being distinctive that it can easily be made up from Chaucer's own writings, or those with which he was certainly familiar."[72] This cautious position is clearly the safest one to take when such poetical conventions as birds, trees, and spices are under consideration.[73]

---

[71] See *Squyr of Lowe Degre*, pp. lv, lvi, and foot-notes.
[72] Ibid., p. lxiii and note.
[73] Mead's examination into the date of the *Squyr*, pp. lii-lxv, in-

And so we will pass by the reference to musical instruments in the *Hous of Fame* [74] with this final observation, that although Chaucer employed in his early work somewhat extended catalogues of one sort or another, he had the intelligence and poetic sense soon to see the ridiculousness of such material outside of an encyclopedia or text-book; and that after *Sir Thopas* he wrote little or nothing of this sort for which his readers could criticise him. Even in the *Hous of Fame* he was probably laughing at himself for his unpoetical enumerations.

(d) *Transitional and Summarizing Sentences*

Several of the transitional lines and couplets that Chaucer uses are compared by Koeppel and Skeat with similar verses in the *Roman de la Rose*. These are listed below:

(a) But flee we now prolixitee best is, (T. ii. 1564) appears to be a literal translation of RR. 19233:

> Bon fait prolixite foïr.

(b) But noght nil I, so mote I thryve
Been aboute to discryve
Al these armes that ther weren . . .
For hit to me were impossible;
Men mighte make of hem a bible
Twenty foot thikke, as I trowe. (HF. 1329-35)

cludes a discussion of the relation of the romance to *Sir Thopas*, and furnishes many parallels from early literature of just the kind of conventions we have been considering.

[74] Ll. 1214-1226. Compare Skeat's note to line 1218 (Vol. III, 268) and Mead's remarks on a similar passage in the *Squyr*, pp. 93-94. As Mead says, "the minstrelsy at feasts is a commonplace of the romances, and the lists of instruments are much alike."

Koeppel thinks that this thought is from RR. 7474-76, and it is true the two passages are not unlike. The expression is common, however; and is one that a poet would naturally use to get out of a long enumeration. Machault has the same sort of thing, if not the same words:

> La maintes paroles deymes
> Que je ne veuil pas raconter;
> Quar trop long seroit a compter. (Tarbé, p. 46)
> Si toutes les volois dire,
> Je ne les te porroie lire,
> Ou conter en un jour et demi. (Ibid. p. 107)

(c) Suffyceth heer ensamples oon or two,
    And though I coude rekne a thousand mo. (A. 1953-54)

In comparing this passage with RR. 17626-27:

> Mes n'en vuel plus d'examples dire,
> Bien vous puet uns por tous soffire,

Koeppel would appear to have taken Chaucer's "oon or two" as equivalent to the French "uns por tous"! Or maybe the poet himself misread the French. However, the two sentiments are sufficiently alike to excite comment and sufficiently ordinary to let us waive it.[75]

(d) Chaucer's beautiful and striking figure—

But al that thing I moot as now forbere.
I have, god woot, a large feeld to ere,

---

[75] If one must have a source for Chaucer's couplet, the following is more satisfactory, for the first line of it is almost literally translated by A. 1954:

> Mil exemples dire en sauroie,
> Mes trop grant conte a faire auroie. (RR. 14204-5)

See also Ovid's *Remedia Amoris*, 461: Quid moror exemplis, quorum me turba fatigat?

And wayke been the oxen in my plough,
The remenant of the tale is long y-nough.   (A. 885-888)

which in all probability was inspired by Jean de Meung's

Ne vous voil or ci plus tenir,
A mon propos m'estuet venir,
Qu'autre champ me convient arer   (RR. 22211-13)

is nevertheless entirely different from the French in its application. Besides, there is no parallel in the *Roman* for A. 887.

(e) Probably this summarizing couplet, which Chaucer used more than twice:

As I have told yow here-tofore;
Hit is no need reherse it more;   (B. Duch. 189-190)

(cf. C. 229-30; F. 1465-66, 1593-94) is a translation of RR. 7995-97, as Koeppel has observed, though this idea, too, is a commonplace.

(f) "There may no tonge telle, or herte thinke" (E. 1341), also T. v. 445, 1321, appears to have come from RR. 2977-79 or 21307-8:

Cuers ne porroit mie penser
Ne bouche d'omme recenser.   (Koeppel)

(g) Koeppel also compares RR. 7155, 21863 and Jean de Meung's *Testament*, 1543 with B. 3900, 3688, and T. v. 1482, respectively. The English lines translate the French literally, but I believe that the phrases were stock formulas. L. 609 anticipates B. 3688, while RR. 3001 has "se la lettre ne ment," instead of "se l'escriture ne ment."

(h) The refrain "in general, this reule may nat fayle" (*Fortune,* 56, 64, 72) resembles the French

> Ceste ruile est si generaus,
> Qu'el ne puet defaillir vers eus,   (RR. 19911-12)

with which Skeat compares it; but the two are not equivalent. *Generaus* means *infaillible,* "absolute." At most, the English line can be no more than a vague recollection of the French couplet or a very natural misunderstanding of it.

(i) Such parallels as "Sitost cum tens et leu verrai"

(RR. 22242)

and

> Whan that she saugh hir tyme, upon a day,   (D. 901) or
> And whan he saugh his tyme, he seyde thus: (F. 966) or
> That shal I seyn, whan that I see my tyme;   (L. 101)

do not appear significant to me. Chaucer uses only "tyme," never "tyme and place" (tens et leu).[76]

(j) Again, we may mention RR. 11448-49:

> En plusors sentences se mistrent,
> Divers diverses choses distrent,

a trick of expression which is translated in the English *Romaunt,* 5813-14, and is used by Chaucer several times:

> Diverse folk diversely they seyde,   (A. 3857)
> Diverse men diverse thinges seyden,   (B. 211)
> Diverse men diversely him tolde
> Of mariage many ensamples olde.   (E. 1469-70)

---

[76] See also T. i 351, ii 1720-21; A. 4050; B. 1128; E. 1114, 1804, 1858, 1936, 2001; F. 1308. (These examples are taken from Kaluza: *Chaucer und der Rosenroman,* p. 210.)

> Diverse folk diversely they demed;
> As many hedes, as many wittes ther been. (F. 202-203)

Dante has the same kind of diction in

> Virtù diversa fa diversa lega
> col prezioso corpo ch' ell' avviva,
> (*Paradiso* II, 139-40)

(k) No one after reading Goddard's delightful and brilliant essay on the *Legend of Good Women* will agree with Koeppel that Chaucer's confession,

> Of trewe men I finde but fewe mo
> In alle my bokes, save this Piramus, (917-18)

was inspired by Jean de Meung's stolid statement:

> Mes moult est poi de tex amans. (RR. 15088)

In commenting on the English lines, Goddard writes: "Only a person in that unwarrantable mood which, as was said at the beginning, is to be studiously avoided in this discussion of the legends, would think of suspecting that Chaucer, by the phrase, 'in alle my bokes,' intends to suggest that the place to look for true men is in real life rather than in literature."

(l) The Knight's gratuitous criticism at the end of his description of the temple of Diana—

> Wel couthe he peynten lyfly that it wroghte, (A. 2087)

is like Guillaume de Lorris's comment on the portrait of Vilanye—

> Moult sot bien paindre et bien portraire
> Cil qui tiex ymages sot faire, (RR. 163-4)

Compare the translation, Rom. 175-176. The context makes the resemblance even closer: both the Knight and l'Amant conclude with the words quoted, after having described paintings on walls. This resemblance has not been recorded hitherto.

By way of summary of this already too long chapter it may be said that while most of the parallels discussed are of little significance as showing *Roman* influence on Chaucer, taken as a whole they furnish excellent illustrations of thirteenth and fourteenth century tendencies of style. They have been treated at some length inasmuch as there is not only fascination but a distinct value in "parallel-hunting." I am not inclined to regard more than eighteen of the correspondences here recorded as standing in the relation of cause and effect; but it must be admitted that with the exception of a few examples, which I have endeavored to show are worthless or exceedingly far-fetched, the parallels are more or less significant. On the other hand, the lines quoted or referred to form a very small portion of the total number of lines of medieval French and English poetry. The larger number of stylistic devices have not been touched upon. Moreover, not a few of those treated of are colloquialisms, for which no literary source need be sought. It is possible that the *Roman de la Rose,* by its use of these, sanctioned them for Chaucer, but we cannot safely infer that what is common to Jean de Meung and the English poet was adapted from the earlier writer by the later. The burden of proof still lies upon those who maintain that the *Roman* had any considerable influence upon Chaucer's style.

CHAPTER V

SITUATIONS AND DESCRIPTIONS

Sandras (p. 36) makes this statement with regard to Chaucer's description of natural scenery: "C'est au point que ce poëte, qui sentait les beautés de la nature, qui savait les peindre, se content souvent dans ses descriptions d'être le copiste de G. de Lorris." If the French critic had said, instead of "le copiste de G. de Lorris," "l'imitateur de l'école de G. de Lorris," he would have expressed himself in such a way that English students could not be offended. To say that a favorite poet is a copyist is to call critics to arms, and the case of Sandras was no exception. But if he had been able to present the array of parallels that have been gathered together since his *Etude* appeared, probably no person fifty years ago, or since, would have challenged his words. Besides, it must be remembered that Sandras did not say *toujours,* but only *souvent,* a very elastic word. All in all, Sandras's general position is not untenable; for if we may trust in strong circumstantial evidence, the young Chaucer did belong to the school of Guillaume de Lorris, as did, for that matter, Boccaccio and Machault.

Before proceeding to the examination of the specific parallels that Skeat and Miss Cipriani have noted, and the discussion of some that have escaped these two investigators, we may recall what Neilson says about sources and source-hunting: "It is necessary, if we are to prove anything with regard to those sources which actually suggested certain features of [the poem under consideration], to find either striking parallelisms in detail which cannot be set aside as commonplaces, or the presence of some distinct feature which in itself is not a regular part of poems of the type."[1] As a corollary to this proposition we may reasonably assume the following: If in a particular poem there appear features common to a certain class of poems and also details that are peculiar to or are emphasized in only one member of that class, the poem which furnished the special details also probably furnished the commonplaces.

Instances of descriptions of nature for which Chaucer is thought to have been indebted to the *Roman de la Rose* may be tabulated as follows. (The list includes all the parallels of this sort that I have been able to find):

B. Duch. 291-3 (S)	RR.	45-47
295-7 (S)		67-74
301-2 (C)		665-68
304-5 (C)		707-10
317 (C)		74-77
318-19 (C)		100-101
340-42 (S)		124-25
410-12 (S)		55-58
406-9 (S)		9176-79
418-20 (S)		1375-76
PF. 122 (S)	RR.	129-131
129-30 (C)		21449-55
		21585-88
204-10 (C)		21327-28
		21491-93
		21518-21
		21589-90

[1] *Court of Love*, p. 228.

Leg. G. W. (Prol. B.):

125-26	(S)	RR.	55-58
128	(S)		125
132-37	(C)		22500-509
148-68	(C)		10563-99
			6460-6520
153-59	(C)		10593-599

To these may be added:

B. Duch. 309-311	RR. 487-493
421-433	1377-1390
414-415	53, 56
PF. 190-191	665-668
192-196	1383-1390
T. iii. 351-354 ⎫ ii. 50-52 ⎬	47-54
L. (b) 139-40	707-708
Sq. T. (F) 52-55	67-73

A few striking facts are disclosed by the data above:

(a) That the references to the *Roman* fall into comparatively well-defined groups;

(b) The fact that all the descriptive passages referred to in the *Book of the Duchess*, with the exception of one, correspond to lines in the French text that are translated in Fragment A of the English *Romaunt;*

(c) That all the references in Chaucer's work, except the stray reminiscence in the *Squieres Tale*, are from poems written before 1386;

(d) The repeated use of the same verses from the *Roman*, especially 54-74, 124-5, 665-668, 708.

The one poem of Chaucer's which appears from the parallels cited to owe the largest amount of its nature description to the *Roman de la Rose* is the *Book of the Duchess.* These passages all fall within one hundred and fifty consecutive lines, or from the opening of the Dream (291) to the end of the description of the animals in the park (442).

For convenience of reference, the details of the situation may be summed up as follows: (1) The poet dreams that he is awakened early one morning in May (291-294) by (2) the sweet singing of birds (295-297), which (3) were sitting and chirping on the tiled roof of his chamber (298-300). (4) They were singing, each in its own fashion, a solemn service (301-302). (5) Some sang high, some low, but all of one accord (304-5). (6) Their music sounded heavenly (306-8). (7) Not for the town of Tunis would the poet have missed hearing them sing (309-11). (8) The whole room began to ring with the harmony (312-16), for (9) every bird was doing its utmost (317-20). (10) The walls of the room were all decorated, the glazed windows had the whole story of Troy worked into them (321-331). (11) On the walls was painted the entire text of the *Romance of the Rose* (332-334). (12) Through the closed windows streamed the sunlight, gilding the bed (335-338). (13) The sky was bright, the air clear, the temperature moderate —neither hot nor cold (339-343). The next fifty-four lines do not concern us. The poet jumps up at the sound of the huntsmen's horn, takes his horse, leaves the room, never stopping until he reaches the open field where the hunters are assembled. The whole crowd rides to the forest. Now follows a brief account of the hunt, which seems to have been unsuccessful. A whelp that has been left behind in the running comes up to the poet and fawns on him as if it knows him. The poet tries to catch the animal, but it flees. (14) In the chase after the whelp the poet is led down through a flowery green full of soft thick grass, and covered with flowers (397-401). (15) He conjectures that Flora and Zephirus made their dwelling there (402-404). (16) So thick are the flowers that the earth seems to vie with heaven and its stars (405-409). (17) Earth had forgotten the poverty and sorrow that winter had made it suffer (410-415). (18) The poet next describes the tall trees, "forty or fifty fadme lengthe," that stood at least "ten foot or twelve" apart (416-422). (19) The leaves and branches so interlaced that all was shadow below (424-26). (20) All around the poet animals were playing—the "herte," hind, fawns, sorrels, bucks, does, roes, and squirrels (427-433), more than Argus even could count.

Such, in rough, are the contents of the dream to the point where the poet meets the Black Knight. In the following discussion the numbers in parentheses refer to the sections of the poem enumerated above.

With (1) Skeat compares RR. 44, 46, and the correspondence is very close. Chaucer's "me thoughte thus" equals "avis m'iere," and "me mette thus" equals "ce songoie." Skeat equates "And in the dawning ther I lay" with "qu'il estoit mains," which appears in Meon's text, *but did not appear in the manuscript which the English translator was following* (compare *Rom.*, 49). But, it may be said, Chaucer found this detail in RR. 88, "Qu'il estoit matin durement," which is prettily translated in the *Romaunt:*

        That it was by the morowe erly.   (94)

(2) and (3) are original situations with our poet. He avoids the confusing dream-within-the-dream of Guillaume de Lorris, and imagines himself awakened by a most natural cause—the early morning chirping of the birds. (4) seems at most only reminiscent of the *Roman de la Rose*. (5) translates RR. 709, but adds the touch "and al of oon acorde," which agrees with RR. 484-485 (*Rom.*, 496-97). (6) seems to paraphrase RR. 667-668 again, and (7) is the same sort of expression that we find in RR. 487-493;[2] though, it may be noted, Chaucer, unlike the dreamer in the *Roman*, does not say that he would not have missed the song of the birds for a hundred pounds; he balances their harmony against the whole town of Tunis. The name of the African city may have been introduced here for the sake of the rhyme. (8) is original with Chaucer, naturally, because (2) is original. As to (9), of the French original lines 100-101 repeat the idea of 74-77, and that is the idea expressed in B. Duch. 317-318, though 319 is original with Chaucer. (10) is a brilliant addition of our poet's, and Skeat's note on these lines is pertinent. The critic remarks: "As stained glass windows were then rare and expensive, it is worth while observing that these gorgeous windows were not real ones, but only seen in a dream." (11) While it might have been suggested by the painted walls in the

---

[2] A similar expression, which Chaucer uses to characterize the Shipman,

"Ther nas noon swich from Hulle to Cartage," (A. 404)

is compared by Skeat with RR. 6099. As *Cartage* is the only word common to the two lines, and as this sort of comparison by elimination is very common in O. F. poetry, I attach no significance to Skeat's parallel.

Garden of Mirth, Chaucer's idea of having not only the "text" but also the glose (which may mean either the commentary or the margin of the manuscript page) of "al the *Romaunce of the Rose*" engraved on the walls of his bedroom is decidedly unique. (12) is a rather pretty touch and is, of course, original, as the situation does not appear in the *Roman de la Rose*. For (13) Chaucer is thought to have used

> Clere et serie et bele estoit
> Le matinee et atempree:

although a similar description of an early morning in spring—

> Et li jours fu attemprez par mesure,
> Biaus, clers, luisans, nes et purs, sans froidure,

occurs in a poem of Machault's that Chaucer certainly used later on in the *Book of the Duchess*.[2a] But if we apply our corollary, we must admit that in this detail of the weather the English poet is following the *Roman* or the *Romaunt;* for "And ful attempre, for sooth, it was" (B. Duch. 341), is almost exactly like "And ful attempre, out of drede" (*Rom.*, 131).[3] (14) has had no source pointed out for it,

---

[2a] *Le Jugement dou Roy de Behaigne* (ed. Hoepffner), 113-114.

[3] In his discussion of the *Book of the Duchess*, Skeat remarks "(Chaucer's) familiarity with the (Roman de la Rose) . . . is such as to prove that he had already been previously employed in making his translation of that extremely lengthy work, and possibly quotes lines from his own translation." (Vol. I, p. 63.) But in a note on the same page the critic "supports" his statement by this additional information (italics mine): "Most of the passages which he quotes are *not extant* in the English version of the Romaunt. Where we can institute a comparison between that version and the

although all the dreamers in the Middle Ages imagined themselves in flowery, grassy meadows (that is, all of *this* sort), and we may consider these lines possibly a recollection of RR. 1401-1409 (cf. *Rom.* 1418-29). (15), as has already been mentioned in Chapter III, seems clearly to come from the *Roman de la Rose*. Sandras suggests as a source for these lines a part of Reason's long allegorical discussion of fortune:

> Les floretes i fait parair,
> Et cum estoiles flamboier,
> Et les herbetes verdoier
> Zephirus, quant sur mer chevauche. (RR. 6674-77)

But the situation in the *Roman* is totally different from that in the *Book of the Duchess*. Besides, nothing is said of Flora. Skeat's parallel, however, names both Flora and Zephirus:

> Cil dui font les floretes nestre, (RR. 9162)

a line which B. Duch. 403 translates literally. In (16) Chaucer introduces his comparison of the flowers and the

Book of the Duchess the passages *are differently worded*. Cf. B. Duch., 420, with R. Rose, 1393.''

To disprove this last statement, I suggest a comparison of B. Duch. 291, and Rom. 49; B. Duch. 304-5 and Rom. 717; B. Duch. 341 and Rom. 131. I do not understand how the ''familiarity'' such as Skeat would have ''Chaucer display with the Roman de la Rose is such as to prove that he had been previously employed in making his translation,'' for the critic is positive that only Fragment A is Chaucer's and ''most of the passages he (Chaucer) quotes are not extant in the English version.'' There seems to me to be clear evidence that Chaucer consulted the *Romaunt* when writing the Book of the Duchess; but I do not believe that his use of the translation necessarily constitutes evidence that he made the English version himself.

stars. Skeat's source for (15) is followed immediately by the undoubted model of B. Duch. 405-9; and it is perfectly clear that the English poet had in mind, if not in sight, Jean de Meung's description of the old-time freedom of the golden age (RR. 9148-79). For the next idea, (17), Chaucer goes back to the first part of the *Roman*. (Notice that here Chaucer uses "povertee," following RR. 57, while the *Romaunt* has "pore estat," 61.) Lines 414 and 415 seem to have been taken over respectively from RR. 53 (*Rom.* 57) and RR. 56 (*Rom.* 60).

As a matter of course, the mention of trees could not be omitted from such a description as this, and the poet, realizing that fact, begins his next paragraph:

> Hit is no need eek for to axe
> Wher ther were many grene greves,   (416-417)

This whole passage (416-442) follows the French very closely. Indeed, we may say that it is direct copying, although a few significant deviations must be noted. Throughout these lines, if we look at all carefully and compare them with the original, we shall see that Chaucer is *intentionally exaggerating every detail*. In 419-20 the poet says that the trees stood one from the other "wel ten foot or twelve"! The French original and the *Romaunt* both have five fathoms or six. Skeat remarks that Chaucer "has treated a *toise* as if it were equal to two feet. . . . In his own translation of the *Romaunt* (1393), he translates *toise* by fadome." Obviously, then, ignorance was not responsible for the change here. Chaucer is saving his "fadome" for line 422, where he gives these wonderful trees a height of from two hundred and forty to three hundred feet, where as the French text says merely:

> Mes li rain furent lonc et haut, (1377)

and the *Romaunt:*

> But they were hye and grete also, (1394)

Chaucer says that the branches and leaves so interlaced that

> They were nat an inche a-sonder, (B. Duch. 425)

while the *Roman* has

> Que li solaus en nesune eure
> Ne pooit a terre descendre, (1380-81)

which the *Romaunt* translates almost literally (1399). The enumeration of the animals in the wood is very modest in the *Roman de la Rose,* for it includes only "daims et chevrions, . . . grant plente d'escoirons . . . and connins" (1383-86). The *Romaunt* follows its original by mentioning only "does and roes . . . squirels . . . conies" (1401-1404). But what does Chaucer do? Not content with merely "many a herte and many a hinde," he tells us that the wood was full of "founes, soures, bukkes, does, . . . and many roes," as well as "squirelles" (B. Duch. 427-431). The rabbits are not mentioned. Finally, it is obvious that Guillaume de Lorris's four lines preceding the statement of how the trees were planted:

> Que vous iroie-je notant?
> De divers arbres i ot tant,
> Que moult en seroie encombres
> Ains que les eusse nombres; (RR. 1369-72)

which are translated in the *Romaunt* (1387-90), inspired B. Duch. 434-441, though these lines are taken over literally from another part of the *Roman* (13731-36), which describes a situation worthy to be recalled. The Duenna (La Vieille) is telling Fair-Welcome (Bel-Acueil) of the lively life she led when she was a girl, and of the fierce contests her lovers had over her.

> If learned Algus, of all men
> The wisest in his reckoning,
> Should his ten wondrous figures bring
> To bear thereon, I doubt if well
> By multiplying he could tell
> The number of the deadly fights
> Wherein my gallants strove o' nights.
> Right fair of face was I, etc.[4]

The exaggeration of this moral derelict is fine satire on the part of Jean de Meung, and Chaucer knew it; so did everyone know it who was as familiar with the French poem as was Chaucer. But in order that there might be no mistaking of the passage, the English poet translated four or five lines literally and then adapted the reference to Argus to the *Book of the Duchess*. The thought was decidedly a clever one; it was introduced with a distinctly humorous intent. And yet Skeat says, "*The Parlement of Foules* is . . . the first of the Minor Poems in which touches of true humor occur"![5]

The *Parlement of Foules*, Chaucer's next dream-poem,

---

[4] Ellis's translation of the *Romance of the Rose*, Vol. II, lines 13486-93.
[5] *Chaucer*, Vol. I, p. 66.

"is remarkable as being the first of the Minor Poems which exhibits the influence . . . of Italian literature." This piece is obviously to be associated in time with *Troilus and Criseyde* and the first draft of the *Knightes Tale*. The *Hous of Fame,* following close upon these three, completes the group which displays Chaucer reveling in his new-found delights of Italian poetry.

In the *Parlement of Foules* he makes considerable use of Macrobius's *Somnium Scipionis,* which he has by this time read for himself; of Boccaccio's *Teseide,* and Alanus de Insulis's *De Planctu Naturae*. Direct traces of *Roman de la Rose* influence are very few, though our poet doubtless saw many of its lines underlying the Italian of the *Teseide*. For instance, stanza 52 of Book VII, which Chaucer followed in PF. 190-196, is obviously taken originally from the *Roman* (1383-90), the same passage that our poet so considerately expanded in B. Duch. 428-433.[6] In the *Parlement,* however, the "conies" are not forgotten. PF. 190-191, where the corresponding Italian lines read:

> Quivi senti pe' rami dolcemente
> Quasi d'ogni maniera ucce' cantare,

seems directly reminiscent of RR. 665-668 or *Romaunt* 669-672. The tree-list has been discussed in the preceding chapter.

Of Miss Cipriani's parallels to 129-130, 204-210, which, it will be seen from the table, are drawn from the last part of the *Roman,* I should throw out 21518-21 as unimportant.

[6] For other parallels between *Teseide,* VII, 51-64, and the *Roman,* see Sandras, *Etude,* etc., chap. iii.

These lines describe the gentle heat and odor produced by the wonderful carbuncle that hangs in the fountain of Genius's park, while Chaucer's describe something entirely different. I believe that PF. 204-5 is merely a recollection carried over from B. Duch. 340-342. Moreover, line 206 recalls rather the grass and spices of Guillaume de Lorris's description; there is no corresponding line in Jean de Meung's. All in all, the only details of Chaucer's picture common with Jean's are the statements that no one ever grows sick in this garden and that night is banished and perfect day rules always (ll. 207-210). Lines 205-7 Chaucer may well have taken from Alanus.[7] Chaucer seems to have forgotten that he put in this last touch about "perfect day," for twice later on in the poem he speaks of the sun going to rest: 266 and 390. Finally, the resemblance between lines 129-130 and RR. 21449-55 and 21585-88 is very slight.

One is tempted to propose the theory that Chaucer, having in mind Genius's comparison of his garden with the Garden of Mirth that Guillaume describes:

>   Car qui du biau jardin quarre
>   Clos au petit guichet barre
>   Ou cil amant vit la karole,
>   Ou Deduit o sa gent karole
>   A cel biau parc que ge devise,
>   Tant par est biaus a grant devise,
>   Faire voldroit comparaison,
>   Il feroit trop grant mesprison, etc. (21211-21218)

[7] *Anticlaudianus*, Bk. I, chap. 3, ll. 20-22. See Ballerstedt, p. 41. The *Roman* has "Sens estres malades ne mortes," 21329, and the *Parlement*, "seek ne old," 207.

decided to combine the two within the one wall and to contrast passionate love, represented by "Cupyde our lord" and his followers (ll. 211-294), with natural love, or love for the sake of procreation, represented by the "noble goddesse Nature" and her charges, the birds (ll. 295ff.). This would explain the significance of the two inscriptions "of ful gret difference" on the gate. Genius, it will be remembered, exhorts the barons of Love not to neglect the great work of man's life; namely, "to repair the gaps made in the human race by the shears of Atropos." But positive evidence for the theory is lacking here.[8] There is no proof at all that when writing the *Parlement of Foules* Chaucer had the *Roman de la Rose* before him. Indeed, even those passages which appear to be reminiscences are scattered and only vaguely recall the French poem.

As for the descriptions of nature in the *Prologue* to the *Legend of Good Women*, almost all that have been attributed to the influence of the *Roman de la Rose* can be traced back to earlier poems of Chaucer, especially the two we have just been considering.

L. 125-126 is to be compared with B. Duch. 410-12, of which it is an echo. The "pore estat" suggests *Rom.* 61. The "atempre" (128) recalls B. Duch. 341.

The lines cited from the *Roman* as the source of L. 132-137, viz., 22500-22509, have little or no resemblance to the

---

[8] Miss Cipriani writes, "Jean de Meung explicitly states the moral he wishes to draw from the Fountain of Life. . . . Note especially in connection with the *Parlement of Foules*, RR. 21559-62, 21569-70, 21582-85." These passages have no particular significance in relation to the English poem, but they set forth Jean de Meung's emphasis of the necessity of procreation in the human race.

English passage, except that the Fr. *sophisme* (22507) is something like Chaucer's *sophistrye* (137). I think we may safely dismiss this parallel.

L. 139-140 is an echo of RR. 707-8 or *Rom.* 715-716.

L. 148-168, Miss Cipriani thinks, is reminiscent of the *Roman,* and it may be that some of Chaucer's description of the repentant birds was remotely suggested by part of the hundred-odd lines the investigator refers us to. But the English passage need go no farther back than the *Parlement of Foules,* or perhaps than B. Duch. 305 for the one line, L. 169. And as to the correlation of L. 153-159 and RR. 10593-99, the diction and situation in the two passages are very little alike.

L. 171-174 looks backward to B. Duch. 402-3 and forward to the Prologue to the *Canterbury Tales* (A. 5-6).

The beginning proper of the second book of *Troilus and Criseyde:*

> In May, that moder is of monthes glade,
> That fresshe floures, blewe, and whyte, and rede,
> Ben quick agayn, that winter dede made,   (ii. 50-52)

furnishes an example of the color enumeration that Chaucer was fond of using; as, for instance, in

Blak, blo, grenish, swartish reed;   (HF. 1647)

And al this hous, of which I rede,
Was made of twigges, falwe, rede
And grene eek, and some weren whyte,   (HF. 1935-37)

Woot I not whether in whyte or rede or grene,   (AA. 146)

For "whyte and rede," see T. i. 158; L. 42; A. 90, 1053.

In the *Roman de la Rose* we find such combinations as

"indes et perses" (63); "blanches et vermeilles . . . jaunes" (1413-14); "Indes, vermaus, jaunes et bis" (21936); "Jaunes, vermeilles, vers et indes" (21952); "De vert, de pers ou de brunete" (21929); "D'armes yndes, jaunes, ou vers" (16978); and "Soit vert, ou cameline ou jauce" (14357). But, as Ballerstedt says, "Diese Farbenhäufung ist noch specifisch mittelalterlich" (p. 43), and we cannot trace Chaucer's use of it to the *Roman de la Rose*.

T. iii. 351-353 is clearly a recollection of RR. 47-54, and iii. 354 is a condensing of RR. 78-80, although this whole passage may have come second-hand through Boccaccio. In the *Squieres Tale* (F. 52-55) we have a late echo again of RR. 67-73.

What are we to conclude as to the influence of the *Roman de la Rose* on Chaucer's descriptions of nature? Certainly less than seventy lines of this sort in Chaucer owe their existence directly to the French poem. The almost servile copying in the *Book of the Duchess* and the sudden falling off of *Roman* influence to a negligible amount in the *Parlement of Foules* are noteworthy. Either Chaucer had some ulterior motive in transferring into the 1369 poem whole sections from Ovid, Machault, Guillaume de Lorris, and Jean de Meung, or else this patchwork was serious art with the poet at the time it was written. Sixteen years later we find him emancipated from these youthful extravagances and turning more to nature and less to books for his descriptions.

The remaining descriptions, other than personal, and the short general situations in Chaucer that have been referred to the *Roman de la Rose,* may be disposed of in a few words. They are the following:

B. Duch.	807-809	(C)	619-20
	835-837	(S)	1689-91
HF.	112-113	(C)	24-25
	1342-53	(C)	6835-40
	1652-54	(C)	6759-64

Kittredge has shown that for a large part of the account of the sorrowing knight in the *Book of the Duchess* Chaucer went to Machault's *Le Jugement dou Roy de Behaigne.* Miss Cipriani's parallel for ll. 807-809, consequently, must be set aside in favor of Kittredge's; although doubtless Machault got his idea of the superlative company of women from Guillaume de Lorris. The lines from *Le Jugement* are:

> Tant qu'il avint qu'en une compaingnie
> Ou il avoit mainte dame jolie
> Jeune, gentil, joieuse et envoisie. (281-283)

See also Machault's *Dit du Vergier* (ed. Hoepffner), 155-158.

The situation in 835-37 only resembles, in no sense translates, RR. 1689-1691.

The opening of the dream in the *Hous of Fame*—

> When it was night, to slepe I lay
> Right there as I was wont to done
> And fil on slepe wonder sone. (112-114)

seems a reminiscence rather of the *Romaunt:*

> I wente sone
> To bedde, as I was wont to done
> And fast I sleep (23-25)

than of the French lines; for besides the situation, we have common to the two passages the rhyme *done: sone,* and the clause "as I was wont to done."

The description of the

> riche lusty place,
> That Fames halle called was,

in HF. 1342-52 has been compared to the picture of one-half of Fortune's house in the *Roman de la Rose* (6835-40):

> Moult reluit d'une part, car gent
> I sunt li mur d'or et d'argent;
> Si rest toute la coverture
> De cele meisme feture,
> Ardans de pierres precieuses
> Moult cleres et moult vertueuses.

The only features that the two houses have in common are gold walls and roof, studded with jewels. But gold and gems in abundance are the materials out of which many a poet has builded an imaginary palace. Even less convincing is Koeppel's equation of HF. 1342-46 with Boccaccio's *Amorosa Visione,* IV, 9-10.

I see no resemblance between HF. 1652-54 and RR. 6759-64, a parallel of Miss Cipriani's.

It is hard to arrive at mutually exclusive sub-classifications of passages of personal description in Chaucer that have been traced to or compared with the *Roman de la Rose;* but if we treat in one section what may be called "generalized personal description," and in another "particularized personal description," we shall be able to discuss all the remaining parallels that fall in this chapter.

CHAUCER AND THE ROMAN DE LA ROSE

The generalized personal descriptions or descriptive touches equated with the French poem are these:

(a)	T. i. 927-928	(C)	RR. 22560-62
(b)	T. ii. 756	(C)	10202-3
(c)	HF. 1710-11	(C)	18380-81
(d)	1732-33 } 1761-62 }	(C)	12254-55
	1758-62	(K)	10602-5
(e)	1780-82	(C)	12270-75
(f)	HF. 1793-95	(C)	RR. 12566-72
(g)	A. 1999	(S)	*Rom.* 7419-20
(h)	C. 79-81	(S)	{ RR. 4529-33 4940-45
(i)	D. 1568	(K)	11049-50
(j)	2001-3 } 1994-95 }	(K)	10547-51
(k)	(D. 2004b, 2004c) }	(S)	17271-73

(a) This expression, "They thought it was better, for fear of failing in one instance, to try all the chances," has a proverbial ring to it. Pandarus twits Troilus, who is experiencing all the pangs of first love, with having in his proud days of "unattachment" characterized lovers thus. The lines in the *Roman:*

> Qu'il fait bon de tout essaier
> Por soi miex es biens esgaier
> Ausinc cum fait li bons lechierres, (22560-62)

are so isolated from any other passages in the French poem that Chaucer appears to have adapted in this first book of *Troilus* that we are not justified in saying that they were the source of the English lines. The only evidence is the agreement of "assayen over-al" and "de tout assaier." But Chaucer uses "assaye" as early as the *Book of the Duchess*.[9]

(b) A closer parallel to the English lines, T. ii. 756—one which combines both ideas of jealousy and masterfulness— is RR. 10171-5:

> Compains, cil fox vilains jalous . . .
> Qui si de jalousie s'emple, . . .
> Et se fait seignor de sa fame, etc.,

in which the Amis adds the moralizing touch to his vivid picture of the jealous husband. Neither of the two passages from the *Roman*, however,—this or Miss Cipriani's quotation,—contains the idea of "loving novelrye."

(c) The best way of justifying this quotation from the French poem as a parallel to the lines in the *Hous of Fame* is by saying that at the time of writing his "dream poem" Chaucer was interested in such subjects as Freewill, Necessity, and Destiny, and that Nature's long confession and discussion in the *Roman de la Rose* (17976-18659) was fresh in his mind. How well these lines (HF. 1702-1712) characterize the noble company of which the "povre Persoun" was a member! But surely Chaucer knew just such persons and might well have drawn the character of this "fifte route" from real life.

(d) (e) (f) We now come to a group of passages which, to judge from Miss Cipriani's citations, were due to consecutive reading by Chaucer in the *Roman*. The French lines, 12254-55, 12270-75, 12566-72, are all a part of Faux-

[9] I do not understand Skeat's glossing *assayen* in T. i. 928 as "to assail."

Semblant's long confession—a section of the *Roman* which Chaucer used in part at least for his characterization of the Friar and the Pardoner—and are translated in Fragment C of the *Romaunt,* 6599-6602, 6613-6622, and 6913-6919, respectively. But I see no particular or even general agreement between Chaucer's "sexte and seventh routes" and Faux-Semblant's denunciation of the Begging Friars. There is absolutely nothing in the English lines to indicate that by this sixth company, who characterize themselves thus:

> We han don neither that ne this,
> But ydel al our lyf y-be

are meant the Mendicant Orders. The next "route" to seek fame is really a part of the preceding;[10] Chaucer represents the members of it as just like the others in order to show the fickleness and injustice of the goddess. Koeppel's parallel for HF. 1758-62; i. e., RR. 10602-5:

> Si se sunt maint vante de maintes,
> Par paroles fauces et faintes,
> Dont les cors avoir ne pooient,
> Lor non a grant tort diffamoient,

when translated literally, after all resembles the English only very slightly. These so-called correspondences, then (d, e, f), are fanciful; the French lines were clearly not the original of the English; and they have little value even as illustrative or elucidative material.

(g) Chaucer's wonderful line:

The smyler with the knyf under the cloke,   (A. 1999)

[10] Cf. 1759-62 with 1796-99.

will suffer from comparison with no parallel or "source" that can be brought forward. It may or may not be a reminiscence of the description of Faux-Semblant, RR. 13030-31 (*Rom.* 7419-20).

(h) The Phisicien's advice to old mistresses in charge of young girls to remember that they have been established as governesses either because they have been pure all their lives or because they have sinned and repented, is very likely an echo of Guillaume de Lorris's character-sketch of La Vieille. The line,

  And knowen wel y-nough the olde daunce, (C. 79)

seems to settle the point. I have no addition to make to Skeat's note to A. 476.[11]

(i) The commonplace statement,

  The carl spak oo thing, but he thoghte another,
               (D. 1568)

might, as a matter of curiosity, be compared with

    car ge fesoie
  Une chose, et autre pensoie

but surely not as a consequence of it.[11a]

(j) and (k) are general observations made by the friar

---

[11] See Vol. V, p. 45.

[11a] If one investigator feels justified in thinking that this idea was taken from the *Roman*, what is to prevent another from maintaining, with equal show of reason, that John Cleveland was following Chaucer when he wrote,

  "that splay-mouthed brother
 That declares one way and yet means another."—

Rupertismus, ll. 11-13 (Poems of John Cleveland, New York, 1901).

in the *Somnours Tale* on the nature of women. Koeppel's parallel for D. 2001-3 is a passage comparing a jealous mistress to a serpent. But in Chaucer, the friar is only preaching to the sick man to avoid strife with his wife, who is admitted to be "holy and meke." As Skeat has shown, the original of Jean de Meung's figure was Ovid's *Ars Amatoria* (II, 376).

The particular individuals for whose description and characterization Chaucer is thought to have been considerably indebted to the *Roman de la Rose* are the knight and the lady in the *Book of the Duchess,* Troilus, Pandarus, the Prioresse, the Frere, the Pardoner, and the Wife of Bath. There is no need in this place of expatiating on these admirable creations of Chaucer's. They are his own notwithstanding the hints he received from various sources; for where he made flesh-and-blood people (except the knight and the lady in the *Book of the Duchess*—they were only dreamfolk), an inferior man, using the same details, would have made a catalogue or a spelling-book. We all admit at the start, then, that Chaucer's character-sketching needs no defense. And even if a hill of sources be heaped up to discredit his originality, he will rise mountain-high above them.

The Knight and the Lady *(Book of the Duchess)*

Commenting on the black knight and the "whyte" lady of this poem, Legouis says: "La moitié des épanchements du dolente Chevalier est remplié d'antithéses banales, et d'un pédantisme qui compromet le pathétique de sa complainte. . . . La bonne duchesse doit sans doute la plupart de ses qualités de corps et d'âme à la Nature, mais elle en doit quelques-unes aussi au Dit du Vergier, à la Fontaine Amoureuse, au Remède de Fortune, et au Jugment du bon roi de Behaigne de Machault.''[12] Clearly, Chaucer had read extensively in Machault before writing the *Book of the Duchess*. Kittredge has pointed out *in extenso* the indebtedness of this poem to *Le Jugement,* which Chaucer appears to have been using from about l. 442 on—the point where the dreamer sees the black knight. Consequently we have to be somewhat skeptical toward the following parallels drawn from the *Book of the Duchess* and the *Roman de la Rose:*

B. Duch.	475-476	(C)	RR.	306-313
	497-499	(C)		200-202
	591-594	(C)		323-326
	758-774	(C)	analogous to 1891-2032
	771-772	(C)		1987 ff.
	858	(S)		537
	874-877	(C)		1237, 1241, 1251
	880-882	(C)		1241-1242
	994-998	(C)		{ 1204-1205 18096-99
	1024-29	(S)		19234-61
	1152-54	(S)		2006-2007
	1211-20	(C)		2403-2414
	1283-84	(C)		1245

475-6 and 497-99 are commonplaces if there ever were any. Miss Cipriani compares the sorrow of the knight with that of Tristesse (RR. 291-338); but it should be noticed that there is a fundamental difference between the two: the

[12] *Geoffroy Chaucer*, p. 72.

grief of Tristesse is violent; she tears her hair and her flesh, and deports herself in general as Criseyde deports herself. (T. iv. stanzas 106, 117.) The knight's grief is more restrained. Besides, it is Avarice whose hue was green (cf. RR. 200 and B. Duch. 497), not Tristesse.

The rhyme *smerte: herte* (593-4) and the general idea expressed, seem to make it probable that Chaucer was thinking of *Rom.* 333-5 (not necessarily RR. 323-6).

As for 758-774, Professor Kittredge remarks: "... almost every word in these lines is accounted for either by Machault *(Le Jugement dou Roy de Beh.)*, vss. 261-73 or vss. 125-133."[13] This statement will dispose of B. Duch. 771-772, of course, as that couplet is included in the longer passage.

We have already seen that golden hair was the conventional thing for beautiful ladies to have; hence line 858 is a commonplace. But 857-858 taken together probably had as their source *Le Jug.* (302-3), not the *Roman*.

874-77, 880-882, 994-998 are no more like the lines quoted from the *Roman* than lines from a dozen other poems describing gentleness, modesty, and wisdom in a mistress. Moreover, 874-877 can be paralleled pretty closely with *Le Jug.*, 328-330. I doubt not that Machault would furnish equivalents for the other two passages.

For the sending of lovers on expeditions, by way of proving them, which was in accordance with the manners of the times, Skeat refers us to RR. 19234-61. He must have misprinted the reference, however, for there is nothing in this passage even remotely to suggest B. Duch. 1024-

[13] In *Mod. Phil.*, April, 1910, p. 468.

29. If Chaucer needed a literary precedent for this idea, he could have found it in Machault's *Dit du Lion.*

Skeat's parallel to 1152-54 is pertinent; the English lines seem to be reminiscent of the French, even though the two situations are quite different.

1211-1220 shows the god of Love's prophecy about the confusion of lovers when they meet their mistresses (RR. 2403-14) come true. Chaucer, when writing his lines, may have been recalling what was said in the French poem about changing color, etc., but his application of it to the case in hand was well made. The poet uses nearly the same words to describe Troilus's situation when he first meets Criseyde (T. iii. 92-98). Of course, blushing, turning pale, stammering, are characteristics of all true lovers in medieval poetry, and those of other times as well!

As for the last couplet, 1283-84, the resemblance to the French lines is not worth consideration. There is no indication of reminiscence of the *Roman* or of dependence on it.

B. Duch. 871-2 is not unlike *Rom.* 543-4 (RR. 531) in phraseology:

> That the goddesse, dame Nature,
> Had made hem [i.e. eyen] opene by mesure. (B.D.)

> And by mesure large were
> The opening of her ijen clere. (*Rom.*)

—a resemblance hitherto unrecorded.

Troilus and Criseyde, in many ways Chaucer's masterpiece—certainly his finest single poem—is said by Miss Cipriani to exhibit, more than any other work of our poet, traces of *Roman de la Rose* influence; but rather the influence of Jean de Meung than that of Guillaume de Lorris. This poem may have been written between 1382 and 1384, but possibly before the *Hous of Fame,* and surely before the *Legend of Good Women.* It is almost the center of a very significant group of pieces—the rest of them being dream-poems, but all displaying a more or less considerable influence from the Italian, as has been said.

By far the larger part of Chaucer's direct borrowings from the *Roman de la Rose* in the *Troilus* are of the nature of proverbs or material for philosophical digressions. But the three principal characters have been said to owe a few features to the French poem,—Pandarus and Troilus more than Criseyde, perhaps.

It has not been shown hitherto, I believe, how close an agreement there is between many of Troilus's traits and the characteristics of the ideal lover as set forth in the first part of the *Roman de la Rose.* How subtly, how insinuatingly, how unconsciously almost, but withal how naturally, Chaucer has applied certain conventional details, cannot be appreciated by reading only single lines, but can be seen in a rough general way by examining the references given below if one looks at them from the point of view of the place of their appearance in the poem. Throughout the story these hints are scattered in such a masterly way that the whole character of the hero unfolds itself as quietly, as smoothly, as imperceptibly, as the most finished artist could make it unfold.

It will be remembered that the god of Love in the French poem holds with the lover a long conversation of nearly seven hundred lines (2082-2776), in which he sets forth his

laws that must be obeyed, enumerates the toils and griefs
which a lover must undergo, and finally bestows on the
lover three gifts which are to help him obtain his desire.

I have listed below the various laws, pains and tortures,
and gifts that the god of Love speaks of, and have cited
lines from Chaucer's poem which show how Troilus fulfils
practically all the requirements which are codified, as it
were, in Guillaume de Lorris's *art d'amors*. The italicized
references are to lines that Chaucer could have taken, and
doubtless did take, from Boccaccio's *Filostrato;* but many
of these were probably due originally to the *Roman de la
Rose*.

The Eleven Commandments of Love, with Parallels from Troilus.

(1) Beware of villainy; villains will not be received
into the service of Love. RR. 2087-2092 (Rom. 2175-2180).

T. i. 901-3, *1030-33;* ii. 840; *iii. 1787,* 1796-99.

(2) Be courteous toward all persons great or small.
RR. 2109-2111 (Rom. 2213-15).

T. i. 1076-78; ii. 187-89, 204-207, 160; iii. 1790, *1800-03*.

(3) Watch thy lips well that they speak no ribaldry or
unbecoming word. RR. 2119-2126 (Rom. 2223-28).

T. iii. *1786, 1789*. [See also A. 70-72, descriptive of the
Knight.]

(4) Serve women; let no one speak calumny against
them. RR. 2127-34 (Rom. 2229-38).

T. i. 817-19; v. 1075-77.

(5) Beware of pride, which is both foolish and sinful;
it has nothing in common with love. RR. 2135-42 (Rom.
2239-46).

T. i. 1084; iii. 1801, *1805*.

(6) Dress as well as your purse will allow, but do not dress beyond your means. RR. 2152-64, 2168 (Rom. 2255-70, 2274).

T. ii. 624-25, 635-37; *iii. 1719.*

(7) Remember that a gay heart inspireth love. RR. 2185-94 (Rom. 2289-96).

T. i. 704-7, 816-17, 856, 890-96, 1072; *iii. 1726-29.*

(8) Practise games and athletics; they bring a man attention and renown. RR. 2199-2212 (Rom. 2305-16).

T. i. 1074; ii. 185-86, 197-203; *iii. 1779-81, 1776-78.*

(9) If you can sing well, do not hesitate to sing when called upon to do so. Make songs and complaints to move your lady to pity. RR. 2213-20 (Rom. 2317-28).

T. ii. 1499-1503; iii. 1254-74, *1716-18, 1743* ff. (The song Troilus sings is from Boethius.)

(10) Avoid the name of miser; lovers should be open-handed and generous. RR. 2221-25 (Rom. 2329-33).

T. i. 958, 1080; *iii. 1718, 1719.*

(11) In order to be true to love, you must set your heart whole in one place. RR. 2250-60 (Rom. 2361-72).

T. i. *537*, 960-62; iii. 103, 133, 134-47, 1298; iv. 1654-57; v. *574, 1695-1701.*

The toils and griefs a lover has to undergo, as the god of Love explains them to the lover.

(1) The lover must cloke his adventures from the eyes of other men; he must make his moan alone. RR. 2281-85 (Rom. 2391-96).

T. i. 743-45, *612-13*, 806; iii. 428-34.

(2) The physical state of the lover—now hot, now cold; now pale, now blushing; now self-forgetful and dumb, now given to much sighing. RR. 2286-2310 (Rom. 2397-2418).

Troilus: i. 441; iii. 94-95.

Pandarus affected: ii. 60.

Criseyde: ii. 645, 652, 698, 809-11 (pointed out by C.), 1256; iii. 1569-70.

(3) The lover will feel the misery of absence. RR. 2311-23 (Rom. 2419-33).

T. iv. 1699-1701; v. *217-245*, 295-332.

(4) Sight of the loved one is the only thing that satisfies; it is a way of lovers to be drawn closer into the fire. RR. 2343-70 (Rom. 2453-78).

T. *i. 442-46, 447-48;* ii. 537-39.

(5) The thought of neglected opportunities will be bitter when you are away from your love; you will curse yourself for having stood as dumb as stone or wood. RR. 2371-84, 2423-28 (Rom. 2480-98, 2545-48).

T. v. *736-43*, 744-49.

(6) A lover's confusion at the sudden sight of his love. RR. 2403-14 (Rom. 2523-37).

T. i. 295-301; ii. 652-58; iii. 80-84 (pointed out by C.).[13a]

(7) A lover's restlessness and sleeplessness at night. RR. 2433-42 (Rom. 2553-2564).

T. iii. 1583-84, *1534-40; v. 222-24*.

Pandarus tortured by love, ii. 57-63.

(8) The lover's further torments, for which he would feel richly rewarded by only one kiss. RR. 2489-92 (Rom. 2609-12).

T. i. 818-819, 810-12.

(9) The lover's anxiety for morning to come. RR. 2504-18 (Rom. 2627-40).

(10) Sometimes he gets up before dawn, draws on his shoes, and through the hail and snow goes to his love's house. RR. 2520-43 (Rom. 2645-70).

The setting of the scene in T. iii. 547-973 has general

[13a] Miss Cipriani also couples with these lines the scene of Troilus lying in bed and rehearsing the speech he is going to make to Criseyde, iii. 50-56. This admirable situation is Chaucer's own; there is no hint of it in either the *Filostrato* or the *Roman de la Rose*.

resemblances to the situation described here in the *Roman*.
Compare also T. iii. 786-88, 792-98; *v. 519-553*.

Love's three gifts to the lover.

(1) Sweet-Thoughts, that assuages the pain of lovers by
bringing before their minds their mistresses and all their
charms. RR. 2655-82 (Rom. 2791-2824).

T. iii. 1541-44, 1548-54; v. 426-476.

(2) Sweet-Speech, or Soft-Speech, which brings ease to
love-smitten knights and ladies. To hear the object of one's
passion praised is refreshing. It lessens the pain and care
to talk over secretly with some one, affairs of the heart.
RR. 2683-97 (Rom. 2825-55).

T. i. 883-89; iii. 1646-66; 1737-42; v. 515-16.

(3) Sweet-Looks, which cannot ease a lover's heart if
he is far away from his love. Therefore every lover should
press always to be in the place where he may see his lady.
RR. 2729-2762 (Rom. 2893-2934).

T. i. 442-46. Cf. esp. Rom. 2899-2900 with i. 445-46:

> Wherefore thou prese alwey to be
> In place, where thou mayst hir se.

> For-thy ful ofte, his hote fyr to cese,
> To seen hir goodly look he gan to prese;

Finally, Love advises the Lover to get above all a trusty
friend and to show him all his "wele and wo," joy and
pain. "Get one," he says, "who can keep thy counsel. If
the friend is one who has suffered the pains of love, all the
better; he will be a good one to give advice. And he will
show thee in turn his whole heart." RR. 2698-2729 (Rom.
2856-92).

Pandarus fulfils all these requirements: he is faithful
to the last, he is always ready night or day to serve Troilus,
whom he loves as a brother and even calls "Brother." Cf.

i. *586-95, 625-30, 646-51, 666-69, 675-76,* 711-14, 771-73, *1051-54, 1058-60,* 1065-71; ii. 57-63.

Miss Cipriani compares T. i. 715-16 with RR. 2719-20.

The kind of adaption of materials that we find in the *Troilus* is very different from that in the *Book of the Duchess;* so different and so superior, in fact, that we wonder what magic course in technic Chaucer took during the thirteen or fourteen years that separated the poems. Where our poet formerly took sections of whole cloth, he now takes threads and weaves them into his web so subtly that it is almost impossible to detect them and trace them. We have compared the *Book of the Duchess* to a patchwork quilt; we may compare *Troilus and Criseyde* to a piece of changeable silk, displaying now this color, now that, according to the angle from which it is examined. Into the warp of Boccaccio, Chaucer, here the masterworkman, has woven the woof of Boethius, Benoit, Guido della Colonna, Guillaume de Lorris, and Jean de Meung and himself.

A few other parallels remain to be considered in this place:

(a) T. ii. 722-723 (C) RR. 8488-89, 10600-601
(b) T. iii. 1544-46 (C) 2247-50
(c) T. v. 551-552 (S) 2251
(d) T. v. 1222 (S) Rom. 368.

(a) I see absolutely no correspondence of thought between the English and the French lines. Criseyde's soliloquy on the character of Troilus is rather reminiscent of some of the many lines of description of true lovers that

Chaucer read in Machault, if, indeed, he needed any literary origin for his remarks.[14] But it should be noted that Criseyde's inventory is very matter of fact; she selects qualities to the point. It is futile to look for sources of lines that are the most natural in the world.

(b) The resemblance between T. iii. 1544-46 and RR. 2247-49, can be seen to be very slight by comparing the English lines with the *Romaunt* 2357-60, which is a fairly close translation of the French.

(c) It is not impossible that Troilus's kissing the cold doors of Criseyde's house was suggested by

> Au departir la porte baise, (RR. 2550)

(d) What Skeat is comparing here is simply the phrase "by potente." RR. 360 has *potance*. La Vieille's description of herself also includes the phrase *a potence:*

> Mon tens jolis est tous ales, (13683)
> Poi me porrai mes soustenir (13685)
> Fors a baston ou a potence.

Pandarus is peculiarly Chaucer's own creation, and I think we may safely say that the poet owed nothing essential for this character, except a few proverbs, to the Lover's Amis, to whom Jean de Meung devotes so many lines. As we have seen, Pandarus fulfils all the requirements which the god of Love said a faithful friend should meet. The Amis of Jean is certainly a striking departure from what Guillaume de Lorris must have had in mind. There are some general resemblances between Pandarus and Reason,

---

[14] Compare, for example, *Le Jug. dou Roy de Beh.*, 135ff., etc.

though there is this fundamental difference, of course: Pandarus does all he can to assist Troilus in his love affair, while Reason does her best to turn the Lover from his. Both Pandarus and Reason, however, laugh at their "charges" now and then, and both discuss fortune. Both, too, are fond of "ensamples" and proverbs. That Chaucer associated Pandarus with Reason may be seen from the following correspondence of setting and diction between T. iv. 432-434 and RR. 5361-5362 (a resemblance not recorded hitherto, I believe).

> But Troilus, that neigh for sorwe deyde,
> Tok litel hede of al that ever he mente;
> Oon ere it herde, at other out it wente.

> Par une des oreilles giete
> Quanque raison en l'autre boute.

For the situation in the French poem, see the translation in the *Romaunt*, 5135-5154. Again, Pandarus may have some of the characteristics of Nature.

Miss Cipriani has made a good deal of the satiric side of Pandarus; but it is a side that I fail to see emphasized by Chaucer. It is true that Pandarus uses raillery and banter to get Troilus to tell him his troubles; he is worldly and somewhat cynical; but after all he is essentially faithful, he undoubtedly has a real affection for Criseyde, and is desirous only that the two young people shall be happy. He is always good-natured, and his remarks, witty as they can be, are ever without a sting. Altogether, there is no one character in the *Roman de la Rose* that approaches him.

We shall see in the next chapter the relationship between Criseyde and Reason. We may note here in passing that Chaucer's constant emphasis of what is Criseyde's most prominent trait, perhaps,—her fear lest people will talk about her, her extreme caution against the poison of wagging tongues—may have been suggested in part by what is said in the *Roman de la Rose* of the villain Male-Bouche, a resemblance hitherto unrecorded, I believe. Compare, for instance, ii. 729-732, 763, 799-805; iii. 274-287; iv. 1555-1582; v. 1058-1064 with RR. 8085-8128, 13117-13186, etc. The similarities are for the most part only general, but they are significant.

Of the immortal group of Canterbury pilgrims, the five whose characters Chaucer derived in part from details in the *Roman de la Rose* are among the most interesting. The poet has not only given us full-length portraits of the Squyer, the Prioresse, the Frere, the Wife of Bath, and the Pardoner, but he has made each one of them tell a story for us. So we have both external and internal evidence of what these persons were.

The character of the "yong Squyer" has been honored by having a famous living model pointed out for him—no less a person than Chaucer himself! M. Legouis writes: "Aussi lorsque le page se mué en soldat et, en novembre 1359, s'en va faire campagne en France, soit dans la suite du duc de Clarence, soit dans celle du roi lui-même, est-il tentant de le voir très semblable au jeune écuyer-poète qu'il a peint dans son Pélerinage, avec ses boucles frisées comme si on les avait mises en papillotes, . . . tout brode comme une prairie de fleurs rouges et blanches, chantant et flûtant tout le long jour, habile à faire des chansons et à les écrire. Tous les deux n'avaient-ils pas alors vingt ans d'âge, n'étaient-ils pas "frais comme le mois de mai?" L'un et l'autre ne chevauchèrent-ils pas pareillement à travers l'Artois et la Picardie? Et pourquoi, comme l'Ecuyer, Chaucer n'aurait-il pas fait prouesse lui aussi pour obtenir les grâces de sa dame? Tenons compte de ce qu'il entre de convention et de réminiscences littéraires dans le portrait de l'Ecuyer;—plusieurs de ses traits viennent de Guillaume de Lorris (*Roman de la Rose*, v. 2185-2221, Edit. Fr. Michel. Le rapprochment, que je sache, n'a pas été signalé) et, à travers Lorris, d'Ovide (*De Arte Amandi*, lib. I. v. 595);—mais il est significatif que Chaucer soit seul à lui attribuer le don de poésie. Les coincidences sont telles qu'en peignant son Ecuyer, il est inimaginable que le poète n'ait pas fait un retour sur lui-même."

Before I read Legouis's admirable little volume on Chaucer, I had noted in my own mind some of the similarities between the Squyer and the ideal lover as Guillaume de Lorris portrays him in the first part of the *Roman*. The young son of the Knight recalls to us, too, the picture of the merry loving Troilus, as he is represented at the end of Book iii:

> In suffisaunce, in blisse, and in singinges,
>   This Troilus gan al his lyf to lede;
> He spendeth, justeth, maketh festeyinges;
> He yeveth frely ofte, and chaungeth wede;
>   And held aboute him alway, out of drede,
> A world of folk, as cam him wel of kinde,
> The fressheste and the beste he coude finde;

> That swiche a vois was of him and a stevene
> Thorugh-out the world, of honor and largesse,
> That it up rong un-to the yate of hevene.
> And, as in love, he was in swich gladnesse,
> That in his herte he demede, as I gesse,
> That there nis lovere in this world at ese
> So wel as he, and thus gan love him plese.
> (iii. 1716-1729)
> And most of love and vertu was his speeche,
> And in despit hadde alle wrecchednesse;
> (iii. 1786-87)
> Benigne he was to eche in general, (iii. 1802).

Although we may hesitate to agree with M. Legouis's ingenious conjecture about the autobiographical echoes in what Chaucer says of the Squyer, we may reasonably admit that not a few strokes in the word-picture of this young gallant are distinctly reminiscences of the *Roman de la Rose* and Chaucer's earlier work. It will be remembered that the Frankeleyn, who admires the Squyer very much, introduces into his own story a squire who closely resembles Chaucer's.[15]

Sandras recorded the similarity between

> Embrouded was he, as it were a mede
> Al ful of fresshe floures, whyte and rede;

and the description of the god of Love, RR. 888-890. Skeat refers us to the English translation:

> His garnement was everydel
> Y-portreyd and y-wrought with floures,
> By dyvers medling of coloures. (Rom. 896-898)

---

[15] Compare the *Frankeleyns Tale*, (F) 925ff.

We might also add that the line

> He was as fresh as is the month of May,

charming and picturesque as it is, was a commonplace not only with Chaucer but also with trouvère poets.[15a]

The last two lines of the portrait of the Squyer:

> Curteys he was, lowly and servisable,
> And carf biforn his fader at the table,   (99-100)

suggest a comparison with RR. 14336-8:

> Et quant ele iert a table assise,
> Face, s'il puet, a tous servise,
> Devant les autres doit taillier.

I admit that it was the custom of squires to carve at the table, and that the parallel I have indicated here may be only a coincidence. As justification for citing the French lines, however, I will merely call attention to the fact that they occur just before the famous description which Chaucer incorporated only thirty lines further on into his picture of the Prioresse.

The Prioresse and the Wife of Bath are the only women in the company whom Chaucer has minutely characterized. We cannot conceive of two individuals more unlike than these two: the Prioresse modest, dainty, tender-hearted, treated with respect by all; the Wife of Bath boisterous, coarse, given to much talking, a good deal of a scold, joked at by the Friar and others of the group. And Chaucer with consummate skill has played a supreme joke on Jean

---

[15a] For references in Chaucer, see L. 613; A. 1037, 1510-11; E. 1747-8; F. 281, 927-8.

de Meung. For from the very section in which La Vieille discloses to Bel-Acueil the wiles used by some women to entrap men and describes the various aids for waning beauty Chaucer has adapted material for eight lines of his description of the winsome Prioresse. (Or perhaps the joke is on the Prioresse herself.) Tyrwhitt first pointed out the indebtedness of A. 127-135 to RR. 14336-37, 14349-62, 14366-73. It is interesting to compare Ellis's translation of RR. 14349-373 with Chaucer's lines:

> 'Tis well she take especial care
> That in the sauce her fingers ne'er
> She dip beyond the joint, nor soil
> Her lips with garlick, sops, or oil,
> Nor heap up gobbets and then charge
> Her mouth with pieces overlarge,
> And only with the finger point
> Should touch the bit she'd fain anoint
> With sauce, white, yellow, brown, or green,
> And lift it towards her mouth between
> Finger and thumb with care and skill,
> That she no sauce or morsel spill
> About her breast-cloth.
>   Then her cup
> She should so gracefully lift up
> Toward her mouth that not a gout
> By any chance doth fall about
> Her vesture, or for glutton rude,
> By such unseemly habitude,
> Might she be deemed.
>   Nor should she set
> Lips to her cup while food is yet
> Within her mouth.
>   And first should she

> Her upper lip wipe delicately
> Lest having drunk, a grease-formed groat
> Were seen upon the wine to float.
>
> (ll. 14117-14140)[16]

"Many of the remarks concerning the Frere," says Skeat, "are ultimately due to the *Roman de la Rose*. See Romaunt of the Rose 6161-7698."[17] These lines in the French poem, it is perhaps needless to repeat, form part of Faux-Semblant's confession before the god of Love, a speech much too long for analysis here. In some respects the Pardoner's character owes more to the *Roman de la Rose* than the Friar's, a relationship that has not been pointed out hitherto, so far as I am aware. On reading the Pardoner's Prologue, we are immediately struck with many resemblances it bears to Faux-Semblant's self-revelation. Like the harangue in the French poem, what the Pardoner has to say takes the form of a confession, and the relation of his personal experiences, impudent, intimate, disgusting, is not a whit overdrawn, as Jusserand says. The Friar makes no confession; but Chaucer makes one for him and attributes to him some of the traits that Faux-Semblant so shamelessly boasts are his own.

To be more specific: Faux-Semblant says that he loves good dishes and wine, and that although he preaches poverty, his bags overflow with coin, and he never makes friends with any poor man (RR. 12154-75). For "poor man" Chaucer substitutes "lazars." The Frere knew all

---

[16] Langlois (p. 163-164) cites a passage very similar to this one from the *Clef d'Amours*, which was undoubtedly Jean de Meung's immediate source.

[17] Vol. V, p. 25.

the taverns and inn-keepers, had no acquaintance with lepers, but dealt with the rich, with merchants. Like Faux-Semblant, too, he did not go about as a poor clerk in thread-bare coat,

> But he was lyk a maister or a pope.

But the Frere and the Pardoner, unlike their French prototype, do not object to have dealings with poor people. Of the first Chaucer says:

> For tho a widwe hadde noght a sho,
> So plesaunt was his *"In principio,"*
> Yet would he have a ferthing, er he wente. (A. 253-55)

And as for the Pardoner—

> But with these relikes, whan that he fond
> A povre person dwelling up-on lond,
> Up-on a day he gat him more moneye
> Than that the person gat in monthes tweye. (A. 701-4)

And in his own Prologue this "noble ecclesiaste" declares,

> I wol have money, wolle, chese, and whete,
> And were it yeven of the povrest page,
> Or of the povrest widwe in a village,
> Al sholde hir children starven for famyne. (C. 448-451)

The Pardoner is without doubt one of the most despicable wretches in literature. And the Frere is a close second, although Huberd has external graces to make him more endurable than the slovenly, repulsive Pardoner. But how closely this precious pair was associated together in the mind of Chaucer may be indicated, perhaps, by the fact that the poet divided one of Faux-Semblant's couplets between them:

> En aquerre est toute m'entente,
> Miex vaut mes porchas que ma rente,   (RR. 12492-93)

The Pardoner says of himself,

> For my entente is nat but for to winne,   (C. 402)

and Chaucer says of the Frere,

> His purchas was wel bettre than his rente.   (A. 256)

while the Frere himself (through Chaucer) puts a similar expression into the mouth of the fiend:

> My purchase is th' effect of al my rente.   (D. 1451)

As Faux-Semblant says that he lives

> Sans james de mains traveillier,   (RR. 12504)

so the Pardoner asserts,

> I wol not do no labour with myn hondes.   (C. 444)

a direct imitation which seems hitherto to have been overlooked.

Like Faux-Semblant, too, the Pardoner preaches against avarice, "Radix malorum est Cupiditas." But, "trowe ye that he wol live in povert wilfully?" He may well say with the other, "Mes ge sui ypocrits," 12163. The Frere's specialty of shriving women was anticipated by Faux-Semblant, RR. 12515 ff., a resemblance not hitherto recorded. Skeat cites as a parallel to the Somnour's contemptuous allusion to the dwelling-place of friars D. 1690-91, a couplet from the *Romaunt:* 7577-78, to which the corresponding line in the French text is 13186. But the phrase seems to have been proverbial.[18]

In these two characters of the Pardoner and the Frere, then, so much alike and yet so well differentiated in personality, Chaucer has mirrored not a little of Jean de Meung's arch-impostor. The friar of whom the Somnour tells a story, Chaucer paints as no different from the Canterbury pilgrim Hubert. Skeat has recorded the similarity of situation between D. 2094-98 and *Romaunt* 6390-98 (RR. 12019 ff.). But the English poet has also reflected much of the actual life and conditions of his day, and it is easy to over-estimate his literary borrowings. Chaucer's clerics are real persons, and they have definite occupations. We do not know what Faux-Semblant is except that he is a very shadowy personification of some sort of ecclesiastic. There is throughout a certain unreality and inconsistency about him. For instance, his fervent arraignment of the Mendicant Friars—Jean de Meung talking! To say that Faux-Semblant is less villainous than the Frere and the Pardoner is not to praise him; he antagonizes us less because he is less actual, less human. Chaucer's triumph in the Canterbury Tales is that he does not intrude himself upon his characters. He gives us their stories, their digressions, as he conceived that the narrators conceived them. This method often leaves us in doubt as to what his own

[18] Rutebeuf, in his *Sainte Marie l'Egiptianne*, ll. 308-9, writes:

    Dame, je qui sui mise el puis
    D'enfer par ma grant mesprison, etc.

feelings were; but on the Pardoner and the Frere, we may safely say, I think, that Chaucer wasted no sympathy or affection.

The character of the Wife of Bath has been made the subject of a somewhat general but informing study by William E. Mead, to some of whose remarks we shall have occasion to refer. But it is not necessary to go over the whole ground again, interesting as the Wife of Bath is at all times. The discussion here will take the form largely of a summary of what has been said about Chaucer's use of the *Roman de la Rose* in the representation of this "worthy woman."

Mead writes in part: "So peculiarly alive is (the Wyf of Bath) that she seems almost to be fashioned after a living model, and this may be to some extent true. Yet closer study shows that in this, as in other cases, Chaucer borrowed all the hints he could get, and that, as usual, he turned to the *Roman de la Rose*. In this particular instance his indebtedness to the French poem is, I think, somewhat larger than has been generally recognized."[19] I am inclined to disagree with this last statement, for on examination of the criticism up to and including Koeppel's article in *Anglia*, XIV, we find that no less than thirty parallels to as many passages in the Wife's Prologue, besides two in the General Prologue, had been pointed out from the *Roman de la Rose*. Lounsbury had remarked that "Chaucer has transfused the quintessence of three works (i. e., Le Roman de la Rose, Valerius ad Rufinum,

[19] *The Prologue of the Wife of Bath's Tale,* by William E. Mead, Publ. Mod. Lang. Assoc., 1901, p. 391.

and Hieronymus contra Iouinianum) upon the subject of Matrimony, into his Wife of Bathes Prologue and the Merchantes Tale."[20]

It may have been Tyrwhitt's general statement that called forth Mead's remark about the underestimate usually made of Jean de Meung's influence on this character. But I do not think that the influence has been underestimated; at least it has not been under-stated. Skeat many times has emphasized the fact that the Wife is modeled largely on La Vieille.

Later on in his article, after he has compared the Wife with Jean's duenna, Mead writes, "Evidently, then, although Chaucer did not attempt to copy the portrait of La Vieille as a whole, he took from her the general suggestion for the outlines of the Wife of Bath. But he modified the figure of La Vieille by making her younger and more vigorous, by giving her as keen an interest in life as she ever had, by representing her as still ready for matrimony whenever opportunity should offer. (Prol. 44-45.) Furthermore, Chaucer transformed the somewhat morose and broken-spirited old woman, entirely out of sympathy with life, into a witty and frisky shrew—good-natured in a way, but still a shrew."[21]

This investigator, however, does not emphasize the fact that the English poet drew from the long discourse of the Amis nearly as much as he drew from the duenna's confession.

A list of the parallels already discovered between the

[20] *Studies*, II, 292.
[21] Op. cit., 394-5.

Wife of Bath's personality and certain features in the French poem may prove instructive, for from it one can see at a glance what parts of the *Roman* Chaucer seems to have been using here. Consequently, I enumerate below such correspondences as may be reasonably said to set forth the Wife's character. (I omit, of course, parallels that are discussed elsewhere in this book.)

A.	461	(S)	RR. 13722
	476	(S)	4545
D.	1-3	(K)	13743-45
	207-210	(K)	14210-14
	227-228	(S)	19071-72
	229-230	(K)	10664-65
	250-252	(K)	9331-34
	248-254	(K)	9328-49
	257 ff.	(K)	9340-49
	263-266	(K)	9348-53
	293-294	(S)	14651
	333-336	(K)	8161-66
	357-361	(K)	{ 15326-29 15338-39
	393-396	(S)	14775-85
D.	407-410	(S)	9839-44
	467-468	(S)	14393-94
	469-473	(K)	{ 13873-79 13865-66
	503-514	(K)	15420-35
	522-524	(K)	14648-51
	552-554	(K)	9777-78
	555-558	(S)	14464-69
	572-574	(S)	14091-96
	575	(K)	14633
	623-24	(K)	9265

662	(K)	10726
929-930	(S)	10692-10708
950	(K)	20152
	(S)	17284-17312
961-963	(K)	17458-67
968	(K)	17304-5

To this list we may add Mead's parallels: D. 534 ff. and RR. 17284-17301. We are also asked to compare RR. 9276-9282, 9310-9357, 9416-9437, though we are not told with what to compare these passages in particular.

Upon examination of the correspondences tabulated above, we may safely say that:

D. 1-2 are imitated fairly closely from the French lines, but are given a new turn with line 3.

207-210 were doubtless inspired by the lines noted. The rhyme *plese: ese* (213-214) recalls the rhyme *plaise: mesaise* (RR. 14212-13).

227-228 are almost a literal translation of the French.

229 is an echo of the Amis's excluding statement after he has told the lover that women are as slippery as eels. We might also compare Faux-Semblant's similar remark, 11783-89, which he prefixes to his tirade against religious pretenders.

250-256 were clearly modeled on the description of the angry, jealous husband whom the Amis depicts in the *Roman*.

257 ff. was probably taken from Theophrastus. See Skeat, V. 298. There is little resemblance to the *Roman*.

293-294, as Skeat points out, are taken from Theophrastus. I do not understand the critic's reference to the

Roman, 14651. There is no resemblance between the English lines and

> Tant le va l'en plus viltoiant.

333-336 and 357-361 are without doubt imitated from the French passages cited.

393-396 may have been suggested by the parallel indicated.

The next three parallels are very close, i. e., 407-410, 467-468, 469-473.

503-514 have strong resemblances to RR. 15420-35, though I should hardly call the passages "parallel," as Skeat calls them.

The next two parallels are close. Indeed, with the whole passage, D. 516-522, we might compare RR. 14644-55. In connection with 558, where the wife says that she used to go to "pleyes of miracles" in order to attract attention, we might note that Ovid says that above all, the playhouse is the place to go to see beautiful women:

> Sed tu praecipue curvis venare theatris,
> (*Ars Amat.* I, 89)

572-574, 575, and 662 are almost translations of the French lines. Skeat, following Koeppel, quotes RR. 9265 in a note to D. 624, without comment. In the absence of any evidence except the English "short or long" and the French "cors ou lons," it cannot be maintained that the French lines were the original of the English.

929-930 may have been inspired by the dozen and a half lines in the *Roman,* but not necessarily.

950 is clearly a translation from the French.

961-963 and 968 represent the particular application by Chaucer of general statements taken from the *Roman*.

Every lover of Chaucer's characters has doubtless at one time or another compared the Wife of Bath with Pandarus; and there is much to justify the comparison. Pandarus—something of a male duenna—is a man who has had experience in love, though Chaucer has gallantly made him refrain from telling of "wo in mariage." But that the poet associated these two characters and had Pandarus in mind while describing the Wife, is suggested by the phrase he uses to characterize each:

But Pandarus, that wel coude eche a del
The olde daunce, and every poynt therinne, (T. iii. 694-5)

Of remedyes of love she knew perchaunce,
For she could of that art the olde daunce. (A. 475-76)

The original of the phrase "the old daunce" appears in Guillaume de Lorris's description of La Vieille, RR. 4545. Pandarus, however, is of a much finer grain than the Wife; besides, he has none of her shrewish nature. He has had several love affairs, as has been said; and as for the Wife—

Housbondes at chirche-dore she hadde fyve,
Withouten other companye in youthe.

But without carrying this comparison any further, let us consider the Wife alone. Her very first word—"Experience"—foretells us that we are going to hear something worth while. *Le malin Chaucer!* In the *Prologue* to the *Legend of Good Women* he tells us that books are all right where we have no other proof. And then he distinctly remarks that he turned to his *books* for the stories of good women! If we pass immediately from that poem to the Wife's Prologue, we see the double force of these lines:

> Experience, though noon auctoritee
> Were in this world, were right y-nough to me
> To speke of wo that is in mariage.   (D. 1-3)

We are, consequently, to hear of matter that is true, the result of experience. But these very lines are taken from one of the "olde bokes!" It should be remembered, however, that Chaucer has given them an application and turn of his own. La Vieille simply says to Bel-Acueil—

> N'onc ne fu d'Amors a escole
> Ou l'en leust la teorique
> Mais ge sai tout par la pratique,
> Experiment m'en ont fait sage.   (RR. 13743-46)

and promises that she will impart to him all the mysteries of the art. Line 3 of the Wife's Prologue is Chaucer's own addition.

With lines 235 ff. Chaucer introduces his observations on marriage and the "fair sex," and he screens himself well by having the Wife, who as much as admits that she is just making talk, accuse her husbands of sarcastic and uncomplimentary remarks about women in general and her in particular. This imaginary conversation, some twenty lines of which appear to have been borrowed from the *Roman de la Rose,* extends to line 378.

But Chaucer is not satisfied to leave all that he has to say of women reported so indirectly. He has the Wife herself confess that

> Deceite, weping, spinning god hath yive
> To wommen kindely, whyl they may live.   (401-402)

and she goes on to show how she possessed her share of the deceit at least. These two devices for bringing into prominence the undesirable traits of women—first by making the Wife report a word-attack her husband made on her, and second by having her show just how she treated her five mates—are separated in the *Roman* by several thousand lines, and form two distinct speeches by two different characters, the Amis and La Vieille. The uniting by Chaucer of the general method of the two is certainly a gain for emphasis and unity.

The Wife of Bath's reference to her lost youth is distinctly pathetic. In this passage Chaucer has greatly improved on his sources—Jean de Meung and Ovid—by the addition of ll. 474 ff. The speech is so perfect and so natural, in fact, that we can fairly hear the Wife pause in the midst of her volubility when she remembers that she is no longer young, that the flour is gone, and that she has only bran to sell. But she suddenly recollects herself, and proceeds gaily with the account of her fourth husband.

The Wife's treatment of her fifth husband's book:

> And made him brenne his book anon right tho,   (D. 816)

has a rather curious literary precedent in Marie de France's lay of *Guigemar,* ll. 234 ff.

In addition to this not uninteresting correspondence, I have noted two more parallels of idea between the Wife's Prologue and the *Roman:*

The Wife's appeal to Scripture in D. 107-110 is exactly the same that Faux-Semblant makes in RR. 12298-301.

Her argument in 115 ff., while decidedly more specific, is the same as Reason's in the *Roman,* 5120-5145, although the Wife's takes an original turn with line 135.

In conclusion, we may glance again at our table of parallels to see how Chaucer used the French poem. In the first place, while a number of the short passages of the English are almost literal translations from the French, Chaucer is not content to follow his model consecutively for any length of time. Often a line taken over bodily from the *Roman* starts in his mind an entirely new train of thought, which he works out originally. In the Wife's Prologue we see that he has chosen striking phrases and ideas from all parts of the *Roman de la Rose,* and has made of them, along with other material, a Prologue which perfectly fits the teller of it. But it is not in his borrowings that Chaucer was greatest, although he displays rare genius for selection, coördination, and adaption of the work of his famous predecessors. It is his realistic, intimate touches of human nature, of real life as he saw it, that make him in the highest and truest sense original.

CHAPTER VI

Proverbs and Proverbial Expressions

Proverbial material is hard to define and classify. Chaucer uses the word "proverb" to characterize a few of the adages in his pieces, but by far the greater number of his proverbs are not formally introduced. The parallels that remain to be considered in this chapter and the next partake of the nature of proverbs and philosophical discussions, if the terms may be intrepreted somewhat liberally. By proverb we shall understand a brief pithy statement of a more or less general truth, regardless of whether it has developed into a popular maxim. By proverbial expressions we shall mean such observations and bits of advice as are distinctly sententious and might easily be turned into genuine adages. More extended discussions of Chaucer's will be reserved for Chapter VII.

It is a commonplace to say that the people of the Middle Ages were fond of proverbs. A timely adage was often more effective than a sword thrust—at least in the stories; a line or two of popular wisdom had more persuasive power than might or right. But proverbs were not used merely as defensive weapons; they were used on every occasion. There was hardly a human situation possible which could not be taken care of by an adage. The universal use of proverbs in medieval literature must not be misinterpreted, however; it is not to be taken as evidence that the age was one of aggressive morality or of serious didacticism. For proverbs either could represent the utilitarian justification of the fable or could enforce the spiritual lesson of the parable. Their employment was, in the main, conventional, habitual.

A study of the proverbs of Chaucer might be conducted in one of two ways. All the proverbs occurring in his work might be collected and then classified into maxims relating to love, speech, silence, fortune, or what not. Or, each character apt at quoting proverbs, as Pandarus or the Wife of Bath or the Pardoner, could be studied as a unit. This method, of course, is the same that we have termed in another place chronological. In an examination of the proverbs which Chaucer is thought to have taken from the *Roman de la Rose* the chronological method is far more instructive than the topical. It is not likely that the poet systematized all the maxims and sententious remarks made in the French poem, indexed them, and pigeon-holed them, so to say, for further use. It is much more reasonable to suppose that when writing up certain situations or when portraying certain characters, he had in mind analogous scenes or personages of other works, and transferred into his own poem what was said elsewhere under similar, or perhaps opposite, circumstances. It is unfair both to Chaucer and to the authors of the *Roman de la Rose* not to examine the setting in which we find parallel passages. To do this logically one must take up either Chaucer's work in complete units or the *Roman de la Rose* in consecutive parts. As we are particularly concerned with the question of the use that the English poet made of the French poem, we may look here at his characters as entities, and from what is said both by the poet and by his personages, attempt to get additional light on the question of the effect of the *Roman de la Rose* on Chaucer.

The Book of the Duchess

The only passage in the Book of the Duchess to be noticed at any length in connection with proverbial material in the *Roman,* is the comparison which the knight makes between his lady and a lighted torch:

> Therto she coude so wel pleye,
> Whan that hir liste, that I dar seye,
> That she was lyk to torche bright,
> That every man may take of light
> Ynough, and hit hath never the lesse. (961-965)[1]

This follows immediately after an enumeration of her physical charms. The simile of the torch, says Skeat, was "a common illustration," and he refers us to RR. 8162. As the French lines are significant, I reprint them:

> Moult est fox qui tel chose esperne,
> C'est la chandele en la lanterne;
> Qui mil en i alumeroit,
> Je mains de feu n'i troveroit.
> Chascun set la similitude,
> Se moult n'a l'entendement rude. (8161-66)

It may have been Jean's very statement that everyone knows this simile that suggested its use to Chaucer. But

---

[1] Chaucer uses the same illustration in the Prologue to the Wife's Tale, 333-335, where the lines have a more decided proverbial ring.

its application by the English poet to what he has said in the lines immediately preceding is not clear. What is the sense of *pleye?* Similarly, Marteau remarks in his note to these lines in the French poem:[1a] "Cette comparaison et la pensée qui précède sont assez obscures, ou tout au moins fort mal présentées. L'auteur veut dire: Jalousie prétend garder pour elle seule Bel-Accueil et ses charmes, comme l'avare son or; c'est sottise. En effet, qui obtient les faveurs d'une femme ne fait tort à personne. Allumer sa chandelle à celle d'un autre, est-ce lui faire tort? Pour un peu, Jehan de Meung dirait: Séduire la femme, c'est faire beaucoup d'honneur au mari. Mais il se contente d'affirmer que ce n'est pas lui faire tort, les charmes de la femme n'augmentant point à ne pas servir, pas plus que l'or au fond d'un sac. Petite économie!"

Three explanations suggest themselves to account for Chaucer's use of the figure of speech in relation to Jean de Meung's: (1) Either the English poet was not thinking of the French poem at all when he wrote the lines, or (2) he had this very passage of the *Roman* in mind, but interpreted it innocently, or (3) he understood Jean de Meung as Marteau understood him, but deliberately changed the application. What he goes on to say about the lady's goodness and virtue seems to accord with this third explanation. One hardly dares suggest that Chaucer implies that the lady's philosophy about granting favors was the same as that of the Amis (who speaks the French lines). It is true that B. Duch. 961 is unfortunate as a transitional line, but we lack evidence for supposing that Chaucer meant any-

[1a] Vol. II, p. 424.

thing more by the comparison than that Blanche, always beautiful, always gracious, without losing any of her charm kindled the hearts of all men that looked on her.

Skeat says that B. Duch. 791-92:

> I chees love to my firste craft,
> Therfor it is with me (y)-laft,

refers to the old proverb that what is learned in youth remains most indelibly fixed in the mind. In his note to these lines (V, 483), after citing the Hendyng form of the adage, he suggests for comparison RR. 13831-34. In the French poem Plato is given credit for the sentiment—

> Car Platon dist, c'est chose voire, etc.[2]

PARLEMENT OF FOULES

The last line of the warning inscription over one side of the gate into the park—

> Th' eschewing is only the remedye. (140)

may be, as Skeat says, from RR. 17553:

> Sol foir en est medicine.[2a]

The French line is spoken by Genius, who is advising men

---

[2] According to Langlois, Plato was known to Jean de Meung and his contemporaries only through Chalcidius's Latin translation of the *Timaeus*. The immediate source of RR. 13830-32 was Chalcidius: "Certusque illud expertus sum, tenaciorem fere memoriam rerum quae in prima discuntur aetate."

[2a] In *Ywain and Gawin* we find the proverb expressed in slightly different words:

> "To fle than was his best rede." (1910)

to fly womankind if they would live in safety. As Genius later describes the kind of garden that lovers should seek as opposed to Guillaume's garden of Mirth, and as Chaucer contrasts in the *Parlement* the two paradises, the use of this proverb here is another bit of evidence for the theory I proposed in the last chapter: that the English poet was intentionally drawing a comparison between Genius's view of love and Guillaume's.

There is nothing to show that Chaucer was thinking of RR. 5453-54 when he lets the "sperhauk" say,

But sooth is seyd, "A fool can noght be stille." (574)

Skeat in his note to this line gives a number of instances of the occurrence of this extremely common proverb.

ANELIDA AND ARCITE

There is no evidence that Chaucer had any part of the *Roman de la Rose* in mind when writing *Anelida and Arcite*. At most, ll. 315-316 are but a doubtful reminiscence of RR. 10660-61.

BOETHIUS

We have already discussed a few of Chaucer's glosses to lines in his translation of Boethius. Three additions of our poet which have a proverbial ring have been credited to his knowledge of the *Roman de la Rose*, and may be noticed here.

In Book II, prose v, ll. 129-131, Chaucer writes, "as who seith, a pore man, that berth no richesse on him by the weye, may boldely singe biforn theves, for he hath not wherof to ben robbed." These lines, Miss Cipriani thinks, are a reminiscence of Jean de Meung:

> Miex porroit uns ribaus de Grieve
> Seur et seul par tout aler,
> Et devant les larrons baler,
> Sans douter eus et lor affaire.   (6001-6004)

The idea is, of course, ultimately from Juvenal, *Satire* X, 22, although Jean de Meung does not mention the Latin satirist's name in this connection. Chaucer clearly knew, at least as early as the Wife's Tale, that the lines were from Juvenal, because he repeats the quotation and credits Juvenal with it:

> Juvenal seith of povert merily, etc. (D. 1192)

He could not have got this information from Jean's text. Moreover, his gloss is by no means a translation of the French: the French has *baler,* while Boethius in the line to which Chaucer's explanation was added has *cantares,* Juvenal has *cantabit,* and the English poet has *singe.* Again, *pore man* does not equal *ribaus.* There is not the slightest reason why Chaucer should have gone outside of Boethius for ll. 129-131. They surely resemble his own translation of "si vitae huius callem vacuus viator intrasses, coram latrone cantares" much more closely than they resemble the lines of Jean de Meung.

In Book II, prose iv, ll. 80-82, we read, "as who seith, thou thy-self, ne no wight elles, nis a wrecche, but whan he weneth himself a wrecche by reputacioun of his corage," which is nothing more than an expansion of the line "and forthy nothing (is) wrecched, but whan thou wenest it."

Miss Cipriani refers Chaucer's expanded explanation to RR. 5767, which merely says:

"Nus n'est chetis, s'il n'el cuide estre."

It is true that Jean de Meung is quoting from Boethius; he says he is. But he translates literally—in this line at least. If Miss Cipriani had cited the next line from the *Roman:* "Soit rois, chevaliers, ou ribaus," which might have suggested Chaucer's "ne no wight elles," her case would have been stronger. However, there is no need at all to suppose that Chaucer was borrowing from a paraphrase of the material he was translating, rather than from that material itself.

In Book IV, prose iv, ll. 205-206, Chaucer translates and explains thus: "For which it bitydeth that, as to the wyse folk, ther nis no place y-leten to hate; *that is to seyn, that ne hate hath no place amonges wyse men.*" Anyone can see that the italicised portion (Chaucer's interpretation) reads exactly like the portion before the semicolon. It seems superfluous to cite as an original for Chaucer's line (206) this from the *Roman:* "Que nule riens hair doie-en," 6495, which is said by Reason in a situation absolutely different from that in the *Consolations*.

We may conclude, then, that none of these three passages cited from the *Roman de la Rose* probably had any influence on Chaucer's glosses.[2b]

[2b] Some of Miss Cipriani's other parallels between Chaucer's *Boethius* and the *Roman* seem to me of even less significance, viz., Bo. V, pr. iii, 125-126 and RR. 18060-61; 127-129 and RR. 18102-3, 18711-13; Bo. V, pr. vi, 113-114 and RR. 18213-15; 205 and RR. 18209-11.

TROILUS AND CRISEYDE

As might be expected from his rôle as adviser, Pandarus leads all the other characters in the *Troilus* in the number of his proverbs. Criseyde follows fairly close behind. Troilus has so many quoted to him by both Pandarus and Criseyde that he has little heart to venture an original maxim. The narrator, Chaucer himself, indulges in a few. When we think of the wealth of regular proverbs that there is in the *Roman de la Rose,* and when we recall the part played by the French poem in helping to shape in Chaucer's mind the characters of Troilus and Pandarus, we should be surprised if Chaucer had not occasionally drawn upon the sententious remarks of the Amis or of Reason for some of the words to put into the mouths of his characters.

Of the parallels pointed out between the *Roman de la Rose* and *Troilus and Criseyde,* fourteen may be considered proverbs or bits of proverbial advice, distributed thus: Chaucer 1, Troilus 1, Criseyde 5, Pandarus 7. The examples discussed below do not include *all* the adages and old saws contained in the poem, of course; Chaucer has pressed into service many sources other than the *Roman,* and has doubtless drawn upon popular wisdom to a large extent. Indeed, our examination of those traced to the *Roman de la Rose* will show that not all of these can be proved conclusively to have been taken from the French poem.

Chaucer's generalized description of the new lover Troilus's condition,

> For ay the neer the fyr, the hotter is (i, 449)

was pretty clearly suggested by RR. 2370:

Qui plus est pres du feu, plus art,[2c]

—spoken by the god of Love after he has told of just such a situation as we find Troilus in. Miss Cipriani seems to have been the first to record the parallel. The expression must have been common, however, for Haeckel cites a number of authorities for it, including two Latin examples.[3] In *Le Jugement dou Roy de Behaigne*, Machault repeats the idea in the same words:

> Et cils qui est plus pres de feu, plus s'art.   (1743)

But he may have been following the *Roman* here as he followed it many places elsewhere.

Troilus does not exactly make the statement that

> Eek som-tyme it is craft to seme flee
> Fro thing which in effect men hunte faste,
> (i. 747-48)

Chaucer says that "al this gan Troilus in his herte cast." We have a right to attribute the thought to the young lover, nevertheless, for it was clearly meant as his own. Koeppel has compared the lines with RR. 8308-9:

> Or doit chacier, or doit foir,
> Qui vuet de bonne amor joir,

a couplet spoken by the Amis. The situations are not identical, and the significance of the parallel appears to me to be slight.

[2c] Translated in the *Romaunt*:
> Who is next fyr, he brenneth most.   (2478)

[3] Willi Haeckel: *Das Sprichwort bei Chaucer* (Erlanger Beiträge, VIII, 1890), p. 17.

Chronologically it was impossible for Criseyde to know the *Roman de la Rose*, but artistically not impossible. Chaucer has studied the poem carefully for her and with remarkable skill has brought her to say what reveals her most intimate self.

When Pandarus is talking with her for the first time about Troilus's goodness and bravery, she replies that she is glad to hear of a king's son conducting himself so well—

> For greet power and moral vertu here
> Is selde y-seye in o persone y-fere.   (ii. 167-168)

a couplet from Lucan quoted by Reason in the *Roman*, 6395-97. And when a little later she is arguing with herself whether or not to accept Troilus's attentions and love, she helps to settle her mind with this reflection:

> In every thing, I woot, ther lyth mesure,
> For though a man forbede dronkenesse,
> He nought for-bet that every creature
> Be drinkelees for alwey, as I gesse.   (ii. 715-718)

another thought taken from Reason's speech (RR. 6479-80). Chaucer could not have summed up Criseyde's character in a single phrase better than he sums it up here by implication: she is *Reason personified*. Whether or not it was divine inspiration that led him to choose this half-capitulating remark of Reason:

> Por ce se ge deffens ivrece,
> Ne voil-ge pas deffendre a boivre,

and put it in Criseyde's mouth, it was certainly more than mere chance.

There are two passages in the *Roman de la Rose* that Chaucer may have had in mind when Criseyde says,

> Our wrecche is this our owene wo to drinke (ii. 784)

one spoken by La Vieille,

> "S'il fait folie, si la boive," (13580)

pointed out by Koeppel, who also compares it with two other lines of Criseyde, iii. 956 and 1035; and one spoken by Faux-Semblant: "Tex gens boivent trop de mesaise," 12460 (*Rom.* 6807). These two names coupled with that of Criseyde sound suspicious; but the proverb was undoubtedly common. It appears in the *Seven Sages:*

> Thou schalt suffre kare and howe,
> And drinke that thou hast i-browe, (1493-94)

and in the *Confessio Amantis:*

> And whoso wicked Ale breweth,
> Fulofte he mot the werse drinke. (III. 1626-27)

two parallels not noted before in this connection. But then, if Chaucer lets Alceste use arguments and proverbs of Faux-Semblant, why should he not let Criseyde?

In Book IV, 1305-6, Criseyde turns god of Love and comforts Troilus with the same words that Cupid uses to cheer the lover in the first part of the *Roman*. For she says,

> But him behoveth som-tyme han a payne,
> That serveth love, if that he wol have joye,

and he says,

> Et plus en gre sunt receu
> Li biens dont l'eu a mal eu.
> (RR. 2613-14. *Rom.* 2740-42)

There is no other resemblance, except their speeches here, between Criseyde and the god of Love; but there is certainly a distinct resemblance between Troilus and Guillaume's lover. Miss Cipriani recorded the parallel passages just quoted, but not the significance of them. The situations are more alike than the mere words.

From these few hints that have been thrown out, it may be seen that a careful comparative study of parallel passages and undoubted borrowings in Chaucer, will reveal in a most startling and interesting way the working of the poet's mind, and will give us—what we feel we often lack—intimate glimpses of the artist in his workshop.

Pandarus, as we have shown, in his general rôle corresponds to the Amis of Jean de Meung, but these two confidants are unlike each other in one important particular: Pandarus stays by Troilus to the last; the Amis drops out of the *Roman* very suddenly, overcome, perhaps, by his own long discourse. Their parts are played in entirely different ways. It is natural, however, that Chaucer should have adapted from the many proverbs and bits of worldly advice that the Amis communicates to L'Amant, a few lines to Pandarus; and so he did adapt them. Chaucer has selected nothing, however, from this part of the *Roman* that would refute our double contention that Jean de Meung's Amis as a whole is totally unlike the friend whom the god of Love commends toward the beginning of the poem, and that Pandarus bears very little resemblance to Jean's Amis and very much to Guillaume's. Of course, here as elsewhere Chaucer has made use of a variety of sources. He does not limit himself for the proverbs of Pandarus to the Amis's speech or even to the *Roman* or the *Filostrato*. He skillfully works in everything he can find to make this great character complete yet consistent.

First we may consider the parallels not taken from the discourse of the Amis.

Koeppel suggests as a parallel to Pandarus's elaboration of the maxim "By his contrarie is every thing declared," i. 638-644, a passage from the very end of the *Roman de la Rose*, ll. 22574-88, the same passage that Miss Cipriani prints as an analogue to Troilus's words to Criseyde, iii. 1212-21. I think there can be no doubt that the French lines inspired the philosophical remarks of Pandarus. The resemblance is very close. But when Chaucer has Troilus say, after he has won the heart of Criseyde—

> O! sooth is seyd, that heled for to be
> As of a fevre or othere greet syknesse,
> Men moste drinke, as men may often see,
> Ful bittre drink; and for to han gladnesse,
> Men drinken often peyne and greet distresse;
> I mene it here, as for this aventure,
> That thourgh a peyne hath founden al his cure.
>
> And now swetnesse semeth more swete,
> That bitternesse assayed was biforn;
> For out of wo in blisse now they flete.
>
> (iii. 1212-1221)

the poet is not turning back to the *Roman* again; he is simply representing the happy lover as recalling the sententious remarks which his friend Pandarus made when Troilus was suffering the tortures of unrequited affection, and as now testifying to the truth of those philosophical remarks. This is a natural, realistic touch of Chaucer's that should not be missed.

Koeppel also showed that these lines of Pandarus—

> What! many a man hath love ful dere y-bought
> Twenty winter that his lady wiste,
> That never yet his lady mouth he kiste. (i. 810-12)

spoken to Troilus in order to rouse him into action from his lethargy of despair, are almost an exact translation of RR. 21878-81,—lines with which Pygmalion temporarily comforts himself in the possession of his cold ivory statue instead of a warm living body. He can at least kiss the statue, he says. This whole episode of Pygmalion, according to Marteau, is a later interpolation into the *Roman de la Rose;* but it is pretty clear from this parallel and one in the *Knightes Tale* that Chaucer's MS. of the French poem contained the story of Pygmalion.

Miss Cipriani suggests as a parallel to Pandarus's statement that "he that parted is in every place is nowhere hool," i. 960-961, three lines of the god of Love's warning, RR. 2250-52. I think that lines 2255-56 furnish a much closer correspondence:

> Qui en mains leus son cuer depart
> Par tout en a petite part.

Compare Rom. 2367-68.

Resemblances have been noted between four ideas that Pandarus communicates to Troilus and four that the Amis imparts to the lover. We may examine these briefly.

If we admit with Miss Cipriani that the proverbial advice which Pandarus gives Troilus,—that he should blot his letter to Criseyde with tears, ii. 1027 was inspired by RR. 8222, we shall have to accept many a faint parallel. There is no identity of situation here: in the *Roman* the friend is advising the lover to weep real (or feigned) tears *in the presence* of his lady. No mention is made of any letter. Pandarus's suggestion is most natural and conventional, and surely does not need to be traced to the French poem.

Again, Pandarus tells his friend that

> . . . wyse ben by foles harm chastysed, (iii. 329)

a line which Skeat, following Koeppel, says that Chaucer took from the *Roman de la Rose*, 8754-55:

> Moult a beneuree vie
> Cil qui par autri se chastie.

The lines in the French poem occur in the friend's long digression about the miseries of poverty, and there is nothing in the setting of the speech or in the wording of the lines to warrant Skeat's dogmatic statement. The context of the one passage is utterly different from that of the other. Moreover, in Book I, Pandarus had already elaborated the idea that "A fool may eek a wys man ofte gyde." (See i. 630-637.) The proverb was certainly well-known. In *Ywain and Gawin,* for instance, occurs the neat little couplet—

> Bot yet a fole, that litel kan,
> May wele cownsail another man, (1477-78)

Miss Cipriani's source for Pandarus's lines of advice to Troilus in iii. 1622-24 and 1634, is reasonable and probable;

viz., RR. 9013-19.[3a] It should be noted here particularly that the lines Chaucer has chosen from the Amis's speech have nothing incongruous with Guillaume's conception of what the confidential friend should advise. Jean de Meung's Amis goes on to tell the lover that women are coquettes. Pandarus does not say this to Troilus; Chaucer lets Criseyde prove by her actions what she is.

THE HOUS OF FAME

Dido was the stock example in the Middle Ages of the deceived mistress, and Aeneas was, as a rule, soundly berated by the poets telling her story. Chaucer's observations in Book I of the *Hous of Fame* on the treachery of lovers and the falseness of men is nothing but poetical orthodoxy. It is altogether unlikely that for these two passages:

> For this shal every woman finde
> That som man, of his pure kinde,
> Wol shewen outward the faireste,
> Til he have caught that what him leste. (279-282)

and

> How sore that ye men conne grone,
> Anoon, as we have been receyved,
> Certeinly we ben deceyved, (338-40)

the poet was skipping about in the *Roman* from ll. 5008-14 to 14080-82, then to 22489-98—portions of the French poem

---

[3a] With these lines compare *Ars Amat.*, II, 11-13. T. iii. 1634, might easily have been taken from the Latin:

> Nec minor est virtus, quam quaerere, parta tueri.
> —*Ars Amat.*, II, 13.

that Miss Cipriani points out as analogous to our quotations.

The couplet about the fleeting nature of time, 1257-58, would seem to have been written with the *Romaunt* in mind. The verbal correspondence of these two lines with *Rom.* 5123-24 (RR. 5344-45) is striking—

| For tyme y-lost, this knowen ye, | For tyme lost, as men may see, |
| By no way may recovered be. (*HF.*) | For no-thing may recured be. (*Rom.*) |

Skeat makes the following remarks on the similarity of the two passages: "As these lines (i. e., Rom. 5123-24) are not in the original, the writer may have taken them from Chaucer's *Hous of Fame*. The converse seems to me unlikely; however, they are not remarkable for originality." (I, 439.) But they are in the original! *Rom.* 5121-22 does not entirely translate the French couplet. Although it is almost impossible to establish the date of the B-fragment of the English translation, it might easily be older than the *Hous of Fame*.

The Man of Lawes reference to the irrecoverable quality of time and his comparison of time with the stream that flows down the mountain and never returns to its source again, B. 20-24, closely resembles the *Rom.*, 369ff., as Skeat has pointed out in his notes. The Clerk makes a briefer statement, E. 118.

PROLOGUE TO THE LEGEND

When Alceste undertakes to defend the poet and to answer the charges that the god of Love makes against him, she uses among other arguments one taken from Faux-

Semblant's answer to the accusations of Male-Bouche against the lover in the *Roman*. Alceste says,

"Al ne is nat gospel that is to yow pleyned," (a) 326,

and Faux-Semblant begins his speech thus:

> Sire, tout n'est pas evangile
> Quanque l'en dit aval la vile, (13215-16)

The comparison of truth with the gospel was doubtless proverbial and is not uncommon in Old French poetry: it occurs elsewhere in the *Roman*, and in Rutebeuf[4] and Machault.[5] But the similarity of situations and of the arguments that follow the lines quoted make it pretty certain that Chaucer had his eye on the *Roman* in this place. Compare also *Romaunt* 7609 ff.

The other proverb that Alceste uses to quiet the wrath of the god of Love—

> For in your court is many a losengeour
> And many a queynte totelere accusour, (b) 352-53

is, according to Skeat, a reminiscence of what is said of the flatterers around Richesse in the early part of the *Romaunt*, 1062-66 (RR. 1052-55). Another parallel might have been suggested, RR. 1973-78 (Rom. 2045-50). It would have been quite a happy thought to have Alceste make before the

---

[4] Compare
> Ausi voir comme est Evangile
> Est ceste chose.
> —*Œuvres*, II, p. 261, ll. 639-640.

[5] Compare
> Sire, il est voirs come euvangile.
> —*Œuvres*, ed. Tarbé, p. 78, l. 11.

god of Love the confession that Cupid makes to the lover in the *Roman de la Rose,* and I am not sure that Chaucer was not thinking of the passage I suggest. Chaucer repeats this couplet later on in the *Nonne Preestes Tale* (B) 4515-4516. The character of Alceste studied from the point of view of the sources of her remarks so far as we can determine them might throw not a little new and interesting light on the meaning of the *Prologue of the Legend.*

THE KNIGHTES TALE

The Knight is fond of proverbs and he commonly introduces those he uses with the clause, "But sooth is seyd." Three of his sayings have been traced back to the *Roman*: (A) 1625-26, 2447-48, 3041-42.

The source of the first,

> Ful sooth is seyd, that love ne lordshipe
> Wol noght, his thankes, have no felawshipe,

has been pointed out by Skeat in his note to l. 1625. The same idea is elaborated in the *Frankeleyns Tale,* (F) 764-66. The lines in the *Roman* corresponding to 1625-26 are 9198-9202.

The source of the second,

> As sooth is sayd, elde hath greet avantage;
> In elde is bothe wisdom and usage,   (2447-48)

is three lines from the Duenna's discourse to Bel-Acueil, and, as Skeat does not print the passage, it may be recorded here:

> Ne fait a foir, n'a despire
> Tout ce qui est en grant aage;
> La trueve l'en sens et usage.   (RR. 13759-61)

The third,

> Thanne is it wisdom, as it thinketh me,
> To maken virtue of necessitee,   (3041-42)

is spoken by Theseus. The idea occurs at least once in the *Roman,* 14960-61, where the words are spoken by La Vieille. The thought is applicable to almost any uncomfortable situation, however, and Chaucer employs it twice elsewhere, T. iv. 1586 and F. 593. But its being put in the mouth of Criseyde when she finds that she has to leave Troy is Chaucer's finest, most appropriate use of it. Who better than Criseyde could "make a virtue of necessity"?

THE MILLER'S PROLOGUE

The drunken Miller's remark to Oswald, "Who hath no wyf, he is no cokewold," (A) 3152, Koeppel compares with RR. 9877-79. As the French lines contain an emphatic reference to the experience of Arnold, the saint of cuckolds, Chaucer may have remembered the passage here. But Chaucer's phraseology sounds like that of a popular proverb, and it is very questionable whether the poet had the *Roman* in mind. The *Miller's Prologue* and *Tale,* as a whole, seems to be particularly free from direct influence of the French poem.

THE REVES TALE

Oswald triumphantly "quits the Miller" with this proverbial flourish at the end of his story of the Miller of Trumpington:

"A gylour shal him-self bigyled be." (A) 4321.

The expression was so common that it is impossible to say

what occurrence of it Chaucer had in mind when he wrote it down here. In addition to Skeat's examples of its appearance in literature a few more might be mentioned.

> Si sachies que cis font bone uevre,
> Qui les deceveors decoivent.   (RR. 8094-95)

> Par barat estuet barater.   (RR. 8139)

> Lobans lobes et lobeurs
> Robe robes et robeors.   (Ibid., 12476-77)

> Et cil lobent les lobeors
> Et desrobent les robeors
> Et servent lobeors de lobes,
> Ostent aux robeors lor robes.
> (Rutebeuf II, p. 18)

Qui simulat verbis, nec corde est fidus amicus;
Tu quoque fac similes; sic ars deluditur arti.
(Cato, *Disticha*, I, xxvi)

PROLOGUE OF THE MANNES TALE OF LAWE

For his discussion of the evils of poverty Chaucer may have used a few details from the discourse of the Amis in the *Roman de la Rose*, 8900-8940. Tyrwhitt noted that this "sentence of the wyse,"

> Bet is to dyen then have indigence.   (B) 114,

occurs in RR. 8928; but Chaucer's "indigence" suggests that his original was the Vulgate, *Ecclus.*, xl, 28.[6]

THE PARDONERES PROLOGUE

Tyrwhitt adduced as a parallel to the couplet,

> For certes many a predicacioun
> Comth ofte tyme of yvel entencioun,   (407-408)

[6] See Skeat's note, V, p. 143.

Romaunt 5763-64 (RR. 5834-35). The same rhymes are found in all three passages, but it is clear from Chaucer's "ofte tyme" that he was following the English translation of the *Roman*. The Pardoner's mention of "veyne glorie" (411), "ipocrisye" (410), and "avarice" are fairly good evidence that Chaucer got other hints for this Prologue from Reason's sermon on evil priests and the misery of avarice (RR. 5792-5839). No one seems to have noted the fact hitherto.

THE PROLOGUE AND TALE OF THE WYF OF BATHE

Whoso that nil be war by othere men
By him shul othere men corrected be. (D. 180-181)

repeats the thought of T. iii. 329. Koeppel suggested RR. 8754-55 as a source of both passages. There is a slight resemblance between the Wife's story of tribulation in marriage, which she tells to the company, and the Amis's story of his wretched poverty, which he tells to the lover. But the parallel does not appear to me conclusive that Chaucer had the lines of the Amis in mind here.

The statement

He that coveyteth is a povre wight, (1187)

has been compared by Koeppel with RR. 19499. Skeat says that lines 1184-1190 are imitated from Seneca's Epistles,[7] and, indeed, Chaucer mentions "Senek" in line 1184. The line in the *Roman* suggested by Koeppel comes shortly before the long passage in which Nature discusses

[7] See note, Vol. V, p. 320.

the question, "Who is a gentleman?" As the Wife has just been expounding "true gentilesse," it appears that Koeppel's citation is perfectly reasonable. Possibly the association of poverty and real nobility of spirit in the *Roman* suggested to Chaucer the general scheme of the Wife's sermon.

The couplet setting forth one advantage of poverty,

> Povert a spectacle is, as thinketh me,
> Thurgh which he may his verray frendes see,   (1203-4)

seems to be rather a reminiscence of Chaucer's own gloss to Boethius, Book II, prose viii, 31: "the knowinge of thy verray frendes," than of *Rom.*, 5551-52, as Skeat suggests. Neither Boethius nor Jean de Meung, however, liken poverty to an optic glass.

The Wife, full of saws as her speech is, appears to owe very few of them to the *Roman de la Rose*. Her proverbs, especially those in the Prologue, are of the popular kind, picked up in daily intercourse with people and not culled from books. Probably there are no literary parallels to be found for many of them.

THE MARCHANTES TALE

The two lines describing the relation of husband and wife:

> O flesh they been and o flesh, as I gesse,
> Hath but on herte, in wele and in distresse,
> (E. 1335-36)

are taken from the *Roman*, says Skeat, following Koeppel. The French lines read:

> Nous fist deus estre en une char;
> Et quant nous n'avons char fors une,
> Par le droit de la loi commune,
> N'il ne puet en une char estre
> Fors que uns cuers a la senestre.   (17366-70)

This argument is used by the wheedling wife who is trying to persuade her husband to tell her his secrets. Jean's roundabout method to express a simple thought as used here seems to fit the verbosity of a coaxing woman. Chaucer has condensed the five lines of his original into a line and a half; for "in wele and in distresse" does not appear in the French.

Lines 1559-61 are also taken from the *Roman*, says Skeat. But I see nothing in the passage he cites, RR. 14798-99, to warrant his assurance. The French text says, in effect, "The one who thinks to possess his wife alone has very little wisdom." The sense of the English line is, "The youngest married man is kept busy trying to possess his wife alone."

The proverb,

> For every labour som-tyme moot han reste,   (1862)

is so common, and must have been so common in Chaucer's day, that it is unreasonable to assert positively that it is from RR. 20663-64:

> Car choses sans reposement
> Ne puet pas durer longuement.

Haeckel[8] cites many authorities for this maxim, and quotes

[8] Page 13.

as almost equivalent to it the line in the *Squieres Tale*, (F) 349:

That muche drinke and labour wolde han reste.

So far as proverbs are concerned, then, the *Marchantes Tale* seems to owe little to the *Roman de la Rose*.

THE MAUNCIPLE'S TALE

The story of Apollo's white crow and the punishment it received may be considered an exemplum illustrating the proverb that the tongue ought to be reined. The Maunciple makes the application, lines 309ff:

Lordings, by this ensample I you preye,
Beth war, and taketh kepe what I seye, etc.

The discussion is by no means short; it extends over more than fifty lines. Koeppel thinks that Chaucer was here following a treatise by Albertano of Brescia, entitled *De arte loquendi et tacendi*.[9] Skeat refers H. 332-333 to RR. 7783 and 7808. The line,

Thing that is seyd, is seyd; and forth it gooth (355),

is ultimately taken from Horace, Skeat says, and adds that Chaucer found it either in Albertano or in the *Roman de la Rose*, 17482-83. But if Skeat had looked one line further in the French and English passages, he would have found proof that Chaucer used the *Roman*. Compare the clause, "though him repente," in the following:

---

[9] *Chaucer und Albertanus Brixiensis*, by E. Koeppel. Archiv für das Studium der neueren Sprache. Vol. 86, pp. 44-46.

> Thing that is seyd, is seyd; and forth it gooth
> Though him repente, or be him leef or looth.

> Et quant dit l'a, si s'en repent;
> Mes parole une fois volee
> Ne puet plus estre rapelee.   (RR. 17481-83)

Moreover, Chaucer goes on to say,

> He is his thral to whom that he hath sayd
> A tale, of which he is now yvel apayd,   (357-358)

which is exactly the lesson that Jean de Meung enforces.

The influence of the *Roman* on this whole digression of the Maunciple is greater than has been recognized. I have examined Koeppel's parallels from Albertano's treatise and am by no means convinced that Chaucer was following the Italian writer. The critic's equation of the introduction of Albertano and that of the Maunciple as indicated by the line,

> But natheles thus taughte me my dame,   (317)

has no weight. The Wife of Bath says:

> My dame taughte me that soutiltee,   (D. 576)

Lines 329-331 are clearly from the French, not the Latin writer. Compare

> My sone, thy tonge sholdestow restreyne
> At alle tyme, but whan thou doost thy peyne
> To speak of god, in honour and preyere.

with

> Que sages est cis qui met paine
> A ce que sa langue refraine,
> For sans plus quant de Diex parole . . .

> Car nus ne puet Diex trop avoer . . .
> . . . ne trop beneir,
> Crier merci, ne graces rendre: (RR. 7786ff)

Lines 332-334 are but a reminiscence of T. iii. 293-94, which in turn was taken from the *Roman,* as Koeppel himself showed in another article. We can conclude nothing from the fact that "Die von Chaucer citierten Autoritäten (ll. 344-345) nennt Albertano sehr häufig." Again, the Maunciple's exposition by no means follows consecutively Albertano's line of reasoning; Koeppel's quotations are taken from all parts of the Latin tractate. Finally, there is only a general resemblance between the closest parallels. They are not close enough to forbid us to assume that Chaucer drew upon the *Roman de la Rose,* the Bible, and his own commen sense for most of his material here. At any rate, Koeppel was mistaken when he wrote that "no one would question the fact that Chaucer had read this little treatise of Albertano's." Chaucer may have known it, but as yet we have no sure proof.

CHAPTER VII

THE INFLUENCE OF THE ROMAN DE LA ROSE ON CHAUCER'S
PHILOSOPHICAL DISCUSSIONS

"All we know or think we know about Chaucer's opinions must be gathered directly or indirectly from his own writings." The task of recreating Chaucer the thinking person, would seem at first sight easy; for we have a large bulk of genuine, varied work of the poet. But as soon as the investigator sits down to a poem and begins to read and to record the lines that express views on significant questions, he finds himself bewildered by contradictions. Suppose, for instance, that *Troilus and Criseyde* is selected to be studied for evidence of Chaucer's philosophy. Pandarus and Troilus, it is soon discovered, have exactly opposite beliefs about fortune, the meaning of dreams and omens, necessity and predestination. In which character, if in either, is the poet revealing his own self? Perhaps the investigator decides that Pandarus's utter contempt for dreams and signs is Chaucer's, and goes on to read the *Hous of Fame*. But here the poet professes ignorance and, unlike Troilus and Pandarus, decides to leave to "grete clerkes" the solution of the causes and significance of dreams. And if the *Nonne Preestes Tale* happens to be the next poem read, the seeker for light finds himself where he started: Chanticler, like Troilus, believes thoroughly in visions, and even uses learned arguments and ancient and modern instances to support his views; Pertelote, like

Pandarus, says contemptuously that there is naught but vanity in "swevenes," and expounds scientifically the cause of bad dreams.

We may ask ourselves, what are the most likely places in which to find an expression of Chaucer's own convictions? (1) In the poems and parts of poems where the poet is speaking directly; (2) in the lines of the characters with whom we feel Chaucer is most in sympathy and is most like; (3) in the passages which, whether spoken by Chaucer himself or by the personages created by him, agree with the beliefs of authors whom the poet, from other evidence, seems to have admired; and (4) in the passages which present a line of reasoning in direct opposition to that of the poet's favorite authors.

It is not a difficult matter to select out of Chaucer's entire work the lines which the poet writes as his own utterances. Such a collection would include, roughly speaking, most of the minor poems, the author's narrative in *Troilus,* large portions of the *Hous of Fame* and the *Legend,* the *Treatise on the Astrolabe,* the *Prologue to the Canterbury Tales,* and various connecting links between the tales themselves, besides *Sir Thopas* and *Melibeus.* But even in judging from these portions, one must bear in mind the author's artistic purpose.

It is much more difficult to pick out with any feeling of assurance the characters most like Chaucer, for in each of his great personages he has given us a more or less complete living being. By a process of elimination we can exclude many who bear no resemblance to the poet. Those whom probably most critics would agree on as embodying one or more attributes of Chaucer himself are Pandarus, Harry Bailey, the Wife of Bath, and the Chanouns Yeman. There are a number of characters who exhibit minor tendencies and express now and then ideas that we associate with the poet; as Criseyde, the goddess Nature (in the *Parlement of Foules*), Pertelote, the Persoun. Then, too, from such characters as the Pardoner, the Frere, and the Sumnour, utterly unlike our poet, we can determine many of the things Chaucer disliked.

The third and fourth groups of passages can be determined by an investigation of the sources of Chaucer.

A full discussion of the nature of Chaucer's mind would fill volumes, and would have to be the result of an examination and a reinterpretation in part of all that has been written on the poet. Our concern here is with specific passages which show the attitude of our poet or of his characters on certain questions treated in the *Roman de la Rose*. In other words, we purpose to make here a comparative study of the beliefs of Chaucer and Jean de Meung (and Guillaume de Lorris, so far as he expresses himself) on definite question of metaphysical or practical philosophy.

FORTUNE

Fortune is an old figure even in classical literature, and appears frequently in Old French and Middle English poetry.[1] In the *Roman de la Rose* Reason refers to the

[1] Richard Rolle's *Pricke of Conscience* contains a discussion of "Dam Fortone" and her wheel. Rolle says that men call her
"noght elles
Bot happe or chaunce, that sodanli falles." (1281-82)
See also many of the poems in Jubinal's collection, *Jongleurs et Trouvères*.

appropriate way the ancients had of representing the goddess as blindfolded:

> Por ce li oil bende li furent
> Des anciens qui la congnurent. (RR. 6909-6910)

Jean de Meung, as is well known, through the mouth of Reason gives a long discussion of the fickle deity (6578-7643). The main sources for this material, besides the historical allusions, were Boethius, Solinus, and Alanus de Insulis—as Langlois has pointed out. The poet has succeeded, in spite of his rambling sermon, which treats of almost every conceivable aspect of the subject, in presenting Fortune as a pretty distinct personage. She is visualized as standing upright, with banded eyes, and as ceaselessly turning her wheel (6637ff.). Her mansion is described picturesquely as situated on a mighty rock in the midst of the sea (6657ff.). Her instability is symbolized by a series of contrasted pictures: the two streams, the two halves of her house, and later the two tuns of Jupiter. Her capriciousness is illustrated by the stories of various princes, both ancient and modern, who fell from the high estate to which they had been raised—an interesting anticipation by over half a century of Boccaccio's *De Casibus*. It should be noted, however, that powerful as Fortune seems to be, Jean de Meung does not identify her with any pagan or Christian deity; he says expressly:

The idea of the unstableness and changeableness of the world is lengthily developed, ll. 1412-1473. (See Morris's and Skeat's *Specimens*, II, pp. 117-119.) Skeat makes no mention of these similarities. For a gorgeous description of the wheel of Fortune, see *Morte Arthure* (E. E. T. S.), ll. 3260-67.

> D'autre part, si est chose expresse,
> Vous faites Fortune deesse,
> Et jusques ou ciel la leves,
> Ce que pas faire ne deves;
> Qu'il n'est mie drois ne raison
> Qu'ele ait en paradis maison;   (6649-54)

The wheel of Fortune had been mentioned by Guillaume de Lorris (4590-99), and Jean de Meung has much to say about it. "It is continually rolling through his verses," to use Skeat's phrase.[2] Two characteristics of the wheel are emphasized by Jean; the ceaselessness and rapidity of its motion (6068-73, 6637-43), and the impossibility of arresting it (7145-48, 7359-62).

The whole trend of Reason's discourse with the lover is this: It is dangerous to trust Fortune; she is capricious, she is unsatisfying. Be wise like Socrates and despise anything Fortune can do to you, for

> S'est moult fox qui s'en desconforte,
> Et qui de riens s'en esjoist,
> Puisque deffendre s'en poist:
> Car il le puet certainement
> Mes qu'il le vueille seulement.   (6644-48)

This long sermon of Reason's seems to have been one of Chaucer's favorite passages. The English poet made constant use of it and of other parts of Reason's discourse on kindred subjects, as appears from the parallels pointed out between the *Roman* and his work. The most elaborate treat-

---

[2] *Chaucer*, II, xxi. Skeat's references to the *Roman* are made to Meon's edition. The corresponding lines in Michel can be determined from the table in Appendix A of this book.

ment of Fortune occurs in the *Book of the Duchess, Troilus and Criseyde,* the *Monkes Tale,* and *Fortune.* The following comparisons have been made between these poems and the *Roman* (or *Romaunt*):

B. Duch. 617-84 (passim), the extended figure of Fortune playing a game of chess with her victim. Compare RR. 7356ff., from which the English lines clearly are imitated. (See Skeat, I, p. 478.)

T. iv. 6-7. Koeppel compares this couplet with RR. 8790-93:

> And whan a wight is from hir wheel y-throwe,
> Than laugheth she, and maketh him the mowe.

>> Tuit cil amis si s'enfoirent
>> Et me firent trestuit la moe
>> Quant il me virent sous la roe
>> De Fortune envers abatu.

The rhymes are the same, but the situations are not. In Troilus, it is Fortune who makes the grimace; in the Amis's discourse it is the former friends. For comparison with this whole first stanza of Book IV, I suggest a stanza from Machault's *Le Jugement dou Roy de Behaigne* (the passage was clearly inspired by the *Roman*):

>> Mais quant Fortune,
>> La desloial, qui n'est pas a tous une,
>> M'ot si haut mis, com mauvaise et enfrune,
>> Moy ne mes biens ne prisa une prune;
>> Eins fist la moe,
>> Moy renoia et me tourna la joe,
>> Quant elle m'ot assis dessus sa roe,
>> Puis la tourna, si chei en la boe.   (684-691)

A little later, in Book IV, Pandarus says,

> Ne truste no wight finden in Fortune
> Ay propretee, hir yeftes been comune. (391-392)

a sentiment which both Reason and the Amis (8774-77) express.

Fortune, 1-4. The mutability of the world is caused by Fortune's error. Cf. *Rom.* 5479-83.—Sk.
9-12. Fortune teaches one to know his true friends. Cf. *Rom.* 5551-52, 5671-8, 5579-81.—Sk.
32. One good friend left. Cf. RR. 8769-73.—Sk.
33-40. Fortune clears the eyes and shows up false friends. Cf. RR. 5672-77.—Sk.

In addition we may note that there are numerous references to Fortune in the *Knightes Tale*. It should be said, moreover, that the two short passages cited from the *Troilus* by no means give an adequate representation of the kinship of Pandarus and Reason as regards fortune. Compare particularly Book I, 834-856, which is but the situation of L'Amant and Reason over again. There is no hint of this in the *Filostrato*.

In his conception of Fortune, Chaucer differs from Jean de Meung in one important detail: the English poet sometimes represents Fortune as the executrix of God's will; e. g., T. iii. 617-23, v. 1541-47; *Fortune*, 65-72. In this respect he is doubtless following Boethius.[3]

But that Chaucer made liberal use of the *Roman* for his

[3] Fortune is also called the sister of Fame (HF. 1547). This is one of the bits of evidence on which W. O. Sypherd bases his theory that Chaucer's goddess of Fame owes many of her traits to previous portraits of Fortune, and among them Jean de Meung's. But Professor Sypherd points out no significant parallels and, to use

references to the fickle goddess no one can doubt. Probably many more short passages of his that have not been discussed owe either their form or their thought to Reason's sensible utterances. And on the whole, Chaucer's attitude appears to have been that of Jean's, as Pandarus's is that of Reason's: Defy Fortune, cease to worry about her gifts, do the work you were put here to do. And he even goes so far as to suggest that she can be made a useful ally:

> Happe helpeth hardy man alway. (L. 1773)

> Thynk eek, Fortune, as wel thyselven wooste,
> Helpeth hardy man unto his empryse. (T. iv. 600-1)

—a more advanced, pragmatic attitude than Jean's entire disregard of Fortune.

DESTINY, FREE-WILL, AND NECESSITY

In RR. 18038-18534 Nature delivers a long sermon on free-will and necessity. She starts by saying that the question of how free-will can coexist with predestination is not one suited for discussion by the laity:

> Mes de soldre la question
> Comment predestination
> De la divine prescience,
> Pleine de toute porveance,
> Puet estre o volente delivre,
> Fort est as gens laiz a descrive,
> Et qui vodroit la chose emprendre,
> Trop lor seroit fort a entendre,

his own statement, "resemblances have no cumulative force if there is no significance in the separate details." See *Studies in Chaucer's Hous of Fame*, pp. 117-122.

>   Qui lor auroit neis solues
>   Les raisons encontre meues. (18038-47)

After stating the objections that one might raise by saying that if God did not know beforehand what was to happen, he would rank no higher than a mortal, she answers them with counter-objections. God is perfect and just to all men, she says, and free-will does exist. If there were such a thing as necessity, men would not work, for they should be provided with everything. Clearly man acts by the prompting of free-will. Other arguments against free-will are considered. But Reason goes on to show that necessity is unreasonable, and in conclusion she proves the freedom of the will. What she says at the end of this discourse of the power of the stars we shall consider in connection with Chaucer's astrology.

This long discussion of five hundred lines forms a part of Nature's confession to Genius, the whole being an exposition of Jean de Meung's ideas of "cosmogony, astronomy, and optics." The poet had difficulty in explaining his views, for his mouthpiece, Nature, jumps many a question she might logically, as God's chamberlain,[4] be able and be

---

[4] Nature says that God made her his "connestable," his "vicaire," 17719. Chaucer uses the same word—*vicaire*—to describe Nature, PF. 379; but, as Skeat says, our poet was probably following Alanus de Insulis. See Skeat's note, Vol. I, p. 521. See also V, 94, where Skeat compares with A. 2991-93 Nature's statement:

>   Si gart, tant m'a Diex honoree,
>   La bele chaene doree
>   Qui les quatre elemens enlace
>   Tretous enclins devant ma face. (RR. 17722-25)

With PF. 380-81 Skeat compares RR. 17898. See also C. 19-22 and RR. 20437-40 (Koeppel).

expected to expound to Genius. Jean attempts to present both sides of the argument, but the reasons he advances for believing in free-will are only a little less unconvincing than those against it. He virtually admits the intricacies that a full discussion of the doctrinal point would involve. His advice to anyone attempting to make the matter plain to unlettered folk,

> Qui bien voldroit la chose emprendre,
> Qui n'est pas legiere a entendre,
> Ung gros exemple en porroit metre
> As gens laiz qui n'entendent letre:
> Car text gens vuelent grosses choses,
> Sans grant sostivete de gloses.   (18328-33)

was more easily given than followed.

Chaucer seems to have been greatly interested in this phase of doctrinal theology—the relation of the freedom of the will to predestination. In the fourth book of *Troilus*, the deserted knight distracts himself for a hundred and twenty-one lines (958-1078) by trying to analyze the diverse opinions of the cunning clerks that have written for and against predestination. But Troilus, fatalist that he is at all times, argues himself into believing finally that

> thus the bifalling
> Of thinges that ben wist bifore the tyde,
> They mowe not been eschewed on no syde.

The conclusion that

> Al that comth, comth by necessitee

agrees with the conclusion we should expect Troilus to reach; but that the poet was making this little digression on his own account and rather forgot his situation (for on what other grounds shall we explain the part line, "now herkne, for I wol not tarie," 1029?) is evidenced by the fact that there is no real occasion for the discussion here. It is entirely lacking in the *Filostrato*. To adapt the discussion to Troilus the poet so arranges his arguments that free-will is denied. Boethius, Dante, and Jean de Meung argued that freedom of the will is granted every human creature. But we cannot say that Chaucer believed in predestination simply because he represents Troilus as so believing. The humorous application of destiny and prescience to the fox's evil designs on Chanticler (B. 4405ff.) appears to be satire on the belief of St. Augustine and Bradwardine in fore-ordination. The Nonne Preest, who is telling the narrative, declares that he cannot enter upon the question that has been disputed by an hundred thousand men—

> Whether that goddes worthy forwiting
> Streyneth me nedely for to doon a thing,
> (Nedely clepe I simple necessitee);
> Or elles if free choys be graunted me
> To do that same thing, or do it noght,
> Though god forwoot it er that it was wroght . . .
> I wol not han to do of swich matere;

for his tale is of a fox. By implication, then, if not by direct statement, Chaucer would seem to be making fun of the doctrine he so elaborates in the *Troilus,* or at least of the expounders of it.

There is no direct evidence to prove what Chaucer really thought of the matter. He seems to have had no more than an intellectual interest in it; and once he had presented both sides of the question (as in *Boethius* and *Troilus*) he was content to let the clerks argue. We are inclined to judge, however, that for practical living the poet believed in the freedom of man to do right or wrong as he chose.

For his argument in the *Troilus* Chaucer appears to have owed nothing to the *Roman de la Rose* (18038-534), which, as Langlois says, is only a translation from Boethius. Reason's discourse in the *Roman* may have suggested the putting of a similar digression in the mouth of Troilus. The English poet used his own translation of the *De Consolatione*.[5] Chaucer's attitude toward Fortune and Destiny might be summed up by the old adage, "God helps those who help themselves."

ALCHEMY AND ASTROLOGY

Chaucer's skepticism clearly asserts itself in regard to these two sciences.[5a]

Jean's position was this: "Alquemie est ars veritable" (17015), but only worthy men can ever hope to practice it successfully. Jean concludes his digression on Alchemy by saying that some men may find out how to turn the baser metals into pure silver,

> Mes ce ne feroient cil mie
> Qui euvrent de sophisterie;
> Travaillent tant cum il vivront,
> Ja Nature n'aconsivront.   (17080-83)

[5] Possibly he took hints from Bradwardine's *De Causa Dei contra Pelagium*. See Morley: *English Writers*, V, p. 197.

[5a] For a succinct statement of his views on alchemy, see Lounsbury, II, 501-3; on astrology, II, 497-499.

Of the stars, Reason (speaking for the poet) says that reason dominates them, although they have a great influence on the life and conduct of man:

> Car autrement puet-il bien estre,
> Que que facent li cors celestre
> Qui moult ont grant pooir sans faille,
> Por que Raison encontre n'aille.
> Mes n'ont pooir contre Raison,
> Car bien set chascuns sages hon
> Qu'il ne sunt pas de Raison mestre
> N'il ne la firent mie nestre.   (18030-37)

Later on, in an interesting passage Reason admits that the stars may be crossed and that men through the will have power to shape and to modify their lives (RR. 18464-79).

Chaucer's relation to Jean de Meung in regard to alchemy and astrology is significant, and has not been pointed out hitherto. Chaucer's skepticism is an evidence of his modernity. Jean's common sense in admitting that Reason is superior to astral influence and in perceiving and stating that there is much chicanery in the practice of alchemy is not to be overlooked. His views are at least in advance of his century.

Chaucer's two references to the music of the spheres (PF. 59-63 and T. v. 1807-13) are probably taken from the *Teseide,* not from the *Roman,* 17886-90. The identity of the rhymes *melodye: harmonye* and *armonies: melodies* is possibly a reminiscence of the French poem.

In L. 2228-30 Chaucer expresses the "Platonic doctrine of forms or ideas." Skeat says that Chaucer is here following Boethius, who in turn follows Plato. Koeppel cites for comparison a similar passage in the *Roman,* 17666-71, lines which Langlois says are imitated from Alanus de Insulis: *De Planctu Naturae.*

Another passage in the *Roman de la Rose,* viz., 17698-709, which was taken from the *De Planctu,* is cited by Koeppel for comparison with these words of the Eagle in the *Hous of Fame:*

> Geffrey, thou wost right wel this,
> That every kindly thing that is,
> Hath a kindely stede ther he
> May best in hit conserved be;
> Unto which place every thing,
> Through his kindly enclyning,
> Moveth for to come to,
> Whan that hit is awey therfro.   (729-736)

In the *Convito,* Treatise III, chap. 3, we find this same idea expressed by Dante, who was doubtless following Boethius, as was Chaucer.

DREAMS AND THEIR SIGNIFICANCE

In the study of Chaucer's attitude toward dreams the following particular parallels between his work and the *Roman* may be noticed:

T. v. 365-368	(K)	RR. 19442-46
HF. 1-52	(S)	19432-47
11	(C)	19116
12	(C)	19143
15-18	(C)	19182-83(?)
		19144
24-31	(C)	19277
		19280-82

33-35	(C)	19292-95
36-40	(C)	19329-37
41-42	(C)	19300-301

To this list we may add for the first time: B. 4112, T. v. 1277 (RR. 1ff).

Compare also, for Chaucer's discussion, T. v. 358-378; B. 4111-4129.

Guillaume de Lorris accepts the belief that dreams foretell good and harm to many a man (RR. 1-20). Troilus and Chanticler are like Guillaume; Pandarus and Pertelote are among those who

> sayen that in swevenynges,
> Ther nys but fables and lesynges.

Chaucer in the opening lines of the *Hous of Fame* clearly followed Jean de Meung, as the many close parallels attest. The discussion in that part of the French poem is carried on by Reason, who, as usual, avoids deciding anything definite:

> Ne ne revoil dire des songes, (19432)
> S'il sunt voirs, ou s'il sunt mensonges . . .
> De tout ce ne m'entremetrai,
> Mes a mon propos me retrai. (19446)

Chaucer likewise says:

> For I of noon opinioun
> N'il as now make mencioun. (HF. 55-56)

But from other passages we may judge that Chaucer's skepticism extended to dreams as well as to alchemy, astrology, and predestination. This doubting attitude is important to bear in mind when one is considering the significance of the dream-poems. Naturally, it would hardly have done for the poet at the beginning of the *Hous of Fame* to have said that he did not believe in dreams. It was artistically necessary for him to assume a wondering attitude toward them. The fact that Chaucer presents Chanticler's dream as coming true is but another case of the poet's ironic concessions to superstitious readers.[6]

HABIT AND NATURAL INSTINCT

The use of the three examples in the *Maunciples Tale* to show the futility of man's trying to restrain the nature of animals is imitated from the *Roman de la Rose*. These illustrations are of the caged bird (H. 163-174), of the cat (175-180), and of the she-wolf (183-186). The example of the caged bird appears also in the *Squieres Tale* (F. 610-620), where Chaucer is clearly following Boethius. In the *Maunciples Tale*, however, he had his eye on the French poem, but Skeat does not emphasize the fact.

The parallels are as follows:

H. 163-174. Skeat says, "From Boethius. It reappears in *Le Roman de la Rose*, 14888-905. It is interesting to see how Chaucer has repeated the passage, and yet so greatly varied the form of it. We find, however, that *silk* and *milk* rhyme in both cases." But an examination of the passages in Boethius and the *Roman* shows *why* the two English

---

[6] For Chaucer's attitude towards common beliefs implying the interposition of supernatural agencies, see Lounsbury, II, 499-500.

appearances of it vary. In the one case (S. T.) Chaucer used the Latin original; in the other (M. T.), the French.

H. 175-180. From RR. 14984-97, says Skeat. Chaucer has varied and reduced his original considerably.

H. 183-186. From RR. 8512-17. As Skeat observes, these lines are taken from a different part of the *Roman* from those about the caged bird and the cat, and are founded on a different argument; viz., the perversity of woman's choice.

It should be noted that Tyrwhitt anticipated Skeat in pointing out these parallels. Moreover, it might be noted that Langlois has found no source for the French passages presenting the examples of the cat and the she-wolf.

In addition to the correspondences cited above I might suggest that L. 2446-51 be compared with H. 161-162, and both with RR. 14972-75—passages which express the thought that animals will stick to the nature of their kind. From the lines in the *Legend* we may judge that Chaucer was interested in the subject of natural instinct and associated it with heredity. Notice also T. i. 218-224; especially the last couplet:

> Yet am I but a hors, and horses lawe
> I moot enduren, and with my feres drawe.

The three illustrations in the *Maunciples Tale* are used in much the same way they are used in the *Roman*. Nature says that men and women desire their ancient liberty instinctively, just as animals obey the nature of their kind (RR. 14906-25). The Maunciple says:

> Alle these ensamples speke I by thise men
> That been untrewe, and no thing by wommen.
> (187-188)

This must have been either direct irony or intentional gallantry on Chaucer's part, for he knew that the lines in the *Roman* were sandwiched in between two accounts of the way in which Venus and Mars disgraced Vulcan—a situation very much like that represented in the *Maunciples Tale,* where Phoebus is deceived. The narrator here, too, makes the woman, as Jean makes Venus, the chief offender.

Nature's statement that men and women love liberty is used by Chaucer in another connection—an indebtedness that I have not seen pointed out hitherto. In the *Frankeleyns Tale* the narrator discusses the nature of love (F. 764-790). "This passage is clearly founded on *Le Roman de la Rose,* ll. 10174-10204," says Skeat. But Chaucer had also another part of the French poem in mind. Compare

>   Wommen of kinde desiren libertee,
>   And nat to ben constreyned as a thral;
>   And so don men, if I soth seyen shal.   (768-770)

with

>   Ansinc sachies que toutes fames,
>   Soient damoiseles ou dames,
>   De quelconque condicion,
>   Ont naturele entencion,
>   Qu'el cercheroient volentiers
>   Par quex chemins, par quex sentiers
>   A franchise venir porroient,
>   Car tous jors avoir la vorroient.
>   Ausinc vous dis-ge que li hon, etc.
>   (14906-14914)

The idea expressed in F. 164-166 had already been presented in the *Knightes Tale,* A. 1625-26 and *Troilus,* ii.

756. These passages have been referred to RR. 9200-9201. Skeat notes that lines 792-796 of the *Frankeleyns Tale* were taken from RR. 10199-10204.

TRUE NOBILITY, OR GENTILESSE

What Chaucer has to say in his ballade on Gentilesse and in the *Wife of Bath's Tale* (D. 1109-1164) agrees in the main with the views of Boethius, Dante, Guillaume de Lorris, and Jean de Meung. Compare the following parallels:

Gentilesse, st.	1.	RR.	19614-19	(Skeat)
st.	2.		19552-67	(Skeat)
st.	3.		19796-800	(Skeat)
W. B. Tale, D. 1158.			2093	(Skeat)
Squieres Tale, F. 483.		Rom.	2187-2238	(Skeat)

Skeat refers to the general discussion of gentilesse in the *Roman*, 7315-28 and 19540-19828, but he notes no further close correspondences than those listed above. We may add, accordingly, the following:

Gentilesse, ll.	2-4	RR.	19644-46
	12-13 ⎱		⎰ 19725-34
	15-16 ⎰		⎱ 19744-59
W. B. Tale, D.	1118-24		19560-67
	1170		19735-38

But Chaucer differs from Jean de Meung in one important respect: the loathly lady in the *Wife's Tale* says:

> Thy gentilesse cometh fro god allone, (D. 1162)

Nature makes no such statement. She says that all men are born potentially noble; but that they must prove themselves by their deeds. How to be noble can be learned from reading and study, and for this reason clerks as a class have far more nobility than kings. But Chaucer and Jean de Meung agree that wealth and renowned ancestors do not make a man noble and gentle; that a poor man may rise to "heigh noblesse" as easily as a king.

APOLOGY FOR PLAIN SPEAKING

In a number of passages in the *Canterbury Tales* the English poet, following Jean de Meung, justifies himself for any coarseness in his diction. The more important are:

A. 725-742, where the poet makes a general apology for plain realistic treatment of the stories to follow.

A. 3171-75, where the poet excuses himself for repeating the offensive language of the Miller.

B. 4450-54, where the Nonne Preest apologizes for recording the cock's censure of woman's counsel.

H. 208-237, where the Maunciple proceeds to justify his use of plain words, particularly the word "lemman."

Both Chaucer and Jean de Meung base their arguments on the words of Plato: "The wordes mote be cosin to the dede," to use Chaucer's statement. In A. 725ff. Chaucer was imitating the *Roman de la Rose*, 16097-16132. The Nonne Preest's apology is taken from the passage immediately following in the French poem, 16133-71. The two other passages in Chaucer have not as yet been referred to the *Roman;* but the Maunciple's justification of himself for using the word "lemman" is not unlike Reason's for using the word "coilles," to which the lover objects (RR. 7730-7935). Chaucer's apology for the Miller is no more than a repetition of the more expanded apology in the General Prologue.

THE FORMER AGE

In *The Former Age* Chaucer was working over the material of his two favorite authors—Boethius and Jean de Meung. The English poet's indebtedness to the *Roman* for material for this poem has been underestimated.

Skeat has suggested these parallels:

FA. 16. RR. 22546, for the word *galentyne*.
FA. 41-48, more or less imitated from RR. 9148-51, 9180-82, 9190-9191.
FA. 49. RR. 9194-97.

To these may be added the following, not hitherto recorded:

FA.	7	RR.	9115-23
	9-10		9132-35
	11		9126
	42		9144-46
	52		10272-73
	53		10279-82
	54		9194-97
	62-64		9105, 10309-16

Chaucer has also used other material, notably the *Metamorphoses*, and has treated all his sources in a fairly free fashion. On the whole, he follows Boethius in the first part of *The Former Age* and Jean de Meung in the last.

CHAUCER'S ATTITUDE TOWARD MARRIAGE AND CELIBACY

Lounsbury interprets the Prologue to the *Wife of Bath's Tale* and the Prologue to the *Monkes Tale* as attacks upon celibacy. What he deduces from Harry Bailey's remarks (B. 3132-3154) is significant:

This one passage is of itself sufficient proof how modern Chaucer was in his way of looking at social questions. It exhibits plainly one side of his point of view. There are other passages that indicate a view of the same subject from another direction. No one, after a careful comparison of all of them, can well escape from the conclusion that against the doctrine of celibacy there was ever present to the poet's mind one most grave objection. This was the double danger with which its practice threatened civilization. If the priest was unfaithful to his vows, if he yielded to the temptations that lie in wait for all, he was not simply bringing a scandal upon his order—he was unsettling the foundations of morality. He was placing an obstacle in the way of the upward progress of humanity. If he remained faithful to his vows —and in this class would necessarily be included the best and the purest—the right to propagate the race would be cut off from the men most likely to transmit to their descendants the highest intellectual and moral qualities. It was the ultimate effect of celibacy, not upon the church, but upon civilization, that was in the poet's thought. It is for that reason he tells us that the world is lost. It is almost impossible to doubt, after reading his words, that he, in the fourteenth century, had leaped to the same conclusion which modern science has at last painfully demonstrated, though it was not permissible for him to express it save after a blunt and even coarse fashion.[7]

Miss Cipriani's view of Chaucer's attitude toward love of kind and, by implication, toward marriage, by no means coincides with Lounsbury's. She writes:

Yet, where the influence of Jean de Meung on Chaucer

[7] *Studies in Chaucer*, II, p. 529.

shows itself most emphatically is in the ethical and religious traits which distinguish the *Troilus* from the *Filostrato*. The attitude in the treatment of the subject-matter is identical; i. e., love, its delights and its drawbacks, are fully described; but this description leads up to the advice of discarding earthly love for the love of Christ, who died for us on the cross. "Love made God incarnate; love made him hang from the cross; love made him hang from it; love brought him the wound in the side." (RR. 5051-54.) To this, of course, may be added the other important passage: "With all your heart and all your soul, I wish that you should love the gentle lady; when love incites you to love her, you must love her with love. Love, therefore, the Virgin Mary. Through love wed yourself to her. Your soul wants no other husband. Through love wed yourself to her," etc. (RR. 5107-5119.)

In this religious and ethical attitude, which it seems to me Chaucer and Jean de Meung have most markedly in common, not only in the Troilus, but through all of Chaucer's works, the difference between the English poet and the two great Italians is most markedly shown.[8]

In particular, Miss Cipriani cites for comparison with stanzas 263 and 264 of the last book of the *Troilus* these lines from the *Roman:* 5335-41, 5019-24, 5045, 5051-58, 5115-19. With the exception of the first reference, all are included in a longer passage (5018-5119), which Meon, Marteau, and Langlois reject.[9] Langlois writes that, although this interpolation is to be found in more than a score of MSS., most of them of the late fourteenth century,

[8] *Studies in the Influence of the Roman de la Rose on Chaucer*, p. 575.
[9] See Meon, II, p. 19; Marteau, II, p. 393; Langlois: *Les manuscrits*, etc., p. 425.

"la langue (de cette interpolation) et la rime diffèrent absolument de celles de Jean de Meung." This scholar might also have added that this extended definition of love in the form of a litany is hardly in the manner of Jean de Meung. Granted even that this passage appeared early enough in the fourteenth century for Chaucer to have been familiar with it before he wrote the *Troilus,* the parallels cited by Miss Cipriani from the *Roman* are not close enough to be of any special significance. The whole passage is lacking in the English *Romaunt of the Rose.* Moreover, her general conclusions as to Jean de Meung's attitude toward earthly love and his advice to his readers to discard earthly love for the love of Christ must be thrown out as incorrect, her whole contention resting on a spurious passage. Even a hasty reading of the last half of the *Roman* will reveal Jean in an entirely other light: in many places he emphasizes man's duty to procreate and to preserve his species.[10] Furthermore, he has something definite to say on celibacy and vows of chastity:

> S'il [i. e., God] vuet donques que virge vive
> Aucuns, por ce que miex le sive,
> Des autres por quoi nel' vorra?
> Quele raison l'en destorra?
> Donc semble-il qu'il ne li chausist
> Se generacion fausist.
> Qui voldra respondre, respoingne,
> Ge ne sai plus de la besoingne:
> Viengnent devin qui en devinent,
> Qui de ce deviner ne finent.   (20551-20560)

[10] Compare, for instance, the long sermon of Genius, ll. 20437ff. See also Chapter V, note 8.

Marteau[11] calls attention to the play on words in the last four lines of the passage, reminds us of Jean's "satire virulente contre la subtilité du clergé en matière de dogmes," and says in conclusion, "Le véritable sens de ce passage, voilé sous une fine ironie, serait plutôt: 'Je laisse les théologiens s'user à débrouiller cette énigme, s'ils le peuvent, car ils s'épuisent en vains efforts.' Aussi avions-nous traduit tout d'abord:

> A l'Eglise laissons le soin,
> S'elle peut, d'eclaircir ce point."

In ll. 20561ff. Genius says that it was never Nature's intention that mortals should "lie barren in cold sterility":

> Mes cil qui des grefes n'escrivent,
> Par qui les mortex tous jors vivent,
> Es beles tables precieuses
> Que Nature, por estre oiseuses,
> Ne lor avoit pas aprestees,
> Ains lor avoit por ce prestees
> Que tuit i fussent escrivans,
> Cum tuit et toutes en vivans.   (20561-20568)

The poet unmistakably through the mouth of Nature's priest defines his position with respect to this point of dogma; and his position is not very far from Chaucer's. But the English poet was philosopher and economist enough to recognize and to insist on the institution of marriage as the great steadier of society. He is not at one with the French poet when Jean makes serious attacks on marriage and paints in glowing colors a world of unrestraint and

[11] Vol. IV, note 61, p. 403.

free love. Chaucer's satire on women and his uncomplimentary allusions to the married state are nothing more than the conventional attitude of fourteenth century wits toward the sex.[12]

Kittredge's recent study of the Marriage Group of Tales in the Canterbury collection[13] furnishes strong evidence against any theory which would make Chaucer a woman-hater and an advocate of bachelorship. "The cynicism of the *Merchant's Tale* is . . . in no sense expressive of Chaucer's own sentiments, or even of Chaucer's momentary mood. The cynicism is the Merchant's. It is no more Chaucer's than Iago's cynicism about love is Shakespeare's."[14] "The Franklin's praise of marriage is sincere. . . . It was the regular theory of the Middle Ages that the highest type of chivalric love was incompat-

---

[12] If we reject Miss Cipriani's general conclusion as to the purpose of the *Troilus*, we still have to account in some way for the apparently religious character of the ending of the poem. A satisfactory explanation and one that does not make Chaucer a teacher of the doctrine of asceticism and celibacy can be found if we but recall the poet's literary interests at the time he was writing the *Troilus*. Boccaccio's *Teseide* furnished the stanzas describing how Troilus after his death was carried to the heavens of bliss, where he realized that "blinde lust . . . may not laste." The *De Consolatione Philosophiae*, I am inclined to think, furnished the general idea of T. v. 1835-48. The hortatory ending of the Latin treatise—the translation of which Chaucer was probably working on at the very time he was writing the *Troilus*—might easily have suggested the lines beginning, "O yonge fresshe folkes." The lines should not be taken to indicate that Chaucer was pleading for love to God and against "love of kind." A didactic, admonitory close for long poems was a medieval convention. In the *Troilus*, Chaucer was merely following this convention.

[13] *Chaucer's Discussion of Marriage*, Mod. Phil., April 1912.
[14] *Op. cit.*, p. 451.

ible with marriage, since marriage brings in mastery, and mastery and love cannot live together. This view the Franklin boldly challenges. Love can be consistent with marriage, he declares. Indeed, without love (and perfect, *gentle* love) marriage is sure to be a failure. The difficulty about mastery vanishes when mutual love and forbearance are made the guiding principles of the relation between husband and wife." The conclusion reached by Professor Kittredge as stated in the last paragraph of his article is this: "We may not hesitate ... to accept the solution which the Franklin offers as that which Geoffrey Chaucer the man accepted for his own part. Certainly it is a solution which does him infinite credit. A better has never been devised or imagined."

We may conclude, then, that Miss Cipriani not only is mistaken in her estimate of Jean de Meung's purpose but incorrectly correlates his work with Chaucer's. It is true that both men thought seriously on many subjects worthy of careful reflection, that both were in advance of their times; but with this difference: Jean de Meung was just far enough ahead of his age to be pessimistic, cynical, destructive; Chaucer was modern enough to be optimistic, charitable, constructive.

CONCLUSION

A recapitulation of the passages in Chaucer, which we may in all reason suppose to have been directly imitated from the *Roman de la Rose,* furnishes us the following partial data on the English poet's debt to the two French poets:

	Chaucer, lines.	RR., lines.
II. Allusions to historical and legendary persons and places	123	194
III. Mythological allusions	22	40
IV. Devices of style	45	71
V. Descriptions and situations	392	524
VI. Proverbs and proverbial expressions	57	77
VII. Philosophical discussions	215	497
Total	854	1,403

Of the lines used from the *Roman,* 379 are from the part written by Guillaume de Lorris, or about 27 per cent of the total. As Guillaume's portion is less than one-fifth of the whole poem, it will be seen that the proportional number of lines borrowed from him is as large as that from Jean. But of these over 300 were used in the characterization of Troilus and Pandarus. Moreover, of the 1,403 lines used from the *Roman,* 43 are from the section corresponding to fragment A of the *Romaunt;* 388 to fragment B, and 16 to fragment C. Statistics and figures are very unsafe to follow closely in determining so delicate a question as relative amount of literary borrowing, and they should not be relied on solely; but in the present instance we may reasonably draw the general conclusion that Lounsbury was inexact when he wrote that "the *Roman de la Rose* is Chaucer's favorite work as regards adaptation only so far as it is the composition of Jean de Meung." Nor need we hesitate to pronounce Van Laun's opposing view as equally wrong. The figures above do not include lines imitated from the *Romaunt,* unless it is pretty certain that Chaucer was also following the original French. Again, they do not fully represent what Chaucer owed to Guillaume, for sometimes in his later work the English poet copied older lines he had written, which in turn were due to the first part of the *Roman*. To Guillaume, then, he was under obligation for not a few touches of outdoor description (as in the *Book of the Duchess*, the *Parlement of Foules*, and the Prologue to the *Legend*, and for many hints in the character of Troilus. Chaucer also took from the first part of the *Roman* some conventional situations and possibly a stylistic device or two.

To Jean de Meung, Chaucer appears to have gone for all kinds of allusions and information. We have seen that Chaucer used the second part of the *Roman* as an encyclopedia of names of persons and places, of proverbs, of philosophy and metaphysics, of history, of mythology. The long discourses of Raison, L'Amis, La Vieille, Nature, and Genius were clearly his favorite passages: Reason's elaborately worked-out allegory of fortune, with a discussion of every side of the question; the Friend's discourse on the hardships and miseries of poverty, on the delights of those good old days when folk lived simply and naturally, on the evils that ensued upon the institution of marriage, with copious illustrations of domestic tyranny and misery; the Duenna's history of her amours, her picture of the follies of women, her stories of famous classical lovers, and her disclosure of the wiles used by some women to entrap men; Nature's discussion of various natural phenomena of the earth and heavens, of alchemy, astronomy, free-will, necessity, destiny, optics, dreams, true nobility and gentility; and Genius's earnest and vigorous exhortation to fecundity, and his promise that if men do their duty in this respect they shall be received into a paradise that exceeds in beauty, beyond power of words to tell, Mirth's Garden of the Rose. To these five long sermons should be added the autobiography of Faux-Semblant, which furnished Chaucer with many details for his characterizations of the Frere and the Pardoner and his attacks on corruption in the clergy, although it is difficult to adduce specific passages to reveal the indebtedness.

In conclusion, briefly to review Sandras's position, we see that the French critic was by no means altogether correct. His statement that Chaucer betrays a reminiscence of the *trouvère* poets on every page, in every line of his writings, is acceptable only under the most liberal interpretation. As well say the same thing of Shakespeare with respect to his predecessors and contemporaries. That Chaucer continually found inspiration in the *Roman* is not to be denied. It doubtless furnished him with new ideas and with new points of view on old ideas. On many a question he may have turned to the poem for guidance. But our evidence does not bear out the statement that he was content *often* in his nature descriptions to be the copyist of Guillaume. Less than seventy lines of this sort were copied from Guillaume, and nearly sixty of these occur in one early poem, the *Book of the Duchess*.

The only portion of Livy's Roman history for which Chaucer was indebted to Jean de Meung is the story of Appius and Virginius; even there only a score of lines were taken over directly from the French—less than one-tenth of the whole narrative.

Sandras's statement that Chaucer grew to old age, always

under the yoke of imitation and having composed scarcely anything but allegorical poems, is inexcusable. As a matter of fact, his greatest single poem, *Troilus and Criseyde,* written when he was but little over forty years of age, is not an allegorical piece; and it surpasses in number of lines all of his verse before 1386, including the *Book of the Duchess, Parlement of Foules, Hous of Fame,* and the *Legend.* As for its being written under the yoke of imitation, a comparison with its sources refutes the charge. Even the four dream poems, conventional as their setting may be, are in their general purport and in many details original. The dream frame-work is all they have in common with the *Roman,* and that device was not original with Guillaume. I am not willing to admit with Sandras that by the school of Guillaume de Lorris Chaucer's taste was formed or debased (altérée). Rather was that school a point of departure for him. As Legouis says, Chaucer was "enclin à sourire des affectations prolongées et du lyrisme qui se guinde." Chaucer does not fill his dream poems with colorless, shadowless allegorical personages; there is an abundance of life, movement, reality, in the *Parlement,* the *Hous of Fame,* and the *Prologue to the Legend.* But it was not so much at the extravagances of Guillaume as at those of his followers—Machault, Deschamps, Froissart—that the English poet smiled. His ten years of apprenticeship between the *Book of the Duchess* and his next dream poem were not years of poetic stagnation; and it is impossible to think of Chaucer writing the *Parlement, Hous of Fame,* and *Prologue to the Legend* in serious rivalry of foreign models. I feel convinced that in these poems he had a deeper, subtler purpose, even though at present I cannot say just what it was.

For Jean de Meung Chaucer seems to have had a continued respect. He freely used in the *Book of the Duchess* Reason's discourse on the fickleness of fortune, and gives evidence even in that early poem of having read large portions of the *Roman,* if not the whole of it. Moreover, the second part of the *Roman de la Rose,* one feels, exerted in a hundred subtle ways an influence on Chaucer that is not demonstrable by the parallel passage method. There was an undeniable sympathetic relationship between Jean de Meung and the English poet that manifests itself unmistakably in their critical, inquiring attitude toward life and its problems, in their tendency to visualize abstractions, in their significant blending of medievalism and modernism, of romanticism and realism. Various sections of Jean's work interested Chaucer deeply at various times; but our examination in chapter seven of the resemblances and differences between the two men has made it clear that the buoyant English pupil was not content to let his cynical French master do his thinking for him. It was not in the school of Jean de Meung but outside of school hours that Chaucer's "esprit" was fashioned. For Jean, no jocund day stood tip-toe on the misty mountain-tops. Can the same be said of Chaucer?

BIBLIOGRAPHY

The works enumerated below were all consulted and made use of in the preparation of this book. The list is not exhaustive, but includes what has been of the most service.

ALANUS DE INSULIS. Planctus Naturae and Anticlaudianus. In Vol. II of Anglo-Latin Satirical Poets (Records Series). Ed. by T. Wright.

— The Complaint of Nature, by Alain de Lille. Trans. from the Latin by Douglas Moffat. *Yale Studies in English,* 1908.

BALLERSTEDT, ERICH. Ueber Chaucers Naturschilderungen. Göttingen, 1891.

BECH, M. Quelle und Plan der Legende of Good Women. *Anglia,* Vol. V.

BOURDILLON, F. W. The Early Editions of the Roman de la Rose. London, 1906. (Printed for the Bibliographical Society.)

CHAUCER. The Complete Works of Geoffrey Chaucer. Edited . . . by Walter W. Skeat. Six volumes; Oxford. Vols. I-V, 2d ed., 1899-1900; Vol. VI, 1894.

— Chaucerian and Other Pieces, being a Supplement to the Complete Works of Geoffrey Chaucer. Edited by Walter W. Skeat. Oxford, 1897.

CIPRIANI, LISI. Studies in the Influence of the Romance of the Rose on Chaucer. *Publ. Mod. Lang. Assoc.,* 1907.

CLASSICAL AUTHORS. Teubner edition of Virgil, Ovid, Horace, Livy, etc.

CONSTANS, L. Chrestomathie de l'ancien français. Paris, 1906.

DODGE, R. E. NEIL. A Sermon on Source-Hunting. *Mod. Phil.*, October, 1911.

GALPIN, S. L. Fortune's Wheel in the Roman de la Rose. *Publ. Mod. Lang. Assoc.*, Vol. XXIV.

GAYLEY, C. M. Classic Myths. Boston, 1911.

GODDARD, H. C. Chaucer's Legend of Good Women. *Jour. of Eng. and Germ. Phil.*, October, 1908; January, 1909.

GODEFROY, F. Dictionnaire de l'ancienne langue française. Eight volumes. Paris, 1881-94.

GOWER, JOHN. The Complete Works of John Gower. Edited by G. C. Macaulay. Four volumes. Oxford, 1899-1902.

HAECKEL, W. Das Sprichwort bei Chaucer. (*Erlanger Beiträge*, viii.) Erlangen, 1890.

HAMMOND, E. P. Chaucer: a Bibliographical Manual. New York, 1908.

HEINRICH, FRITZ. Ueber den Stil von G. de Lorris und J. de Meung. In *Ausgaben und Abhandlungen aus dem Gebiete der roman. philologie*. Part XXIX. Marburg, 1885.

JORET, CHARLES. La Rose dans l'antiquité et au moyen âge. Paris, 1892.

JUBINAL, A. Jongleurs et Trouvères. Paris, 1835.

KALUZA, MAX. Chaucer und der Rosenroman. Berlin, 1893.

— The Romaunt of the Rose, from the Glasgow MS., parallel with its original, *Le Roman de la Rose*. Part I. *Chaucer Soc. Publ.*, 1891.

KITTREDGE, G. L. Chaucer's Medea and the Date of the Legend of Good Women. *Publ. Mod. Lang. Assoc.* Vol. XXIV.

— On the Romaunt of the Rose. Vol. I in *Studies and Notes in Philology and Literature*. Boston, 1892.

— Chaucer's Discussion of Marriage. *Mod. Phil.*, April, 1912.

— Chauceriana. *Mod. Phil.*, April, 1910.
KING HORN. Edited by Joseph Hall. Oxford, 1901.
KOEPPEL. Chauceriana. *Anglia,* XIV (1892).
— Chaucer and Albertanus Brixiensis. In *Archiv für das Studium der neueren Sprache.* Vol. 86.
LANGLOIS, ERNEST. Origines et sources du Roman de la Rose. Paris, 1890.
— Les manuscrits du Roman de la Rose. Lille-Paris, 1910.
LEGOUIS, EMILE. Geoffroy Chaucer. (*Les grands écrivains étrangers.*) Paris, 1910.
LOUNSBURY, T. R. Studies in Chaucer. Three volumes. London, 1892.
LOWES, J. L. The Prologue to the Legend of Good Women. *Publ. Mod. Lang. Assoc.* Vols. XIX, XX.
— The Date of Chaucer's Troilus and Criseyde. *Publ. Mod. Lang. Assoc.*, 1908.
MACHAULT, GUILLAUME DE. Œuvres de Machault. Edited by Tarbé. Paris-Rheims, 1849.
— Œuvres. Edited by Hoepffner. (*Soc. des anc. textes franç.*) Vol. I.
MARIE DE FRANCE. Lais. Edited by Warnke. 1900.
MEAD, W. E. The Prologue of the Wife of Bath's Tale. *Publ. Mod. Lang. Assoc.*, 1901.
— The Squyr of Lowe Degre. Edited by William E. Mead. Boston, 1904.
NEILSON, W. A. Origins and Sources of the Court of Love. Vol. VI in *Studies and Notes in Philology and Literature.* Boston, 1899.
NEW ENGLISH DICTIONARY ON HISTORICAL PRINCIPLES. Edited by J. A. H. Murray and H. Bradley. Oxford, 1884, etc.
PARIS, GASTON. Mediaeval French Literature. (In the *Temple Primers.*) London, 1903.
PARIS-LANGLOIS. Chrestomathie du Moyen Age. Edited by G. Paris and E. Langlois. 4th ed. Paris, 1904.

OWL AND THE NIGHTINGALE. Edited by John Edwin Wells. Boston, 1909.

PETIT DE JULLEVILLE. Histoire de la langue et de la literature française. Paris, 1878-1900. (Langlois gives an account of the *Roman de la Rose* in Vol. II, pp. 105-160.)

PUBLICATIONS DE LA SOCIÉTÉ DES ANCIENS TEXTES FRANÇAIS. Paris, 1875—

RITSON, J. Ancient Engleish Metrical Romanceës. Edited by J. Ritson. Three volumes. London, 1802.

ROMAN DE GUILLAUME DE DOLE, publié . . . par G. Servois. (In *Société des anciens textes français*.) Paris, 1893.

ROMAN DE LA ROSE. Edited by Francisque Michel. Two volumes. Paris, 1864.

— Edited by P. Marteau. Five volumes. Orleans, 1878-80.

ROMANCE OF THE ROSE. Englished and edited by F. S. Ellis. (*Temple Classics*.) London, 1900.

ROOT, ROBERT K. Chaucer's Legend of Medea. *Publ. Mod. Lang. Assoc.* Vol. XXIV.

RUTEBEUF. Œuvres complètes. Edited by A. Jubinal. Three volumes. Paris, 1874.

SANDRAS, ETIENNE GUSTAVE. Etude sur G. Chaucer considéré comme imitateur des trouvères. Paris, 1859.

SPECIMENS OF EARLY ENGLISH. Vol I edited by Morris; Vol. II edited by Morris and Skeat. Oxford, 1898.

SYKES, FRED HENRY. French Elements in Middle English. Oxford, 1899.

SYPHERD, WILBUR OWEN. Studies in Chaucer's Hous of Fame. *Chaucer Soc. Publ.*, 1907.

TATLOCK, J. S. P. The Development and Chronology of Chaucer's Works. *Chaucer Soc. Publ.*, 1907.

TEN BRINK, B. Chaucer: Studien zur Geschichte seiner Entwicklung. Münster, 1870.

— Early English Literature, Vol. II. Translated from the German by W. Clarke Robinson. New York, 1892.

WARREN, F. M. On the Date and Composition of Guillaume de Lorris's Roman de la Rose. *Publ. Mod. Lang. Assoc.*, 1908.

WEBER, H. Metrical Romances of the 13th, 14th, and 15th centuries. Edited by H. Weber. Three volumes. Edinburgh, 1810.

YOUNG, KARL. Development of the Troilus and Criseyde Story. *Chaucer Soc. Publ.*, 1908.

APPENDIX A

Comparative Table of Meon's, Michel's, and Marteau's Numbering of the Lines of the Roman de la Rose

Michel	Meon	Marteau	Michel	Meon	Marteau
100	100	102	2700	2700	2776
200	200	210	2800	2800	2882
300	300	310	2900	2900	2982
400	400	410	3000	3000	3094
500	500	510	3100	3100	3196
600	600	612	3199	3200	3306
700	700	712	3300	3300	3410
800	800	822	3400	3400	3514
900	900	924	4100	3500	3618
1000	1000	1024	4199	3600	3722
1100	1100	1130	4299	3700	3826
1200	1200	1230	4399	3800	3926
1300	1300	1340	4499	3900	4032
1400	1400	1440	4599	4000	4132
1500	1500	1552	4699	4100	4318
1600	1600	1652	4799	4200	4418
1700	1700	1760	4903	4300	4522
1800	1800	1860	5003	4400	4622
1896	1900	1960	5205	4500	4722
2000	2000	2068	5305	4600	4822
2100	2100	2176	5405	4700	4922
2200	2200	2276	5505	4800	5026
2300	2300	2376	5605	4900	5126
2400	2400	2476	5705	5000	5226
2500	2500	2576	5795	5100	5316
2600	2600	2676	5905	5200	5426

CHAUCER AND THE ROMAN DE LA ROSE

Michel	Meon	Marteau	Michel	Meon	Marteau
6005	5300	5526	9411	8700	8992
6105	5400	5626	9511	8800	9092
6205	5500	5726	9611	8900	9192
6311	5600	5826	9711	9000	9292
6411	5700	5938	9810	9100	9396
6512	5800	6038	9910	9200	9496
6612	5900	6138	10008	9300	9596
6711	6000	6242	10110	9400	9696
6812	6100	6342	10212	9500	9800
6912	6200	6448	10312	9600	9904
7012	6300	6552	10416	9700	10012
7112	6400	6652	10515	9800	10112
7212	6500	6756	10615	9900	10212
7312	6600	6860	10715	10000	10312
7412	6700	6960	10814	10100	10420
7512	6800	7060	10914	10200	10520
7611	6900	7160	11014	10300	10620
7711	7000	7260	11114	10400	10726
7813	7100	7360	11219	10500	10832
7913	7200	7460	11329	10600	10946
8014	7300	7564	11429	10700	11046
8114	7400	7664	11529	10800	11146
8214	7500	7764	11633	10900	11250
8313	7600	7864	11730	11000	11350
8413	7700	7964	11830	11100	11450
8513	7800	8064	11930	11200	11550
8613	7900	8168	11991	.....	11617
8713	8000	8272	12028	11300	11654
8813	8100	8372	12094	.....	11722
8912	8200	8476	12128	11400	11754
9011	8300	8576	12229	11500	11854
9111	8400	8676	12329	11600	11954
9211	8500	8784	12431	11700	12056
9311	8600	8888	12534	11800	12156

Michel	Meon	Marteau	Michel	Meon	Marteau
12635	11900	12256	16036	15300	15722
12734	12000	12356	16136	15400	15830
12834	12100	12456	16235	15500	15930
12934	12200	12556	16335	15600	16034
13033	12300	12660	16435	15700	16134
13134	12400	12766	16534	15800	16238
13234	12500	12868	16633	15900	16346
13335	12600	12976	16733	16000	16454
13436	12700	13076	16834	16100	16564
13536	12800	13180	16934	16200	16664
13636	12900	13280	17034	16300	16764
13737	13000	13384	17134	16400	16868
13837	13100	13484	17235	16500	16972
13937	13200	13584	17335	16600	17078
14037	13300	13688	17435	16700	17178
14137	13400	13794	17535	16800	17282
14237	13500	13894	17635	16900	17382
14337	13600	13994	17735	17000	17484
14437	13700	14094	17835	17100	17584
14537	13800	14194	17935	17200	17684
14637	13900	14294	18035	17300	17786
14743	14000	14394	18135	17400	17886
14843	14100	14498	18235	17500	17986
14943	14200	14600	18335	17600	18086
15043	14300	14700	18435	17700	18186
15143	14400	14800	18535	17800	18286
15243	14500	14900	18635	17900	18390
15343	14600	15000	18735	18000	18490
15443	14700	15100	18835	18100	18590
15544	14800	15200	18935	18200	18690
15644	14900	15300	19035	18300	18790
15744	15000	15410	19135	18400	18890
15835	15100	15514	19235	18500	18990
15936	15200	15618	19335	18600	19090

Michel	Meon	Marteau	Michel	Meon	Marteau
19433	18700	19190	21232	20500	21016
19533	18800	19290	21332	20600	21116
19633	18900	19394	21432	20700	21216
19733	19000	19494	21532	20800	21316
19832	19100	19594	21632	20900	21416
19932	19200	19694	21732	21000	21520
20032	19300	19794	21832	21100	21622
20132	19400	19894	21932	21200	21716
20232	19500	19994	22032	21300	21816
20332	19600	20098	22132	21400	21916
20432	19700	20202	22232	21500	22016
20532	19800	20308	22332	21600	22130
20632	19900	20408	22432	21700	22230
20732	20000	20512	22543	21800	22330
20832	20100	20612	22643	21900	22430
20932	20200	20712	22779	22000	22534
21032	20300	20816	22777	22074	22608
21132	20400	20916			

Michel's careless editing is the cause of the confusion of the numbering of the last two hundred lines. His lines 22773-22817, which are misplaced, should follow l. 22741

APPENDIX B

Table showing corresponding lines in Ellis's translation of the *Roman de la Rose*, the Middle English *Romaunt of the Rose*, and Marteau's edition of the original French text.

Marteau	*Ellis*	*Romaunt*	*Marteau*	*Ellis*	*Romaunt*
100	99	104	2000	2004	1981
201	195	201	2105	2107	2113
300	298	300	2200	2200	2228
400	398	400	2300	2301	2332
500	498	502	2402	2404	2435
600	599	597	2503	2520	2546
700	697	697	2600	2613	2648
803	809	793	2700	2722	2758
899	904	883	2800	2829	2888
999	988	985	2900	2926	2998
1100	1107	1085	3000	3024	3112
1200	1207	1188	3100	3124	3214
1300	1306	1280	3200	3225	3328
1400	1409	1377	3300	3324	3430
1500	1506	1474	3400	3423	3536
1600	1612	1570	3500	3526	3648
1700	1712	1676	3601	3627	3753
1730	1740	1705	3700	3726	3870
			3800	3830	3998
End of Fragment A of the *Romaunt*.			3902	3938	4106
			4000	4039	4196
1800	1809	1768	4100	4141	4328
1899	1910	1868	4203	4234	4432

CHAUCER AND THE ROMAN DE LA ROSE

Here ends the work of Guillaume de Lorris. The next eighty lines in Marteau and Ellis give a sort of conclusion to Guillaume's part of the *Roman*. They are not translated in the *Romaunt*, and are found in only one or two manuscripts.

Marteau	Ellis	Romaunt
4291	4321	4433
4400	4439	4566
4500	4550	4671
4599	4643	4791
4700	4742	4924
4800	4844	5050
4900	4952	5176
5000	5058	5300
5100	5157	5422
5200	5254	5560
5300	5366	5684
5396	5470	5810

End of Fragment B of the *Romaunt*.

5500	5567
5600	5670
5700	5767
5800	5864
5900	5959
6000	6064
6100	6166
6200	6267
6300	6376

Marteau	Ellis
6400	6474
6500	6582
6600	6682
6700	6786
6801	6889
6900	6988
7000	7096
7100	7194
7200	7288
7300	7382
7400	7479
7500	7580
7600	7680
7700	7782
7800	7883
7901	7990
8000	8086
8100	8188
8200	8296
8300	8400
8400	8497
8500	8590
8603	8703
8700	8801
8800	8895
8901	8987
9000	9088
9100	9187
9200	9295
9300	9395
9400	9499
9500	9610
9600	9719
9701	9823

Marteau	Ellis	Romaunt	Martin	Ellis	Romaunt
9800	9916		12600	12704	7358
9900	10012		12700	12798	7458
10000	10120		12800	12904	7558
10100	10216		12900	13008	7668
10200	10309		12932	13042	7698
10300	10407				
10398	10504				
10500	10612				

Here ends Fragment C of the *Romaunt*.

Marteau	Ellis	Romaunt
10600	10706	
10700	10806	
10800	10909	
10900	11005	
11000	11103	

Here begins Fragment C of the *Romaunt*.

11061	11163	5811
11100	11199	5846
11200	11301	5944
11300	11400	6048
11400	11505	6148
11500	11607	6248
11600	11710	6344
11700	11805	6430
11800	11901	x6502
11900	12002	6622
12000	12101	6728
12100	12202	6822
12200	12298	6926
12300	12397	7038
12400	12495	7148
12500	12596	7258

xRR. 11703-728 are not translated in the *Romaunt*.

13000	13108	
13100	13209	
13200	13306	
13300	13407	
13400	13507	
13500	13615	
13600	13716	
13700	13812	
13800	13911	
13900	14013	
14000	14110	
14100	14209	
14200	14308	
14300	14410	
14400	14510	
14500	14607	
14600	14709	
14700	14807	
14800	14908	
14894	15004	
15000	15095	
15100	15193	
15200	15302	
15300	15400	
15400	15501	
15500	15602	

Martin	Ellis	Romaunt	Martin	Ellis	Romaunt
15600	15702		19000	19118	
15703	15799		19101	19227	
15800	15896		19200	19324	
15900	15895		19301	19425	
16000	16100		19400	19528	
16100	16198		19499	19625	
16200	16296		19600	19730	
16300	16393		19702	19834	
16400	16494		19800	19930	
16500	16588		19900	20038	
16600	16694		20000	20138	
16700	16798		20100	20242	
16800	16898		20200	20342	
16900	17011		20300	20444	
17000	17118		20400	20543	
17100	17222		20500	20644	
17200	17326		20600	20743	
17300	17428		20700	20838	
17400	17532		20800	20939	
17500	17630		20900	21038	
17600	17722		21000	21140	
17700	17826		21100	21248	
17806	17922		21200	21350	
17900	18016		21300	21454	
18000	18114		21400	21560	
18100	18218		21500	21658	
18200	18314				
18300	18410				
18400	18522				
18500	18618				
18600	18716				
18700	18814				
18800	18916				
18900	19020				

Ellis does not translate the French text beyond line 21504 with the exception of the story of Pygmalion, RR. 21593-21964. See his translation, Vol. III. pp. 215-227.

INDEX OF PASSAGES FROM CHAUCER'S WORKS AND THE ENGLISH ROMAUNT OF THE ROSE, QUOTED OR REFERRED TO IN THE TEXT

Romaunt of the Rose (Ref.)	(Page)
23-5	139
49	127, 130n
57	131
60	131
61	131, 136
94	127
128	136
131	129, 130n
175-6	122
212	87n
333-35	147
368	154
369ff	192
454	87n, 93
496-7	128
528-94	85
543-4	148
546	91n
669-72	134
715-16	137
717	130n
819	87n
855-6	89n
862	91n
896-8	159
928	87n
974	87n
1010	87n
1013	87n
1062-6	193
1182ff	95
1387-90	133

(Ref.)	(Page)
1214	87n
1393	130n, 131
1394	132
1399	132
1401-4	132
1418-29	130
1556-57	87n
2045-50	193
2175-80	150
2187-2238	221
2205-12	41
2213-15	150
2223-8	150
2229-38	150
2239-46	150
2255-70	151
2274	151
2289-96	151
2305-16	151
2317-28	151
2329-33	151
2357-60	155
2361-72	151
2367-8	189
2391-6	151
2397-2418	151
2419-33	152
2453-78	152
2478	184n
2480-98	152
2523-37	152
2545-8	152
2553-64	152

(Ref.)	(Page)
2609-12	152
2627-40	152
2645-70	152
2740-42	186
2791-2824	153
2825-55	153
2856-92	153
2893-2934	153
2899-2900	153
5123-4	192
5135-54	156
5479-83	209
5551-2	198, 209
5579-81	209
5671-8	209
5763-4	197
5813-4	120
6029-30	59
6390-98	165
6599-6602	143
6613-22	143
6807	186
6913-19	143
7419-20	141, 144
7577-8	165
7069ff	193
7608-66	72

The Compleynt Unto Pite

92	51

Anelida and Arcite

20	96
146	137
269	75n
315-6	180
323-4	97

Book of the Duchess

189-90	119

(Ref.)	(Page)
284-9	13
291	126, 130n
291-3	124
291-433 passim	126-127
295-7	124
301-2	124
304-5	124, 130n
305	137
309-11	125
317	124
318-9	124
319	128
331	40
340-2	124, 135
341	108, 130n
341	129, 136
402-3	53, 137
405-9	131
406-9	124
410-12	124, 136
414-15	125, 131
416-17	131
416-42	131
418-20	124
419-20	131
420	130n
421-33	125
422	131
425	132
427-31	132
428-33	134
434-41	133
435-40	37
475-6	146
497	147
497-9	146
570	40
572	41
591-4	146, 147
599-616	112
617-84	208

CHAUCER AND THE ROMAN DE LA ROSE

(Ref.)	(Page)
628-9	92
633-37	93n
636-41	93
654	108
660-61	100
671	75n
717-9	38, 39
718	75n
724-31	42
732-3	41
735	40
735-7	54
738-9	31n, 40
758-74	146, 147
771-2	146, 147
791-2	179
797-8	85
807-9	139
821-6	87
835-7	139
849	108
857-8	147
858	146, 90n
871-2	148
874-7	146, 147
880-82	146, 147
887	75n
939ff	92n
961-5	177, 178
981-3	101
994-8	146, 147
1024-9	146, 147
1045	110
1057	33
1058	41
1075-6	110
1080-81	38
1080-85	38
1115	110
1121	41
1152-4	146, 148

(Ref.)	(Page)
1211-20	146, 148
1237	75n
1283-4	146, 148

The Parlament of Foules

59-63	215
114	58n
122	124
129-30	124, 134, 135
140	179
148-51	95
176-82	114
190-91	125, 134
190-96	134
192-6	125
204-5	135
204-10	124, 134
205-7	135
206	135
207	135n
211-17	72n
211-94	136
261	59n
266	135
267	90n
277	57 and note
295ff	136
298-301	89n
316	20
330-64	115
337-64	102
343	115n
359	94n
379	211n
380-81	211n
390	135
456-8	45n
501	75n
574	180

Boethius de Consolatione Philosophiae

(Ref.)	(Page)
II prose iv:80-82	181
II prose v:129-31	180
II met. vi:5-6, 8, 12-3, 15-6, 19	26
II prose viii:31	108, 198
III prose viii:26	108
IV prose iv:205-6	182
V prose iii:125-6	182n
V prose iii:127-9	182n
V prose vi:113-4	182n
V prose vi:205	182n

The Former Age

7	223
9-10	223
11	223
16	223
41-48	223
42	223
49	223
52	223
53	223
54	223
57-9	55
62-4	223

Fortune

1-4	209
9-12	209
17-20	40
32	209
33-40	209
36	120
65-72	209

Gentilesse

1 stanza	221
2 stanza	221
3 stanza	221

(Ref.)	(Page)
ll. 2-4	221
12-13	221
15-16	221

Merciles Beaute

29	75n
39	75n

Compleynt of Mars

126	75n

Troilus and Criseyde

Bk. I.

6	50
158	137
218-24	219
295-301	152
351	120n
441	151
442-6	152, 153
445-6	153
447-8	152
449	183
537	151
586-95	154
612-13	151
625-30	154
630-37	190
638-44	188
646-51	154
666-9	154
675-6	154
704-7	151
711-4	154
715-6	154
743-5	151
747-8	184
752-6	39
771-3	154

(Ref.)	(Page)	(Ref.)	(Page)
806	151	635-7	151
810-12	189, 152	645	152
816-7	151	652	152
817-9	150	652-8	152
818-9	152	698	152
834-56	209	715-8	185
856	151	722-3	154
883-9	153	729-32	157
890-6	151	754	99
901-3	150	756	141, 142, 221
927-8	141	763	157
928	142n	784	186
946-52	111	799-805	157
958	151	809-11	152
960-1	189	840	150
960-2	151	1027	190
969	96	1256	152
1030-3	150	1499-1503	151
1051-4	154	1564	117
1058-60	154	1720-1	120n
1065-71	154		
1072	151	Bk. III.	
1074	151	50-56	152n
1076-8	150	80-84	152
1080	151	92-8	148
1084	150	94-5	151
		103	151
Bk. II		133	151
50-52	125, 137	134-47	151
57-63	152, 154	274-87	157
60	151	293-4	202
160	150	320	75n
167-8	185	329	190, 197
185-6	151	351-4	125, 138
187-9	150	428-34	151
193-4	95	547-973	152
197-203	151	617-23	209
204-7	150	694-5	171
436	50	725	57
537-9	152	786-8	153
624-5	151	792-8	153

(Ref.)	(Page)	(Ref.)	(Page)
854	75n	Bk. IV.	
900	75n		
936	75n	6-7	208
956	186	22-4	50
1035	186	24	51
1161	75n	106 stanza	147
1167	75n, 77n	117 stanza	147
1212-21	188	222 stanza	46
1254-74	151	391-2	209
1255	59n	432-4	156
1282	85n	519-20	94
1298	151	586	75n
1534-40	152	595	75n
1541-4	153	600-601	210
1544-6	154, 155	684	75n
1548-54	153	958-1078	212
1569-70	152	1029	213
1583-4	152	1305-6	186
1603	75n	1356	95
1622-4	190	1397-8	75n
1634	190, 191n	1546	52
1646-66	153	1553	46
1716-18	151	1555-82	157
1716-29	159	1586	195
1718	151	1591	53
1719	151	1654-7	151
1726-29	151	1699-1701	152
1737-42	153		
1743ff	151	Bk. V.	
1776-8	151	7	52
1779-81	151	208	57
1786	150	217-45	152
1786-7	159	222-4	152
1787	150	263-4 stanza	225
1789	150	295-332	152
1790	150	358-78	217
1796-99	150	363	75n
1800-3	150	365-8	216
1801	150	426-76	153
1802	159	445	119
1805	150	460-1	97

CHAUCER AND THE ROMAN DE LA ROSE 255

(Ref.)	(Page)	(Ref.)	(Page)
515-6	153	338-40	191
519-53	153	343-4	45n
551-2	154	363	75n
574	151	379	42
638-41	101	388-96	45
655	53	388-407	42
736-43	152	392	45, 46
744-9	152	397-404	42
813-4	92n	518	57
882	75n	609	72n
1058-64	157	617	72n
1075-7	150	668	72n
1222	154	729-36	216
1277	217	916-8	38
1321	119	1022	41
1373-9	112n	1183	78
1482	119	1213	94
1541-7	209	1214-26	117n
1590	72n	1257-8	192
1695-1701	151	1271-4	42, 43
1807-13	215	1329-35	117
1828-32	102	1342-53	139, 140
1835-48	228	1387	90n
1849-54	102	1413-4	41
		1547	209
The House of Fame		1571	49 and note
1-52	216	1647	137
11	216	1652-4	139, 140
12	216	1702-12	142
15-18	216	1708	75n
24-31	216	1710-11	141
33-5	217	1732-3	141
36-40	217	1758-62	141, 143
41-42	217	1759-62	143n
55-6	217	1761-2	141
103-8	29n	1780-2	141
112-3	139	1789	49
117-8	38	1793-5	141
137-8	72n	1796-9	143n
239ff	41	1875	79
279-82	191	1935-7	137

(Ref.)	(Page)
1960-76	112
1961-76	102

Prologue to Legend of Good Women

(a)

273-4	11
292-3	45
311-2	100
326	193
529	100

(b)

29-35	11
42	137
73-82	67
75-77	67
78-80	67
101	120
125-6	125, 136
127	99
128	108, 125
132-7	125, 136
139-40	125, 137
148-68	125, 137
153-9	125, 137
160-2	85
169	137
171-4	53, 137
215-17	92n
226-40	63, 67
237-49	71
249	37, 63
279-80	63
290	63
311	71
315-8	64
338	59n, 66
338-40	64
352-3	193

(Ref.)	(Page)
377-80	65
400-402	65
410-411	72
475-7	65
507-9	65
535	66
548-51	66

Legend of Good Women.

600	59n
609	119
613	160n
655	93
741	75n
917-8	121
1672	90n
1715	108
1747	90n
1773	210
2228-30	215
2250	52
2252	51
2434	107
2446-51	219
2497-2500	46
2493	81

Canterbury Tales A.

5-6	137
70-72	150
90	137
99-100	160
127-135	161
152	90n, 91n, 92n
177	75n
182	75n
253-5	163
256	164
281-2	107
404	128n
431-2	41

(Ref.)	(Page)	(Ref.)	(Page)
461	168	2670	79
475-6	171	2921-3	114
476	144, 168	2991-3	211n
675	90n	3041-2	194
701-4	163	3089	85n
725-742	222	3152	195
781	79	3171-5	222
885-8	119	3245-6	91n
1037	160n	3312-4	37
1037-8	89n	3314	90n
1049	90n	3672	75n
1053	137	3756	75n
1155	106n	3857	120
1165	79	3974	91n
1510-11	160n	4000	75n
1558	75n	4041	79
1570	75n	4050	120n
1625-6	194, 220	4056	75n
1817	59n	4099	79
1928-9	85	4172	80, 81n
1930	86	4192	75n
1936-7	57	4295	108
1940	85	4321	195
1940	59n		
1944-6	42	*Canterbury Tales B*	
1951	59n	20-24	192
1951-2	58	72-4	42, 44
1953-4	118 and note	94	75n
1963-6	72n	114	196
1999	141, 143	211	120
2083-6	53	295ff	21n
2087	121	360	93n
2112	106n	404	93n
2166	90n	701-2	100
2178	90n	1128	120n
2222	56	1178	79
2233-7	59n	1341	78
2235-6	59n	1360-61	75n
2388-90	60	1519	106, 107
2447-8	194	1537	106
2452	56	1559	94n

(Ref.)	(Page)	(Ref.)	(Page)
1581	106, 107	3931	29
1933	106n	3934-8	29n
1950-61	116	3940-5	29
1957	94n	3941	29n
2120	75n	3947	29
2526	75n	3948	29n
3127	79	3949-50	28, 29
3132-54	224	3953-6	30n
3185-6	30n	3980	74, 75n
3253	31	4004	75n
3253-7	31	4098	81
3261-2	31	4098-4101	81
3281-4	31	4111-29	217
3326	30n	4112	217
3379	30n	4131	104
3431-5	30n	4280	75n
3537	30n	4405ff	213
3587	30n	4450-4	222
3635-6	30n	4460	94
3653-3740	24	4515-6	194
3655	24	4633	100

Canterbury Tales C

(Ref.)	(Page)
3669ff	26
3669-70	27n
3672-5	27n
3677-82	27n
3688	119
3699-3700	27
3701-4	27n
3705-8	27
3719-24	27n
3725-8	27n
3732-3	27n
3735-9	27n
3740	30n
3756	75n
3773	30n
3851-2	30n
3900	119
3917-56	28
3917-22	29n
3918	28, 29

(Ref.)	(Page)
1	33
16-18	40
19-22	211n
32-4	89
79	144
79-81	141
105ff	35
135-8	33
139-64	34
165	33
168-9	33, 34
184	33, 34
203	33, 34
207-253	34
229-30	119
255-76	33, 34
262-6	34
402	164

(Ref.)	(Page)	(Ref.)	(Page)
407-8	196	555-8	168f
410	197	572	75n
411	197	572-4	168ff
444	164	575	168ff
448-51	163	576	201
863	75n	604	59n, 67
		611	59n

Canterbury Tales D

(Ref.)	(Page)
618	59
1-3	168f, 172
623-4	168f
107-10	174
659	75n
115ff	174
662	169ff
170-1	96
677-8	37
180-81	197
708	75n
182-3	21n
721-3	40
207-10	168f
724-6	40
227-8	168f
816	173
229-30	168f
901	120
235ff	172
929-30	169ff
248-54	168f
949	75n
250-2	168
950	169ff
257ff	168f
961-3	169ff
263-6	168
968	169
293-4	168f
1067	105
304	90n
1109-64	221
324-7	21n
1112	75n
333-6	168ff, 177n
1118-24	221
347	75n
1158	221
357-61	168ff
1162	221
393-6	168ff
1170	221
401-2	173
1184-90	197
407-10	168ff
1187	197
467-8	168ff
1192	181
469-73	168ff
1203-4	198
474ff	173
1234	104
483	79
1451	164
484	97
1512	104
503-14	168ff
1568	141, 144
516-22	170
1690-1	165
522-4	168
1961	75n
534ff	169
1994-5	93n, 141
552-4	168
2001-3	141, 145

(Ref.)	(Page)
2004b-c	141
2094-8	165
2289	41

Canterbury Tales E

118	192
880	93
999	75n
1114	120n
1263	75n
1335-6	198
1341	119
1350	75n
1421	75n
1469-70	120
1559-61	199
1567	75n
1730	53
1747-8	160n
1777	58n, 59n
1804	120n
1854	75n
1858	120n
1862	199
1936	120n
2001	120n
2031-3	20n
2058-64	93
2265	79
2303-4	75n
2322	94
2379-80	45n
2393	79

Canterbury Tales F

52-5	125, 138
57	99
95	41
164-6	220
202-3	121
228ff	36

(Ref.)	(Page)
232-3	36
281	160n
349	200
483	221
548	110
555	75n
593	195
610-20	218
764-6	194
764-90	220
768-70	220
792-6	221
795	110
925ff	159n
927-8	160n
951-2	54, 55
966	120
1045	53
1132	75n
1308	120n
1465-6	119
1593-4	119

Canterbury Tales G

3	85
19	104
511	75n
633	75n
698	75n
795	75n
925	75n
1028-9	45n
1150	75n
1185	78

Canterbury Tales H

14	75n
68	104
161-2	219
163-74	218
175-80	218, 219

(Ref.)	(Page)
183-6	218, 219
187-8	219
208-37	222
254-5	75n
309ff	200
317	201
329-31	201
332-3	200
332-4	202
344-5	202
355	200
357-8	201

Canterbury Tales I

601	75n
711	104
714	85

Index of Passages From The *Roman De La Rose* Quoted or Referred to in the Text.

(R. R.)	(Page)
1ff	217
1-20	217
7-10	14
24-25	139
45-47	124
47-54	125, 138
53	125, 131
55-58	124, 125
56	125, 130
57	131
63	138
67-73	125, 138
67-74	124
74-77	124, 178
78-80	138
88	127
100-01	124, 128
124-25	124
125	108, 125

(R. R.)	(Page)
129-31	124
163-4	121
200	86, 147
200-02	146
291-338	146
306-13	146
323-26	146
360	155
445	93
484-85	128
487-93	125, 128
527	90n
529	91n
530	91n
581	148
533	91n
537	146
539-40	92n
554	86
584	59n
619-20	139
647-74	115
665-68	124, 125, 128, 134
675-78	94
707-08	125, 137
707-10	124
709	128
747-48	108
808	86
811	91n
844-45	89n
849	91n
850	91n
869-988	61
880-907	67
888-90	159
906-907	68
918	86
964	86
1000	87
1000-1002	88

(R. R.)	(Page)	(R. R.)	(Page)
1003	87	2119-26	150
1005	87, 89n	2127-34	150
1052-55	193	2135-42	150
1108-9	92n	2152-64	151
1164ff	95	2168	151
1199	87	2185-94	151
1200-1	92n	2185-2221	157
1202	91n	2199-2212	151
1204-5	146	2213-20	151
1237	146	2221-25	151
1241-2	146	2247-50	154, 155
1245	146	2250-52	189
1246-48	88	2250-60	151
1251	146	2251	154
1338-68	113, 114	2255-56	189
1369-72	132	2273	75n
1375-76	124	2275-2568	62
1377	132	2281-85	151
1377-90	125	2286-2310	151
1380-81	132	2311-23	152
1383-86	132	2343-70	152
1383-90	125, 134	2370	183
1401-09	130	2371-84	152
1413-14	138	2403-14	146, 148
1447ff	54, 55	2403-14	152
1535	87	2423-28	152
1581	91n	2433-42	152
1689-91	139	2489-92	152
1884-85	61	2504-18	152
1891-2032	146	2520-43	152
1973-78	193	2550	155
1987ff	146	2609	79
2004	79n	2613-14	186
2006-7	146	2655-82	153
2018-20	97	2683-97	153
2082-2776	149	2698-2729	153
2087-92	150	2719-20	154
2087-2274	62	2729-62	153
2093	221	2862-64	58
2103-4	41	2977-79	119
2109-11	150	3001	119

(R.R.)	(Page)	(R.R.)	(Page)
3113-14	107	5785-88	102n
4030-31	58	5792-5839	197
4032	58	5834-35	197
4034-36	58	6001-6004	181
4040ff	58	6019	75n
4505	108	6060	75n
4529-33	141	6062	75n
4545	168, 171	6068-73	207
4590-99	207	6099	128n
4747-48	75n	6128	19n
4894	79n	6270-75	56
4910-27	102n	6276	56
4910-51	112	6277	57
4940-45	141	6324-27	32
5008-14	191	6325	34
5018-58	112	6329	19n
5018-119	225	6329-30	33
5019-24	225	6331-33	33
5045	225	6335-36	34
5051-54	225	6335-38	33
5051-58	225	6339-44	33
5074-79	102n	6347-49	33
5095-5100	102n	6359-65	33, 34
5107-19	225	6369	19n
5115-19	225	6371-93	33
5120-45	174	6395	19n
5151	19n	6395-97	185
5335-41	225	6460-6520	125
5344-45	192	6479-80	185
5361-62	156	6481	75n
5379	75n	6495	182
5395-96	75n	6574	40
5453-54	180	6578-7643	206
5469	19n	6581-82	75n
5600	87	6581-86	39
5672-77	209	6637ff	206
5682-83	108	6637-43	207
5717	75n	6644-48	207
5757-61	12n	6649-54	207
5767	182	6657ff	206
5775	75n	6674-77	54, 130

(R. R.)	(Page)	(R. R.)	(Page)
6678-80	99	7315-28	221
6709-14	115n	7329	29
6759-64	139, 140	7356ff	208
6811	108	7357-58	29
6826	108	7359-62	207
6835-40	139, 140	7373-81	15n
6870-71	75n	7388-89	99
6893-94	107	7400	108
6909-10	206	7474-76	118
6911-87	24	7480-82	93
6926-27	27n	7488	79n
6928	26n	7510-73	37
6929-42	27n	7516	19n
6930-32	26n	7549-56	96
6940-42	27	7652-53	75
6944	25, 27	7652-54	39
6947-49	27	7730-7935	222
6952-58	27	7781	19n, 22n
6975-81	27n	7781ff	21n
6984-86	26n	7783	19n
7091	19n	7783	200
7118-19	94	7786ff	202
7118-43	95	7808	200
7145-48	207	7846	19n
7155	119	7852	19n
7163-70	27n	7995-97	119
7171-72	27n	7998	82n
7173-79	27n	8056	104
7183-88	27n	8085-8128	157
7194	19n, 24	8094-95	196
7225-27	29n	8139	196
7225-7358	28	8152	80n
7226-30	29n	8161-66	168, 177
7243-45	29n	8179-80	107
7247-48	29	8222	190
7249-50	29n	8300-8305	101
7255	75n	8308-9	184
7277-83	29	8440-41	75n
7283	29n	8488-89	154
7290-91	75n	8512-17	219
7303	75n	8617	41

(R. R.)	(Page)	(R. R.)	(Page)
8737	19n	9404-05	38
8754-55	190, 197	9416-37	169
8769-73	209	9438	78
8774-77	209	9438-39	102
8776	110	9440	20n
8790-93	208	9444	79n
8822-23	75n	9458	19n
8900-40	196	9470	20n
8928	196	9472-73	95
9013-19	190	9478	20n
9030	80n	9486	19n
9038	19n	9507	20n
9063-64	108	9554	20n
9105	223	9582-87	38
9115-23	223	9583	41
9126	223	9656-62	92
9129-30	107	9680-86	102n
9132-35	223	9692-95	36
9144-46	223	9698	36n
9148-51	223	9700	19n
9148-79	131	9758	19n
9160-63	54	9777-78	168
9162	130	9839-44	168
9176-79	124	9877-79	195
9180-82	223	9891	19n
9190-91	223	9926	75n
9194-97	223	9933	41
9198-9202	194	9941	41
9200-201	221	9945-56	31n, 41
9239	75n	9948	41
9265	168, 170	9953-56	31, 40
9276-82	169	9954-55	75n
9310	19n	9956	31
9310-57	169	10052	79n
9328-49	168	10084-85	75n
9331-34	168	10168	20n
9340-47	102n	10171-75	142
9340-49	168	10174-204	220
9348-53	168	10199-204	221
9358-61	38	10202-3	141
9365	19n, 38	10272-73	223

(R. R.)	(Page)	(R. R.)	(Page)
10279-82	223	12460	186
10309-16	223	12476-77	196
10413-14	75n	12492-93	164
10518-20	75n	12504	164
10547-51	93n, 141	12515ff	164
10563-99	125	12515-21	102n
10593-99	125, 137	12566-72	141, 142
10600-601	154	12751-62	89n
10602-5	141, 143	12897	75n
10660-61	180	13030-31	144
10664-65	168	13117-86	157
10692-708	169	13162-3	75n
10726	169	13186	165
10845-46	94	13215-16	193
11049-50	141	13215-64	72
11135	79n	13456	108
11198	62	13523	79n
11208-9	62	13563-64	75n
11208-19	84n	13580	186
11388-91	53	13683	155
11396-99	96	13685-86	155
11438	80n	13700-701	96
11448-49	120	13722	168
11559ff	58	13731-36	133
11592	59n, 66	13731-37	37
11592-95	57	13743-45	168, 172
11664-65	59	13759-61	194
11688-89	72	13792-93	75n
11783-89	169	13830	19n
11816	79n	13831-34	179
11822-24	75n, 77n	13859-60	75n
11836-40	102n	13865-66	168
11986	100	13873-79	168
12019ff	165	13965	75n
12154-75	162	14080-82	191
12163	164	14091-96	168
12174	75n	14115ff	41
12239	19n	14152-55	
12254-55	141, 142	14154	45, 46
12270-75	141, 142	14163	75n
12298-301	174	14166-67	46

(R. R.)	(Page)	(R. R.)	(Page)
14170	.....	15326-29	168
14198-203	44	15338-39	168
14204-5	118n	15342-45	43
14210-14	168f	15349-52	43
14219	105	15350-54	43
14277	59	15401	75n
14336-7	161	15420-35	168
14336-8	160	15429-30	75n
14349-62	161	15481-82	75n
14357	138	15513-14	75n
14366-73	161	16046-47	59n
14393-94	168	16097-132	222
14464-69	168	16133-71	222
14560	19n	16179-80	18
14560-61	75n	16199	110
14578	19n, 22n	16558-59	93
14576-79	22n	16596-604	58
14633	168	16712-13	58n, 75n
14644-55	170	16871-74	101
14648-51	168	16895-96	41
14651	168, 170	16897	41
14652	75n	16913ff	102
14676	78	16967	94
14714	106, 107	16978	138
14775-85	168	17015	214
14785-815	60	17080-83	214
14798-99	199	17103	110
14817	37	17107	41
14888-905	218	17113ff	40
14906-14	220	17132	19n
14906-25	219	17178-80	87
14960-61	195	17262	19n, 30n
14972-75	219	17271-73	141
14984-97	219	17274	19n
15034	110	17284-301	169
15088	121	17284-312	169
15100-129	60	17304-5	169
15152-53	75n	17366-70	199
15162-63	97	17369	82n
15218	79	17407	75n
15255	75n	17458-67	169

(R. R.)	(Page)	(R. R.)	(Page)
17478-637	31	19132	19n
17481-83	201	19143	216
17482-83	200	19144	216
17523	19n	19182-83	216
17528	93n	19182-87	37
17553	179	19233	117
17614-25	30	19234-61	146, 147
17614-26	31	19277	216
17626-27	118	19280-82	216
17666-71	216	19292-95	217
17698-709	216	19300-301	217
17719	211n	19302-4	38
17722-25	211n	19329-37	217
17872-3	50	19432-47	216, 217
17886-90	215	19442-46	216
17898	211n	19499	197
17976-18659	142	19502-9	22n
18030-37	215	19506	19n
18038-47	211	19525	75n
18038-534	210, 214	19540-828	221
18060-61	182n	19545	105
18096-99	146	19552-67	221
18102-3	182n	19560-67	221
18167	75n	19614-19	221
18209-11	182n	19644-46	221
18213-15	182n	19682	75n
18328-33	212	19725-34	221
18380-81	141	19735-38	221
18464-79	215	19744-59	221
18711-13	182n	19784-85	75n
18843-4	75n	19796-800	221
18858-59	75n	19911-12	120
18941	49	19995	19n
18966	19n, 36	20101	19n
18969	36	20152	169
18969-71	37	20327	75n
18979-81	37	20437ff	226n
18996-19024	60	20437-40	211n
19007	87	20551-60	226
19071-72	168	20561-68	227
19116	216	20663-64	199

(R. R.)	(Page)	(R. R.)	(Page)
20701	52	21878-81	189
20702-3	52	21929	138
20767-9	50	21936	138
20771	51	21952	138
21016	105	22004-5	53
21027-32	56	22080	59n, 66
21042-46	56	22087-94	59n
21113	19n	22211-13	119
21211-18	135	22234	57
21307-8	119	22242	120
21327-28	124	22289	80n
21329	135n	22327	19n
21449-55	124, 135	22365	40
21491-93	124	22437	19n
21518-21	124, 134	22443	19n
21559-62	136n	22489-98	191
21569-70	136n	22500-509	125, 136
21582-85	136n	22507	137
21585-88	124, 135	22546	223
21589-90	124	22560-62	141
21715	106n	22574-88	188
21818-19	40	22816-17	86
21863	119		